CRAFTING A
TIBETAN TERROIR

Culture, Place, and Nature
STUDIES IN ANTHROPOLOGY AND ENVIRONMENT
K. Sivaramakrishnan, Series Editor

Centered in anthropology, the Culture, Place, and Nature series encompasses new interdisciplinary social science research on environmental issues, focusing on the intersection of culture, ecology, and politics in global, national, and local contexts. Contributors to the series view environmental knowledge and issues from the multiple and often conflicting perspectives of various cultural systems.

CRAFTING A TIBETAN TERROIR

WINEMAKING IN SHANGRI-LA

BRENDAN A. GALIPEAU

University of Washington Press | *Seattle*

Crafting a Tibetan Terroir was made possible in part by a grant from the Association for Asian Studies First Book Subvention Program.

Additional support was provided by the Samuel and Althea Stroum Endowed Book Fund.

An earlier version of chapter 4 was published in the *Journal of Agrarian Change* in 2021. A version of chapter 5 was previously published as "Resisting Modernity and Indigenising the Future: Living with Pollution and Climate Change in a Sacred Landscape in Southwest China" in *China Perspectives* 135 (2023).

Design by Ani Rucki | Composed in Arno Pro

Photographs by the author unless otherwise noted.

Maps by Matthew Hartzell.

UNIVERSITY OF WASHINGTON PRESS | uwapress.uw.edu

LIBRARY OF CONGRESS CATALOGING-IN-PUBLICATION DATA

Names: Galipeau, Brendan A., author.

Title: Crafting a Tibetan terroir : winemaking in shangri-la / Brendan A. Galipeau.

Description: Seattle : University of Washington Press, [2024] | Series: Culture, place, and nature | Includes bibliographical references and index.

Identifiers: LCCN 2024014075 | ISBN 9780295753355 (hardback) | ISBN 9780295753362 (paperback) | ISBN 9780295753379 (ebook)

Subjects: LCSH: Wine industry—China. | Tibet—Economic conditions. | Capitalism—China.

Classification: LCC HD9386.C52 G35 2024 | DDC 338.4/7663209515—dc23/eng/20240716

LC record available at https://lccn.loc.gov/2024014075

♾ This paper meets the requirements of ANSI/NISO Z39.48-1992 (Permanence of Paper).

For Bodhi and Ma Yi

Contents

Foreword

K. SIVARAMAKRISHNAN

Crafting a Tibetan Terroir examines the transfer and then embrace of the imported craft of viticulture. The author uses this developing winemaking culture to offer a study of how enterprise at the local level allows Tibetan people in Southwest China to participate in patterns of economic development that blend state socialism and state-led capitalism. Viticulture also provides an original and perceptive window into the shaping of Tibetan ethnic identity.

Scholarship on the production of modern forms of culture and agriculture in a distant part of China has been a burgeoning area of work for a few decades. Brendan A. Galipeau takes discussion of other kinds of modernity in refreshing new directions.[1] He also contributes to an understanding of how ethnic minorities in China have navigated new patterns of incorporation into Chinese society. Government processes that both celebrate and seek to manage ethnic difference have caused non-Han people to grapple with their own sense of identity. They have assessed and selectively seized opportunities provided by the arrival of new commercial activities into their homelands, where both their livelihoods and traditions are exposed to commodification.[2] Galipeau discusses this as indigenizing modernity, a concept he elucidates through examination of how the imported craft of winemaking acquires, over several decades, a distinct Tibetan terroir.

Studies of the import of crops and long histories of their production in countries and climates quite foreign to them, what the environmental historian Alfred W. Crosby referred to as ecological imperialism, have well documented the botanical transfers accelerated by European expansion in modern times. Less frequently, scholars have traced the ways in which imported cultivars and foods come to define regional cultural identity. Galipeau provides a vivid ethnographic account of such an outcome in Southwest China, with grapes and wines.[3] He situates this work through a subtle evocation of Kham in northwestern Yunnan as a particular kind of Tibetan region that has a history different from that of other areas of China inhabited by Tibetans, including the Tibetan Autonomous Region.

Important to his argument is how the region becomes a "zone of convergence" between Chinese efforts to promote tourism in the area to experience Tibetan culture in a place quite deliberately named and exoticized as Shangri-La and the opportunities provided to the people in the area to develop viticulture through their earlier contact with Swiss missionaries and later receipt of Chinese government support. The book remains carefully situated in southern Kham, where farmers of Tibetan origin gradually incorporated viticulture into much older traditions of barley and wheat cultivation. Galipeau does not make broad what might have been unsustainable claims about an enduring Tibetan world contrasted to increasing Chinese influence. Equally, he perceptively notes that the adoption of viticulture was both an act of village-level entrepreneurship and a program actively sponsored by the Chinese state in the late twentieth century, in a terrain where the flavors and enticements of winemaking had arrived via the hand of missionary winemakers.

Winemaking and its promotion also enter a terrain where the Chinese state, having already renamed the region Shangri-La, was actively promoting ethnic tourism. Such investments also create pressures for crafting local culture into a commodity that is embodied in farms, homes, sartorial styles, music or art, and public rituals residents exhibit for their visitors. Studies in Asia, but also in Latin America and sub-Saharan Africa, have analyzed the performance of indigeneity and local cultures that get reified in the service of tourist industries. Ethnic minorities, hill peoples, and frontier areas have often been the target of such endeavors. In southern Kham, broader regional and geopolitical histories show the many factors that led to its depiction in literature, film, and travelogue as Shangri-La. This longer view of the processes underway suggests colonial influences undergird what became a Chinese project. Galipeau is aware of the broader anthropological scholarship on ethnic tourism and the historical layers of imagination and intervention that shaped the outcomes in Yunnan. His own research dwells in the ethnographic details that elucidate the local debate on these issues of performance and presentation.

Chapters reveal the contestation within the Kham Tibetan community on how residents may work with wine production in the region in the project of indigenizing modernity. Galipeau resists the dichotomization of such relations between winemaking and identity formation to show the diversity of approaches that emerge as Tibetans in the area grapple with a growing wine industry and how it may be stamped indigenous on their terms. Such discussion centers on a fascinating account of terroir as divergent histories of grape growing and winemaking in the region result in different kinds of claims to terroir with respect to the wine manufactured in the region. Such nuanced arguments emerge from fieldwork undertaken over more than a decade since 2007 that informs the way Galipeau came to know and study winemaking in Shangri-La. Along the way, he has conducted in-depth research in one village, more regional studies, and archival inquiries in France and Switzerland to trace the connections that brought winemaking to Northwest Yunnan.

Inevitably, such a project demands comparison with another prominent commercially harvested product in the area—caterpillar fungus—and Galipeau provides that. As with matsutake mushrooms (although their harvest and production is dispersed across the globe), wine from Kham works with a globalized food culture as the basis for local economic and cultural expression in layered struggles over identity, modernity, and social change.[4] Among other factors at work here is the revival of interest in Tibetan healing and Buddhism, and the confluence of those interests with food culture, performed traditions, and the charm of remote, scenic landscapes in addition to the imaginative work done by tourism boosters.

Galipeau also examines the rise of environmentalist responses to the ecological degradation that is created by the rapid expansion of commercial viticulture. What emerges, then, is a multilayered study of the production of wine and identity among the Tibetans of this region of Kham and the effects of commoditized and globalized winemaking on the regional economy, ecology, and society. There is a lot to learn from this book for those interested in food studies, surely. But the work done by Galipeau also provides analysis of the agrarian transformation wrought by commodity crops. He offers insight into the negotiated agency and process of identity making that is at work among people living in an ethnic frontier of China. This is a book that is, in short, as well crafted as the wine that inspires its wide-ranging travels and its subtle, patient recovery of food culture and enterprise.

Notes

1. See, for example, Lisa Rofel, *Other Modernities: Gendered Yearnings in China after Socialism* (Berkeley: University of California Press, 1999).
2. A spate of studies have emerged since the early work spearheaded by Stevan Harrell. See Stevan Harrell, ed., *Cultural Encounters on China's Ethnic Frontiers* (Seattle: University of Washington Press, 1996).
3. See Alfred W. Crosby, *Ecological Imperialism: The Biological Expansion of Europe, 900–1900*, 2nd ed. (Cambridge: Cambridge University Press, 2004).
4. For the case of matsutake mushrooms from China, see Michael J. Hathaway, *What a Mushroom Lives For: Matsutake and the Worlds They Make* (Princeton, NJ: Princeton University Press, 2022).

Acknowledgments

I began spending time in Tibetan Northwest Yunnan in 2007 as an undergraduate student, taking part in an environmental and cultural field studies program, during which I first visited many of the communities and met the people featured in this book. In subsequent years, I worked for a nongovernmental organization (NGO) in tourism development and as a teaching assistant for the same study program, continuing to interact with the region long before officially beginning this research. I am grateful to everyone in the villages of Cizhong, Meilishi, Adong, Bu, and elsewhere for opening their homes and sharing wine, food, and their lives with me. I especially wish to thank and recognize Wu Gongdi, Hong Xing, Azu, Hong Bao, Api, Ani Dom, Zhouma, and Li Weihong. I thank Chris and Tingting Carpenter and Thanit Kunkhajornphan for first introducing me to Yunnan Province many years ago. The three of them changed my life forever. My friend and colleague Sun Fei (Apu) provided incredible field assistance on multiple occasions between 2013 and 2016, and I was fortunate to collaborate with him to publish a photo essay on winemaking in Cizhong. He has also gone on to become quite the local wine expert in Shangri-La.

Others in Shangri-La who participated in and contributed to the research in various ways include Songtzen (Sonny) Gyalzur, Huang Zong, and Yves Roduit. In Shangri-La, the Richmond family, Kevin and Lynn Skalsky, Jason Lees, Joel Simbrow, Ashu, Gonpo, Tsebho, Adong, Neil and Wendy Kirkland, Jop, Ells, Guillaume de Penfentenyo, Qi Lian, Amy Wright, Constantin and Phoebe de Slizewicz, and Frank at Flying Tigers Café were always wonderful companions and hosts. I am also grateful to other friends and fellow scholars working in the region including Ben Hillman, Eric Mortensen, Dasa Mortensen, Denise Glover, Hannah Klepeis, and Wang Bo. Other friends and colleagues to whom I owe a debt for commenting on or contributing to this book in various ways include Loretta Lou, Michael Hathaway, Dan Smyer Yü, Jean Michaud, Ralph Litzinger, Ling Zhang, Mindi Schneider, Joseph Bosco, Brian Eyler, Edwin Schmitt, Adam Liebman, Karlis Rokpelnis, Derek Sheridan, and Alex Nickley. David Atwill provided helpful comments on the entire manuscript, and Eugene Anderson read multiple drafts, offering much-appreciated expert suggestions and ideas. My gratitude goes to all my teachers, administrators, and friends at the University of Hawai'i at Manoa, including Hong Jiang, Miriam Stark, Christine Yano, Fred Blake, Elaine Nakahashi, Marti Kerton, Eric Cunningham, Adam Lauer, Brian Lane, Sovatha Ann, Tony Alvarez, Phoebe France, Zakea Boeger, Maura Stephens-Chu, Piphal Heng, and Michelle Daigle.

At Rice University, colleagues in the Transnational Asia Research Initiative in the Chao Center for Asian Studies gave me great encouragement and kept me moving forward in this project. These wonderful individuals included Brianne Donaldson, D. Mitra Barua, Ka-Kin Cheuk, Alex Lee, Maria Hwang, Sohoon Yi, and Han Sang Kim. Sonia Ryang served as my mentor and always provided invaluable and kind support and encouragement, which continues today. I greatly value her friendship and guidance as a leading senior scholar in Asian anthropology. Other faculty and administrators at Rice who provided great assistance and advice include Steven Lewis, Haejin Koh, Hae Hun Matos, Dominic Boyer, and Amber Szymczyk. At National Tsing Hua University (NTHU), my former department, the Institute of Anthropology, provided continued support in finishing this project. I thank the director of the institute, Cheng-hwa Tsang, and former director Shu-min Huang for their unwavering guidance of a junior colleague. My two fellow hires at NTHU, Haoli Lin and Ellen Hsieh, along with other colleagues in Tawain—including Kerim Friedman, Franco Lai, Kunhui Ku, Shirley Ho, Yen-ling Tsai, Jeffrey Nicolaisen, Yiling Hung, Courtney Work, Ian Rowen, Chris Upton, Dana Powell, and Chu-wen Hsieh—have provided encouragement in various ways. For considerable help with new research and ensuring that everything, including finances to complete this book, was in order, I thank two of my students in Taiwan, Flora Huang and Sabrina Lin.

In China, I was hosted for research from 2014 to 2015 by Shen Haimei, a professor at the Yunnan Ethnological Research Institute of Yunnan Minzu University, who also helped with my visa and research permits. In 2016, Liu Zhiyang, a professor of anthropology at Sun Yat-sen University, provided support for my fieldwork and arranged for me to give a lecture there for graduate students. Portions of my research also took place in archives in Paris, France, and Martigny, Switzerland, and I must thank the archivists at each location for providing me with great support and hosting me graciously. In Paris, at the Missions Étrangères de Paris, Lucie Perrault and Ghislaine Olive provided invaluable assistance in helping me arrange my visit and locating various materials. In Martigny, the archivist Jean-Pierre Voutaz, canon of the Congrégation du Grand-Saint-Bernard, warmly welcomed me for ten days and provided open access to materials and invaluable assistance, uncovering many treasures for my research. I thank him and his colleagues for their hospitality and the honor of joining them at lunch each day during my research and for the opportunity to experience the annual Feast of Saint Bernard. In 2016, I greatly benefited from funding provided by the Confucius China Studies Program. I also received a Foreign Language and Area Studies (FLAS) fellowship from the US Department of Education and the University of Hawai'i at Manoa in summer 2013. An earlier version of chapter 4 appeared in the *Journal of Agrarian Change* in 2021, and an earlier version of chapter 5 was published in *China Perspectives* (issue 135) in 2023 as an article titled "Resisting Modernity and Indigenising the Future: Living with Pollution and Climate Change in a Sacred Landscape in Southwest China." I thank both journals for their invaluable peer review process.

The manuscript benefited from the generous comments of three anonymous readers. The third reader's particularly insightful suggestions about content and structure and line-by-line editorial comments challenged and encouraged me to make the book significantly better. At the University of Washington Press, Lorri Hagman stuck with me for many years, never giving up on this project, and provided her continued expert advice with the text even after her retirement. I cannot thank her enough for her support and encouragement. Others at the press including Marcella Landri, Joeth Zucco, Jane Lichty, and Beth Fuget were also instrumental in guiding the book through publication. I also thank K. Sivaramakrishnan for including and curating this book as part of his series Culture, Place, and Nature. Freelancer Karla Armbruster was a wonderful editor who helped me guide the book to its current form, and I am immensely thankful for her insightful advice and attention to detail and presentation. I am also grateful to my friend and colleague Matthew Hartzell, who made the book's maps, and to Ben Joffe for providing the translations of the Tibetan poems that appear as epigraphs in chapters 1, 4, and 5.

I have benefited from working with several scholarly mentors over the years, each of whom I thank for their advice, patience, and encouragement. Jonathan Padwe's attention to fine details in writing and his argument framing and theoretical chops in environmental anthropology and anthropological theory have been invaluable. I am thankful for his guidance and friendship. Alex Golub has also been a constant source of support and has encouraged me to stay true to argument, theory, and presentation in my work. Ty Tengan has made me aware of my role as an ethnographer and the power, responsibility, and importance that anthropology holds today for indigenous peoples. I also continue to benefit from friendship and advice from Bryan Tilt as a scholar of contemporary China, anthropology, and the environment.

Last but certainly not least, I thank my family. My parents, Steve and Tia Galipeau, have been supportive and a constant source of love and care for my entire life in more ways than I can ever say. Without them this book would never have been possible. I cannot thank them enough and know that much of my curiosity about nature, culture, people, and the world comes from them. My mother sadly left us in May 2024, but I am so pleased that she was able to read the final draft and see the book's cover before her passing. Thanks also to my brother, Owen, for always being there, even though we do not get to talk as often as we should. For years my wife, Ma Yi, has been a continual source of love, inspiration, support, and encouragement. Despite her own struggles and difficulties, she has been a rock of faith and belief in me and this project. She also played an invaluable role in helping me to negotiate bureaucratic processes in China and at my host university, where she assisted with paperwork for visas and research permits, among a variety of other frustrating procedures. She was closer to this project than was anyone else, and I love her so much for everything she has done for me. To our son, Bodhi, thanks for reminding me every day what is most important and keeping me smiling.

Conventions

Language and Translations

This book is based on ethnographic research conducted primarily in standard (Mandarin) Chinese, or *putonghua*, along with associated local dialects used in Yunnan. Tibetan words and names used in conversations are sometimes noted in the text, along with Tibetan place-names. When not obvious from context, Chinese and Tibetan terms are distinguished by "Ch" or "T." Chinese terms and names are transliterated using the standard pinyin system, except in cases where individuals chose to romanize their own names. Historical spellings according to previous romanization systems are sometimes provided in parentheses following the current pinyin spelling. Tibetan words are transliterated using the Wylie system. In most cases, place-names are introduced using the Chinese names, as these are the terms local residents most commonly use. Local Tibetan dialects in Northwest Yunnan are quite different from other eastern Tibetan or Kham-based dialects, and even more so from what might be called standard Lhasa Tibetan, to the point that many locals have told me they cannot even communicate with people speaking Lhasa dialects. As a result, standard Chinese and local Chinese dialects are the lingua franca in the region. One often hears villagers speak a mix of Chinese and Tibetan words in a single sentence. Unless otherwise noted, readers may assume that all translations from Chinese are my own or those of my local research assistant in Yunnan, Sun Fei.

Pseudonyms and Naming

Names of individuals are given as pseudonyms, except in cases where the persons discussed are easily identifiable public figures, government or company officials, people who have already been written about by name in other publications or news media, or individuals who requested to be identified by their real name.

Equivalents

One Chinese *mu*: 1/6 of an acre

One Chinese yuan (¥), or renminbi (RMB): approximately .14 US dollars ($) (as of February 2024)

CRAFTING A
TIBETAN TERROIR

Introduction

The master put grapes in an earthen jar
The grapes began to rot in the dark
The grapes exploded and vociferated
Opening wide their grape-like eyes
Experiencing their own dying, their own rotting away.
In their exhaustion their aspect changed.
Now anyone can drink that wine
The grapes are completely forgotten.
As if it is that easy to forget one's past
Forever.

"Wine, June 22, 2001," by Jangbu, contemporary Tibetan poet

June 2016. I sat at lunch with several elderly Catholic priests from the order of Great Saint Bernard in the picturesque town of Martigny in the Swiss Alps. Surrounded by mountains and vineyards, for ten days I had been conducting archival research on former Saint Bernard missionary activity in Southwest China and Tibet. The priests' hospitality had been wonderful, including lunch every day with wine, followed by chatting over coffee and local Swiss chocolates. In reciprocation, I pulled a bottle of white ice wine (a sweet dessert wine) out of the bag I had carried around Europe for several weeks. One of the fathers with whom I talked most days at lunch was ecstatic about this wine. Having been a viticulturalist and winemaker in his younger days, he was keenly interested in my work on winemaking in

Tibet. All the priests found the ice wine delightful, but this man, a cousin of Maurice Tornay, a missionary killed by Buddhist lamas in Tibet and later martyred and granted sainthood, was particularly impressed, even suggesting that there in Valais, Switzerland's oldest and most famous wine region, they should take lessons in mountain winemaking from Tibetans. I explained that this bottle of wine came from an ethnic Naxi community in Weixi, where his cousin and many other missionaries from his order had been stationed more than fifty years before. He was happy to learn that, in many ways, this wine had begun with a tradition introduced by fellow members of his order.

What brought me to Switzerland with a bottle of Tibetan/Naxi wine that so evoked such meaning and emotion from a Catholic priest there? Drinking wine can be like tasting history, and doing so may summon memories and sensations. Wine can evoke feelings about place, weather, land, and human relations. Wine may speak to politics and global relations between nations and cultures. It is "more than a manufactured agricultural product, it's something closer to a miracle," says the eminent filmmaker and vineyard owner Francis Ford Coppola in reference to drinking wine from the era of the French Revolution (Ross and Roach 2013). Discussing wine and the vineyard landscapes it creates may illustrate much about land ownership and territory and the people who grow the grapes, make the wine, and consume it. Through wine and vineyards, the story of more than a century of entanglements between Tibet, China, and Europe has blossomed over the past several decades to completely transform rural landscapes and livelihoods in a small corner of Southwest China on the border with Tibet.

As the anthropologist John Osburg (2013b) points out, many people tend to view post-1978 Chinese capitalism through one of two monolithic lenses: either free-market individual entrepreneurialism or moderated free-market economics controlled by a neo-Marxist or socialist state. Osburg, however, reminds us that viewing global capitalism in China in such a dichotomous way may be unproductive and that we should see China as a model of hybridity and contradictions. Acknowledging this perspective with regard to Southwest China, *Crafting a Tibetan Terroir* illustrates how in the construction of the wine landscape and winemaking there is a mix of individual entrepreneurial talent along with state- and corporate-based schemes. These hybrid forms of production work to formulate multiple ways of being and of expressing Tibetan and other ethnic identities in the face of modernity. Landscapes are formed, re-crafted, and transformed through numerous spheres of influence. With invocations of history, tradition, religion, and "culture," wine landscapes are also inherently temporal and human (Ingold 1993, 2000). While we most often see landscapes as a backdrop to human action, they are also actors within the stories we tell, and we should attempt to move them into the forefront of these narratives. As the anthropologist Anna Tsing put it, "Landscapes are working assemblages of coordinations within a dynamic history" (2015a).

In contrast to locales such as Burgundy and Bordeaux, where since before the time of the Roman Empire wine has dominated the landscape and made it human and "artificial" (Latour 2015), wine landscapes in Tibetan Southwest China are relatively new creations, appearing only over the past 150 years. However, they are overlaid with conversations about colonialism and global capitalist development, and as human and agricultural landscapes they are just as old as those in France, with agricultural relations having existed for thousands of years between Tibetans, barley, and wheat. By placing landscapes, people, and commodities together into a conversation as actors across space and time, this book about wine tells the story of rural Tibetan people adapting to and melding themselves in a process of "indigenizing modernity" (Sahlins 1999; Turner, Bonnin, and Michaud 2015). They draw on exterior influences and forces, including colonial Catholicism, capitalist agrarian change, and state power, to craft a terroir, or "taste of place," for the wines they produce. In doing so, they carve out their own space, place, and regional ethnic identities and roles as caretakers of local landscapes both within and beyond the confines of the economic transformations occurring around them. These forms of ethnicity and identity in Southwest China—involving both historical and contemporary flows of religion, capital, and conceptions of ecology and landscapes—are unique and previously unknown (Harrell 2014).

Northwest Yunnan, Kham, and Diqing

Yunnan Province is in Southwest China, nestled between Tibet and Myanmar to the west and Laos and Vietnam to the south, with other mountainous and ethnically diverse provinces to the east and north. Yunnan is inhabited by over twenty-five distinct ethnic and cultural groups, with tropical rainforests in the south of the province leading north into deep narrow canyons through which three of Asia's largest rivers flow, surrounded by high snowcapped peaks on the edge of the eastern Himalayas. In rugged and mountainous Diqing Prefecture and Deqin County in Northwest Yunnan, the landscape is distinctive. The Mekong and Yangzi Rivers, known locally as the Lancang and the Jinsha, flow through deep, dry, and arid canyons flanked by forested mountains and high glacier-covered peaks. Along the flatlands on the banks of these rivers and their tributaries are scattered Tibetan villages, identifiable by a common yet surprising sight—vineyards. In recent years, grapes and wine have become significant in the livelihoods and daily agricultural life of local Tibetan villagers in this region. These industries build on a small colonial missionary history in a few Catholic villages, combined with state schemes to improve local livelihoods and promote commodities for tourism development.

My observations throughout this book focus on Tibetan people as an ethnic minority and an indigenous population living in Diqing Prefecture and the Tibetan cultural region known as southern Kham (southeast Tibet), and more specifically the Tibetan-named areas of Rgyalthang and Dechen. This study does not intend to make any wider observations about the larger Tibetan cultural region or its populations outside of Southwest China. This area is different from other parts of Tibetan Kham in that it has moved in and out of Chinese political control far longer and today does not suffer from the same political and social instability experienced in other parts of Kham in neighboring Sichuan Province, Gansu Province, and the Tibetan Autonomous Region. Diqing remains unique due to a long-standing relationship with the Chinese state dating back several centuries, its location along major historical trade routes between Tibet and China, and its significant ethnic diversity, consisting of many minority populations beyond Tibetans. While inhabited by a majority of Tibetans, the region remains an ethnic and cultural melting pot. As the religious studies scholar and longtime visitor to and expert on the region Eric D. Mortensen (2019) demonstrates, framing Rgyalthang merely as a Sino-Tibetan borderland tends to discount how local Tibetans view themselves, given that they are neighbors of multiple different ethnic groups to the south, including Naxi, Lisu, and Yi, and not only Han. For Mortensen, Tibetans in Rgyalthang see themselves as being at the center of a variety of other cultures, ethnicities, and polities as indigenous people of Rgyalthang. Indeed, the very idea of nativeness, the vernacular term closest to *indigeneity* among Tibetans, directly translated as "born of this soil and rocks" (*sakyé dokyé*), typically refers to belonging to a particular village or region rather than a broader category of collective identity (Yeh 2007a; cited in Gros 2019c). These characteristics are part of what has allowed the region to develop economically the way that it has, in many cases without the same political and social struggles that other Tibetan regions in China have faced (Hillman 2010). Life for Tibetans in Diqing remains distinctive economically and socially.[1]

Recent scholarship has worked to highlight the particularities of broader Kham within Tibetan and Chinese studies, centering this region and the Sino-Tibetan borderlands rather than simply viewing them as peripheries of China and Tibet. The importance of the region within historical and contemporary identity formation and political dynamics continues to play out in various ways, including through the promotion and development of the region for transnational winemaking projects (Gros 2019b). In this vein, this book also sets out to capture the broader importance of the region and its peoples in worldmaking. Kham and Diqing Prefecture are neither simply Chinese nor Tibetan but are perhaps viewed more effectively as a "third space" on their own. This is due in part to their being governed differently than other Tibetan regions in China, including the Tibetan Autonomous Region. Diqing is separated not only by an internal Chinese border but also by administrative policies that have created different opportunities and ways for local people to view and think about themselves in the context of being Tibetan and Chinese (Gros 2019c; Hillman 2010). Herein I highlight the ways in which wine production, landscape formation, and identity construction relate to the character of Diqing as a meeting place between multiple worlds (Tibetan, Chinese, and European). In doing so, I draw on Stéphane Gros's (2019c) call to take Kham as being in both Tibet and China, alongside other scholarship that points to the Sino-Tibetan borderlands as zones of "convergence" (Jinba 2017) and "symbiosis" (Smyer Yü 2017).

"Shangrilazation," Ethnicity, and Landscape

The name Shangri-La originated in British author James Hilton's famous 1933 novel *Lost Horizon* and the subsequent Hollywood film directed by Frank Capra. Both the novel and the film depict Shangri-La as a mystical paradise hidden deep in the Himalayas near a towering snowcapped peak, where people age slowly and Tibetan Buddhism, Chinese philosophies, and Western Catholicism have blended together. The contemporary manifestation of "Shangri-La" as a physical place in Northwest Yunnan and Diqing and the role of ethnicity, the state, and a various motley crew of actors and ideas in this process are central to the story I tell in this book.[2] In 2001, the city and county originally named Zhongdian in Chinese and Rgyalthang in Tibetan were officially renamed Shangri-La (transliterated in Chinese as Xianggelila) by the government for the explicit purpose of promoting Tibetan (and other) ethnic tourism.[3] This renaming involved an elaborate process in which the government called on academics to prove that Zhongdian City and Zhongdian County, one of three counties along with Deqin in the Diqing Tibetan Autonomous Prefecture, were indeed the actual places described by Hilton. Of course, this claim was pure fantasy and speculation. Although Hilton never visited Tibet, the prefectural government was able to outcompete another "Shangri-La" in neighboring Sichuan and gain national naming recognition from Beijing.

All of Diqing Prefecture is now often broadly referred to as Shangri-La beyond the official county and city, and I often refer to it as such. Outside of the official Shangri-La, the Chinese state has also been working to craft the entirety of the Sino-Tibetan borderlands in the four provinces of Yunnan, Sichuan, Gansu, and Qinghai as a "greater Shangri-La tourism zone" (Coggins and Yeh 2014; Klingberg 2014). Urban Han tourists and foreigners alike view this larger Shangri-La as a borderland region of difference, cultural diversity, and ecological wonders ripe for exploration. As the anthropologist Stevan Harrell (2014, vii) frames this transformation: "The imagined space that was really nowhere has become real (or at least the imagination of that space has been projected on a real place), while at the same time the real space of the Sino-Tibetan borderlands has been imagined—as a place of difference, a place of conservation, a place of abundant resources, a place of aesthetic pleasure."

Emily T. Yeh and Chris Coggins, in their edited volume *Mapping Shangrila* (2014a), frame the creation of this region as a physical space and landscape as "shangrilazation," a process of corporate marketing and statecraft reconfiguring ethnicity and landscapes. Many of the ethnographic and literary endeavors throughout the volume pertain to the landscape reconfigurations and ethnic identities that I suggest wine production and its influences from global capitalism work to create. In *Mapping Shangrila*, Coggins and Yeh (2014, 8) explain in their introduction that part of their own intellectual pursuit is thus "to investigate the multiple landscape and identity effects of the marketing of these borderlands as reified representations of Tibetan culture."

Ethnic identity continues to locate itself in new forms of expression, as it has done with wine, in response to new forms of governmentality based around Shangri-La:

Work[ing] diligently to increase its soft power in the region, [the
state has been] encouraging transnational and local cooperation
in the development of natural and cultural landscape resources.
. . . Indigenous cultural landscapes . . . have thus become marketable commodities . . . in a global trade network that alternately
(and sometimes simultaneously) commercializes, exploits,
re-creates, and protects desirable landscapes while restructuring,
to varying degrees, the space of everyday life and subjectivity.
Since the establishment in 2001 of Shangrila County in Diqing
Prefecture, Yunnan, the state, NGOs, and local people have become increasingly engaged in the physical and symbolic transformation of landscapes throughout the Sino-Tibetan borderlands.
(Coggins and Yeh 2014, 13–14)

Landscapes in Shangri-La are incontrovertibly real and simultaneously
products of visible and invisible sociocultural contests and media representations. The practices that imbue these landscapes with meaning and
with a capacity for agency cannot be understood without paying attention
to the subject positions of those who live and work within them (Yeh and
Coggins 2014d). *Crafting a Tibetan Terroir* provides a powerful illustration
of such subject positions through the story of wine.

"Shangrilazation" as transformation of ethnic identity, landscapes, and
immaterial meaning is neither hegemonic nor complete, but always in the
process of formation, as a particular civilizing project in the Sino-Tibetan
borderlands (Yeh and Coggins 2014d, 25). Globalization and tourism have
opened new modes of inquiry and identity formation. While the region
is now readily accessible, its name defines the people who live there, the
people who visit, and the relationship between the region and the Chinese
state. Local people have begun to recognize an importance in speaking
for themselves in what some view as a crisis facing their indigenous traditions. They have drawn from images of the local environment, including
the mountains and rivers, to redefine their place-based identities on their
own terms rather than on those of outsiders. Here "landscape is not only

a subject to be written about; it is an agent that can and does express itself historically and politically. . . . Landscape plays an important role in imaginative constructions of identity" (Ying 2014, 49). As indigenous culture is further treated as a marketable resource in the governmentality of Shangri-La, Tibetans and other minorities are working to restore, revive, and reinvent indigenous places and cultural practices and identities within these new frameworks of global capitalism (Yeh and Coggins 2014c). With wine, Tibetans and other ethnic groups are specifically indigenizing modernity in the context of capitalist development on their own terms. As Coggins and Gesang Zeren suggest: "The colonized, or those who would be converted, often resist these efforts, engendering 'new forms of conversation with the landscape, including re-enchantments, religious syntheses, [and] reassertions of the landscape's potency'" (2014, 211; quoting Allerton 2009).

As the anthropologist Ralph Litzinger (2014) also reminds us, one cannot think about Shangri-La as a place or a cultural construct without referencing history, from British colonialism and the geopolitics of the Great Game in Central Asia between China, Russia, the United States, and Europe to Hollywood and literary mythmaking. However, today Shangri-La has been reborn in China through wine production and consumption and Chinese and Western encounters with Tibet (Litzinger 2014). Transnational engagement with Shangri-La and its impact on the lives of local people has also changed significantly since the contributions made by the Yeh and Coggins volume. While Tibetan livelihoods, ecology, and sacred landscapes became heavily entangled with conservation work among transnational NGOs through the 2000s, a unilateral ban on foreign NGOs working in Tibetan areas after 2008 led to significant changes, including the opening up of Shangri-La to more direct forms of foreign investment and capital for economic development through wine.[4] Via transnational corporations and entrepreneurs, wine and winemaking now play prominent roles in "shangrilazation" through production of a place-based Tibetan commodity. Wine's "cultural biography" (Kopytoff 1988) involves multiple histories, actors, flows, turns, and stories.

Why Wine?

The geographer Jennifer Dinaburg makes an important observation regarding agriculture and natural resources in Shangri-La, noting how in recent years Tibetans in the region have been described as "cultivators of plants and as self-entrepreneurial subjects who are instructed to be motivated by the promise of development benefits but who are not actually granted any control or ownership over the means of production" (2008, 99). With grapes and wine, this is not always the case. While some communities have been economically "crunched" (Wilk 1997) by the commodification of grapes and wine (Galipeau 2015), others in fact have managed to take better advantage of the state's development schemes and landscape transformation as citizens of Shangri-La. In the Catholic community of Cizhong Village, agentive household smallholders have made themselves distinct as historical Catholic winemakers. In another situation, involving a large French luxury conglomerate, villagers in this region have played a role in directly negotiating the outside use of their own land for the first time in China's post-reform era. That villagers do possess considerable individual agency over their household lands, as Yeh and Coggins (2014b) are keen to point out about this region, is useful in framing how they are now using commodification to indigenize modernity on their own terms and in their own images.

In Shangri-La, wine is also part of a much larger trend of "re-internationalization," where commodities are made for both national and transnational consumption (Hathaway 2014). Many of the actors involved in winemaking arrived in Shangri-La from abroad, reestablishing the region's historical connections with France and Switzerland. Like the matsutake (Japanese; *song rong* in Chinese), a mushroom collected by villagers in Shangri-La and exported as a luxury gift to Japan, more and more wine produced in Shangri-La is being exported for foreign consumption, tying Shangri-La and its peoples to China's wider globalization.

Tibetan Indigeneity and Indigenizing Modernity

The Chinese state has a complicated attitude toward indigeneity (a concept not acknowledged domestically), framing its many ethnic groups as minorities, or *minzu*.[5] *Crafting a Tibetan Terroir* is, in great part, the story of how rural Tibetans in Diqing think about and practice indigeneity through winemaking. Within anthropological scholarship, there has been a strong and growing interest in indigeneity, particularly with regard to access and ownership over land and natural resources.[6] Tibetan identity in Diqing connects to the production of wine as a commodity from a specific location on land inhabited by Tibetan people. Indeed, during my early research in Shangri-La in the late 2000s, one of the major points people stressed about their economic well-being was their access and customary rights to a particular set of natural resources and the economic opportunities provided to them by these lands and resources. These rights include access to caterpillar fungus (*Ophiocordyceps sinensis; dong chong xia cao* or simply *chong cao* in Chinese and *yartsa gunbu* in Tibetan), a valuable fungus collected in Tibet, worth more than its weight in gold, and consumed by Han as a luxury and gift, and access to wine grape markets. Both of these resources and commodities depend on availability and demand, in large part because of the "Tibetan" image inscribed by the state-given name of Shangri-La. For villagers, their Tibetan identity connects with these resources and their ownership of them.

More broadly, in the case of Tibetans living in China, Emily T. Yeh (2007b), a geographer, has provided a useful analysis of how the formation of indigeneity as a process and construct may be illustrated through the collection of the caterpillar fungus. She argues that while commodification of the caterpillar fungus and large sales of it to Chinese consumers is a recent phenomenon, Tibetans' possession and ownership of the land on which the fungus grows is not. As demand for this resource continues to grow, more non-Tibetans have begun to seek access to its collecting grounds, while local Tibetans, including those with whom I spent time, have started to assert their rights to such collecting grounds as indigenous inhabitants and owners of customary land rights. However, as Yeh further highlights, to avoid agitating against the Chinese state by asserting any sort of sovereignty, Tibetans have had to be cautious in terms of framing these access rights as a purely ethnic issue based on Tibetanness.

As local Shangri-La Tibetans have begun to enter wider markets through the collecting and selling of "Tibetan"-marked natural and agricultural resources, including caterpillar fungus and matsutake, and winemaking, they have also begun to assert themselves as indigenous peoples through their ownership of or rather usage rights over the lands on which these resources are found or grown, for example, through rigorous community organizing to manage access to fungi collecting grounds. This important factor in commodity production informs individual and group identities among Tibetan people in Northwest Yunnan through wine, caterpillar fungus, and other valuable resources and products. The following chapters focus ethnographically on the links between agricultural production of wine and peoples' descriptions of this process in relation to being Tibetan individuals. This argument draws from work by the anthropologist Marshall Sahlins in his discussion of "indigenizing modernity," a methodology by which indigenous peoples are "tak[ing] cultural responsibility for what has been done to them" by colonialism and capitalism (1999, i): "Unified by the expansion of Western capitalism over recent centuries, the world is also being re-diversified by indigenous adaptations to the global juggernaut. In some measure, global homogeneity and local differentiation have developed together, the latter as a response to the former in the name of native cultural autonomy. . . . What the self-consciousness of 'culture' does signify is the demand of the peoples for their own space within the world cultural order. . . . The project is the indigenization of modernity" (ix–x).

In work applying Sahlins's framework, the geographers and anthropologists Sarah Turner, Christine Bonnin, and Jean Michaud (2015) explore how local markets and products, including traditional liquor and alcohol, have been developed and utilized by highland Hmong ethnic minority communities in southern Yunnan and Vietnam, providing a means through which to maintain their ethnic and indigenous identities while also engaging with states and modern market economies on their own terms, often only when and if they choose to. As the authors explain in framing modernity and commodity markets with respect to highland ethnic minority communities living in Yunnan:

> Modernity incorporates a convergence of institutional arrange-ments—such as a market economy and bureaucratic state—along-side a "divergence . . . of lived experience and cultural expressions of modernity that are shaped by what is variously termed the 'habitus,' 'background,' or 'social imaginary' of a given people" (Gaonkar 1999, 16). . . .
>
> The vast majority of Hmong households in these uplands are busy with daily agricultural and rural livelihoods. Some are eager to take up new opportunities and diversification strategies that might make life easier, such as new farming techniques, high-yield crop va-rieties, cash crops, and trading networks extending beyond custom-ary ethnic circles. . . . Like any other minority group in these uplands, Hmong individuals are adopting market economic opportunities and state policies and programs as they see fit. However, these cre-ative adaptations do not signal a straightforward acquiescence with modernization's wishes. (Turner, Bonnin, and Michaud 2015, 8–9)

Tibetan winemaking in its various forms represents this same mode of indigenizing modernity, at times accepting but also refusing or alter-ing government frameworks and modern capitalist markets. There are, though, also contradictions in how various actors in this story go about indigenizing modernity. Some directly engage with the state and modern market economies through wine, while others are vehemently opposed to the new viticulture economy and push back against its rapid expansion. Various middle-ground methodologies also exist, in which village farmers and wine companies work with markets but do so beyond the direct arm of the state, organized more coherently around Tibetan culture or other ideals. This book contributes further to thinking about this methodology of indigenizing modernity among Tibetans in Shangri-La by illustrating how in one locale and among predominantly one ethnic or indigenous group, with one commodity form, it can be deployed in a variety of contrasting ways.

With respect to Tibetans, Yeh (2007b) suggests that a growing interest among urban Chinese in various aspects of Tibetan culture, including medicines, may lead to more awareness within China of Tibetans as indigenous peoples, though without specific reference to indigeneity given the term's problematic political nature in China. John Osburg (2020, 2013a) and Dan Smyer Yü (2012, 2015) have pointed in particular to an urban Chinese uptake of Tibetan Buddhism and culture and travel to Tibetan regions as a means of finding fulfillment and overcoming the emptiness of urban China's hyper-capitalist lifestyle. In conjunction, Smyer Yü (2012) frames the revival of Tibetan Buddhism occurring among Tibetans themselves in the context of larger global indigenous movements. In many ways, the desire among Chinese and foreigners to consume wine and other goods and services from Shangri-La, including religion, gives local Tibetans a means through which to identify themselves through economic production and promotion of their local landscape.

Terroir

Terroir as a project or methodology in identity construction for agricultural and natural products provides a means by which Tibetans and others can indigenize modernity. In the most traditional sense, terroir has typically referred to geographical features associated with wine, such as soil, climate, and geology. Anthropologists and social scientists have expanded the term to include ideas of history, ethnicity, and methods of production among winemakers and other agricultural producers (e.g., Besky 2013; Demossier 2011, 2018; Trubek 2009). These semiotic contextualizations of terroir as constructions of both product and place are key among the communities, the state, and the corporate actors that utilize and create terroirs for their wines. Each uses various aspects of these ideals of terroir to create wines that reflect who they are and the landscapes from which their wines are made.

Terroir is also a concept of branding and identity tied to the production, cultural traits, and placiality of consumable commodities. Anthropologists have engaged with terroir in terms of providing agency to commodity producers and farmers involved in the creation of specific place-based products, tying the concept back to political ecology and Marxist critiques of capitalism (e.g., Ulin 1995, 2002). For winemakers and grape growers in Shangri-La, the use of terroir is both agentive and alienating. Some, particularly Catholic smallholders, give their wine a place-based and historical contextualization tied to France and Switzerland to create terroir. For grape growers elsewhere in the region, the picture varies, with some simply providing their grapes to state and corporate wineries that use the image of Tibetans to market wine. In this arrangement, farmers are alienated from the product, whereas in other situations farmers take some part in the transformation of grapes into the final commodity.

In France, where terroir's use began with wine, the concept's original meaning has evolved from being almost purely about geography to being very much a question of territory, identity, history, and cultural practices. Prominent wine regions such as Bordeaux and Burgundy have been classified with reified regional specificity to mark the wines produced in different areas and the microclimates and histories surrounding them (Demossier 2018; Ulin 1995). Winemakers originating from and trained in these regions, who at times have worked with and taught local Tibetans, have exerted a particular influence on place and taste making in Shangri-La. There, wineries have begun to highlight vintages and varietals produced using specific Tibetan village names to reflect their small niche terroirs within the larger wine landscape of the region. In this particularly powerful Burgundian form of terroir, village and community are mobilizing forces within an increasingly competitive and complicated global wine economy (Demossier 2018). In Burgundy, individual farming villages are known to coalesce around their wines, just as farmers in Shangri-La are being influenced to do. In this way, the terroirs of wines in Shangri-La are increasingly being crafted through both historical and contemporary foreign associations and influences to create distinction. This practice is exemplified by flavor profiles unique to grapes grown in Shangri-La and not found anywhere else. There are French winemakers, for example, who, in the physical place conceived by China called Shangri-La, are making wine to export to the West. They see special opportunities in the distinct "Tibetan" flavors and terroirs they are creating to appeal to consumers in China and abroad.

With respect to China and the Chinese cultural conceptualization of terroir, a vernacular term, *fengtu*, has surfaced with the two characters representing wind and earth, or a relationship between climate and soil, to imply "taste of place" (Zheng 2019, 283). This terminology has not entered mainstream use among average Chinese wine consumers in the way that *terroir* has abroad. Wine producers in Shangri-La, however, frequently make use of the original French term *terroir* to describe their wines in marketing materials online and through personal narratives. As an analytic tool, terroir has been used a great deal in exploring food commodities in China and elsewhere in Asia, particularly tea, which has entered heavily into global discourses on regional and place-based production, taste, labor, and quality (Besky 2013; Chan 2012; Zhang 2014). Terroir has become a major force in studies of landscapes and food in the Chinese cultural world through tea and the translation of the term into Chinese cultural constructs related to flavors and other sensory aspects. Given its native application to wine in France, uptake in tea production and consumption among Chinese, and the cultural constructs surrounding wine in Shangri-La, terroir lends itself perfectly to capturing the particularities of the region's wine economy.

Methodology and Reflexivity

I spent several years in Shangri-La and Diqing Prefecture, dating back to 2007. Primary data collection took place beginning in summer 2013, when

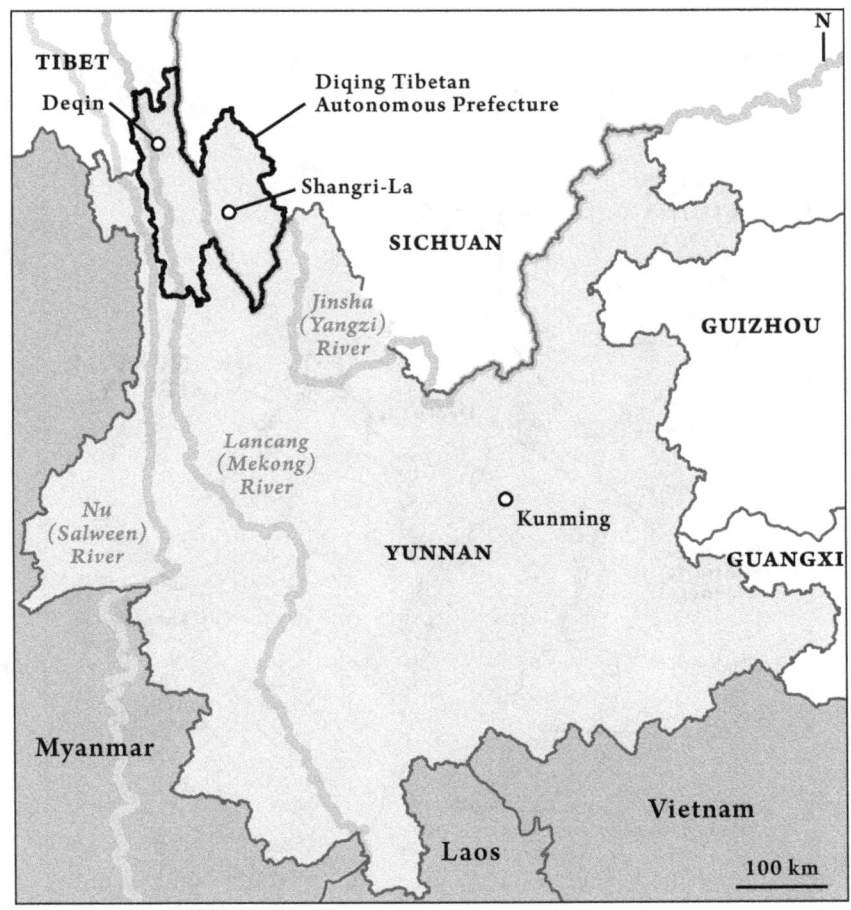

MAP 1. Yunnan Province

I first visited Cizhong Village. I followed that stay with long-term field-work in a variety of locales in the region from fall 2014 through summer 2015, with a six-month follow-up visit and one month spent in Europe for archival work during spring and summer 2016. A return trip took place in summer 2018. Living side by side with my study subjects and engaging in their daily lives was by far the most useful of my methodological approaches, and I was constantly taking notes and observing events and

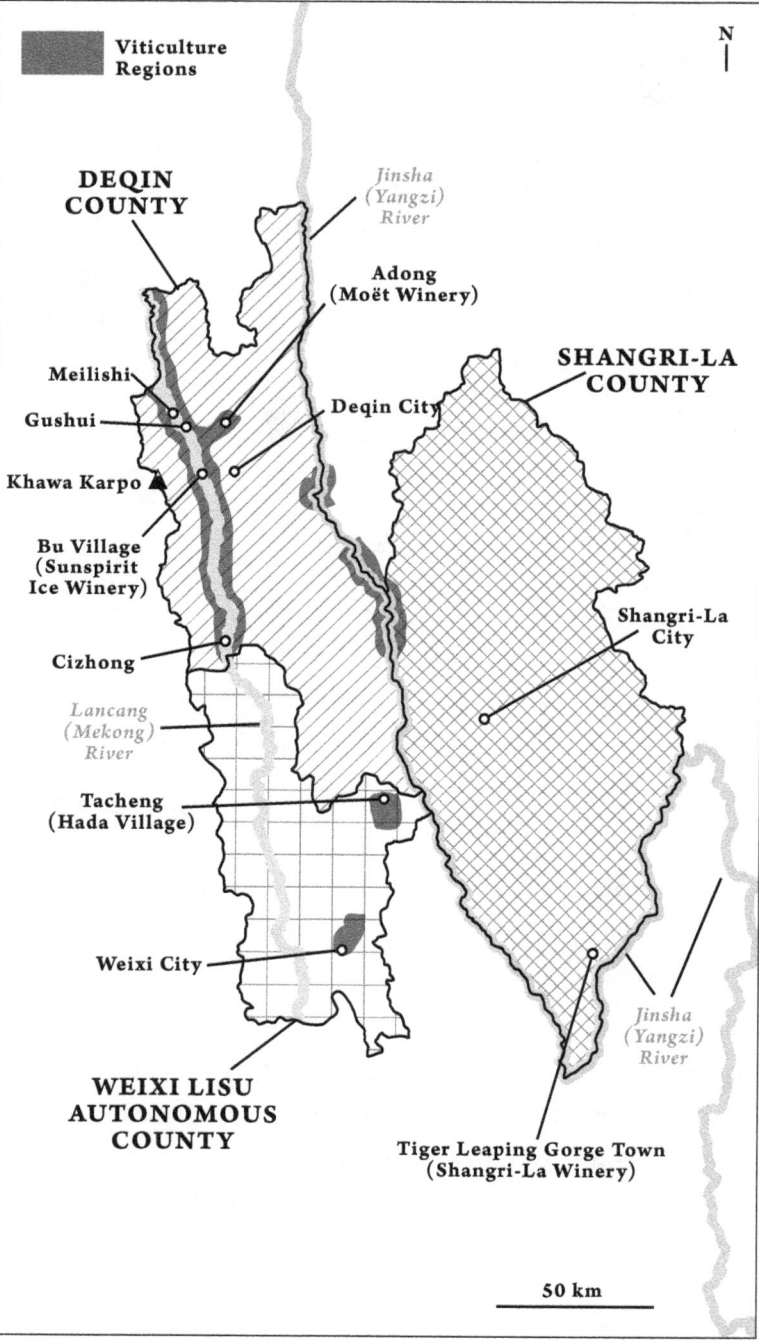

N

Viticulture
Regions

DEQIN
COUNTY

Jinsha
(Yangzi)
River

Adong
(Moët Winery)

SHANGRI-LA
COUNTY

Meilishi
Gushui
Deqin City

Khawa Karpo

Bu Village
(Sunspirit
Ice Winery)

Shangri-La
City

Cizhong

Lancang
(Mekong)
River

Tacheng
(Hada Village)

Weixi City

WEIXI LISU
AUTONOMOUS
COUNTY

Jinsha
(Yangzi)
River

Tiger Leaping Gorge Town
(Shangri-La Winery)

50 km

activities as they occurred so that I could later interpret them. Robert M. Emerson, Rachel I. Fretz, and Linda L. Shaw point out that "if substance ('data,' 'findings,' 'facts') are products of the methods used, substance cannot be considered independently of the interactions and relations with others that comprise these methods " (2011, 15). I recognize that much of what I have written in this book comes from my own understanding and interpretations as an ethnographer, while both attempting to understand and interpret the events in the lives of my study subjects and stretching factors such as my own linguistic abilities.

When I first conceived my plan to conduct the research for this book, I envisioned a "traditional" ethnographic experience, that is, residing in one or two rural Tibetan villages over time, living with a local family, and simply "being there" while conducting interviews and observing and taking part in daily life. This vision was based on earlier fieldwork and observations in Shangri-La over how deeply ingrained vineyards and grapes had become in rural livelihoods. I was particularly interested in learning about the impact of this industry in one or two rural communities. Certainly, this type of activity still made up most of my time, but my overall approach changed to emphasize conducting a multisite regional ethnography in several villages, along with visiting wineries, breweries, and restaurants, interviewing government officials, and hosting and organizing my own local wine tasting at a French friend's restaurant in Shangri-La. I also found myself traveling as far as Paris, France, and Martigny, Switzerland, for over a month to delve more deeply into the archival history of viticulture in Shangri-La and the Sino-Tibetan borderlands.

Opposite MAP 2. Diqing Prefecture. Diqing is administered as a Tibetan autonomous prefecture, meaning that Tibetans make up the majority of the population and lead the government; however, the prefecture is in fact incredibly diverse in terms of ethnicity. While in two of Diqing's three countries, Shangri-La and Deqin, Tibetans are the majority population, in the third, Weixi, Lisu predominate and oversee the county's government and administration. For ease of identification, the area of each county is shaded with different line textures.

As the project developed, I found there were so many stories in different locations related to the idea and development of Shangri-La's wine economy. Given these discoveries, I decided that it would serve the goals of my study and the people and topic I was studying to further explore these tales and the individuals and communities who wished to share them. Therefore, I ended up spending significant "field" time in Cizhong Village, as well as time in other villages with wineries or where individuals were involved in various winemaking projects or wine and viticulture-related activities, such as environmental activism against pesticide use. This approach, together with archival materials and interviews with government officials and other important figures, has produced, I believe, a much more cohesive and compelling story. In Cizhong and other village locales, my participant observation activities often involved planting grape vines, plowing, weeding, fertilizing, pruning, harvesting, and winemaking.

Certainly, one of the primary barriers to conducting fieldwork in China remains language. After years of effort, I can speak standard Chinese with a strong level of efficiency. However, throughout China, people converse in local dialects, which are not found in any language textbook, though standard Chinese has certainly become increasingly accessible throughout China via schooling and activities such as watching national television. Except for elders who had no formal schooling before the 1950s, everyone in Deqin and Shangri-La today is at least partially proficient in standard Chinese. Another complication is that in Tibetan communities, daily conversations are conducted in local Tibetan dialects or a combination of Tibetan and the Yunnan dialect of Chinese. Formally studying the Tibetan language for work in Yunnan is practically out of the question, because the dialects spoken there differ so much from the Lhasa dialect taught in universities that the two are almost mutually unintelligible. Luckily, however, two of my primary informants in Cizhong Village—my host father, a prominent Catholic leader, and one local historian and elder who knew French and Swiss missionaries before 1949—both were highly proficient in standard Chinese, allowing me to converse with them with ease. Over time, my own proficiency in understanding and comprehending local dialects significantly improved.

Conducting official or formal research in rural China remains a difficult and complicated bureaucratic process. Many foreign researchers simply arrive in the country on a tourist visa and conduct their work unofficially or with only some local government approval established through *guanxi*, or "relationships," sidestepping the formal process of securing the correct visa and required higher-level approvals. However, doing so has become increasingly difficult in China's Tibetan regions, with Yunnan remaining one of the few locales where foreigners are able to conduct research among Tibetan communities. Fortunately, I was able to secure the proper permits and approvals, through affiliation with a host university in the provincial capital of Kunming and then working with the university to secure a formal research permit from the provincial Foreign Affairs Department. Having heard many stories about failed research projects and permissions in China, I was quite reassured to receive a permit with the official red stamp indicating the government formally approved of and supported my project. For me, this form of approval also meant, importantly, that I as a researcher was responsible to my study subjects. If one does not have formal permission to conduct research in a rural community (or anywhere in China, for that matter), one's study subjects may face retribution from the state for speaking to and interacting with an unapproved foreign researcher. Therefore, as a responsibility to my study subjects, I pursued and received such approval, which then also permitted access to and contact with important government officials and company representatives involved in Shangri-La's wine industry, opportunities that would not have been possible without potential consequences had my project not been officially approved.

Many of my relationships in Shangri-La were also cultivated through the consumption of local alcoholic spirits during evenings spent with members of the community—a rather common occurrence through which bonds can be formed in anthropological research (Bernard 2011; Fiskesjö 2010), and in which, in my experience, some of the best relationships are often built in rural China. Anthropologists have long engaged with the topic of drinking during fieldwork and with the study of drinking behaviors (Douglas 1987). The opportunity to inquire about various topics during fieldwork and have one's subjects open up and welcome one into the fold of their community often goes hand in hand with engaging in social drinking. In some cases, the ethnographer's willingness to engage with locals in such practices helps to alleviate his or her position as an outsider (Bernard 2011; Fiskesjö 2010). As an anthropologist studying wine and winemaking and conducting work with Yunnan Tibetans who tend to drink a lot, particularly as a social act, I found myself joining in the practice often throughout my fieldwork.

Engaging in "participant intoxication" (Fiskesjö 2010) perhaps warrants further reflexive analysis. In the context of working among the Wa, an ethnic minority in southern Yunnan and Myanmar, the anthropologist Magnus Fiskesjö highlights one of the fine needles that foreign anthropologists must seek to thread when working with local communities and participating in socialized drinking. We find ourselves in the ambivalent position of wanting to ingratiate ourselves with the communities we study, through drinking if it is what is socially accepted and expected, while also hoping to maintain a polite but acceptable escape route from intoxicating situations. However, at least in the Wa context (which is similar, in my experience, among some Tibetans), declining to drink places one immediately on unequal grounds with hosts and marks one as an outsider who refuses local social norms while insisting on imposing one's own. These are dilemmas that I often found myself negotiating.

Also of note is that while I sometimes write about wine and taste in this book, I am by no means an expert in this area and possess no formal training as a sommelier. I grew up in California with wine-drinking parents and have lived there and in Oregon's Willamette Valley for several years at a time, learning about wine as an amateur drinker. Perhaps my most formal training came from my time spent in Shangri-La, particularly interacting with foreign winemakers, and generating an at least better than rudimentary understanding of wine taste, quality, aesthetics, and so forth. I did at times spend evenings and afternoons speaking with and learning from a trained French chef and sommelier at a popular French and Tibetan fusion restaurant owned by friends in Shangri-La City. He helped me develop a more thorough repertoire of wine language and understanding, which I have used in my writing.

CHAPTER 1

Wine in Tibet from Catholic Colonialism to Global Capitalism

Fearing thirst, I sought out drink

-

The drink I found was the
Chang-nectar of Mindfulness
Now I have no fear of thirst.

Milarepa (Tibetan saint and poet, 1052–1135 CE)

Winemaking as a form of indigenizing modernity in Shangri-La reflects transnational histories that began with colonial Catholicism in the nineteenth century. While not all contemporary winemakers link their wine with earlier French and Swiss Catholic missionaries, many, particularly in Cizhong Village, do. Others, such as the French luxury conglomerate Moët Hennessy, mention in their marketing materials and interaction with media that wine arrived with the French. Without European introduction and influence, would Shangri-La be a landscape of vineyards and wine today?

Colonialism and Global Capitalism in the Development of Chinese Wine

Europe's initial attempts to introduce goods in China during dynastic rule were useless. China believed itself to be the core of civilization, while everywhere else was the periphery and "the other," just as Europe viewed China as "the other" (Wang 2009, 2004). Paying tribute from the periphery to the Chinese empire did not grant the right to trade with China but rather was an obligation. Most European powers were unaware that the Chinese and Mongol emperors had been hoarding an array of Western riches since the Yuan/Mongol (1279–1368) and Ming (1368–1644) dynasties. Whenever the West desired something from the Chinese, particularly tea, which Western populations craved in vast amounts as a stimulant, silver currency was the only form of payment accepted. This trade system was in place until Europeans managed to connect more of the Pacific region in their trading network and first introduced Hawaiian sandalwood, which was desired as a luxury good in China, followed by their own intoxicant, opium (Sahlins 1994, 2010). Thus began a long process of opening China up to a variety of European colonial endeavors, two of the most prevalent in this discussion of global economic reach being intoxication and proselytization. China continued to resent these encroachments on its sovereignty but was forced to capitulate after the opium wars with Britain and the Treaty of Nanking in 1842. Other treaties followed with France, including the Treaty of Tientsin in 1860, which allowed the entrance of French (especially Catholic) missionary endeavors into China, further marginalizing China within a global system in which it had viewed itself as the center (Kilpatrick 2015; Sahlins 1994).

The West had initially desired stimulants (tea) from China, but with the introduction of opium to China, a new stage of commodity flows within the global system began in which China became "the intoxicated" (Smith 2012), rather than the intoxicator. Opium opened the door for other European intoxicants, including wine, which until that time had seen relatively little consumption in China compared to grain alcohols, which were more at the center of Chinese ritual and culture. These exchanges continue in both directions, with wine production and consumption in Shangri-La and across China as a whole expanding at a rapid pace. Today, China is producing, exporting, and consuming this intoxicant.

However, making wine from grapes was not entirely nonexistent in early China. Archeological finds from the Han dynasty (202 BCE–220 CE) show that winemaking existed by at least 103 BCE, when the Han court began diplomatic relations with central and western Asia, where grape wine was common. The popularity of grape wine reached a peak during the Tang dynasty (618–907 CE), when it remained an exotic foreign item consumed mostly by the elite, with production centered around the Tang capital, Xi'an, in Shaanxi, and in neighboring Gansu. Thereafter, its influence declined among Chinese consumers until the arrival of Europeans, who played a major role in the establishment in the 1800s of Changyu in Shandong, still one of China's largest wineries and vineyard operations.[1] While "true" grape wine originated during Han trading relations, with the Eurasian wine grape variety *Vitis vinifera*, China may in fact be the source of the world's oldest alcoholic beverage, which contained local wild grapes dating back to the Neolithic period, between 7000 BCE and 6600 BCE (McGovern 2009, 28–59). This drink, traces of which were discovered on ancient pottery found at the Jiahu archaeological site in today's Henan Province, in central China, contained fermented rice (possibly the first domesticated in the world), honey mead, and fermented juice of both wild grapes and hawthorn berries. The Jiahu example remains a peculiarity in the development of wine in that the practice of fermenting wild grapes in China disappeared thereafter despite an abundance of local grape varieties, many of which remain undomesticated. Relevant to this story, Tibetan documents suggest that Tibetans may also have domesticated wild grapes for consumption and winemaking to a limited extent in the southeast part of the country at least as early as the eighteenth century (see more below, under "Viticulture and Winemaking in Tibet"; Stein 1972, 25).

Tibet and in particular the Sino-Tibetan borderlands also interacted with China through trade in a stimulant, tea, with some of the brick tea primarily produced in Sichuan passing through today's Deqin and Shangri-La, along the ancient Tea Horse Road (Freeman and Ahmed 2011; Fuchs 2008). Southern Yunnan was also a center of production for brick-form teas, including the recently famous luxury commodity Pu'er tea, which was also sold to Tibet via mule trains through and across Yunnan.

As the historian Patrick Booz explains, after the Tibetans first encountered tea around the eighth century, "they took to the new beverage with great enthusiasm [and] it became a central element of social and economic life as well as being the indispensable daily drink for reasons of hydration, nutrition, social interaction, hospitality and religious functions. Proverbially considered one of the 'four pillars of life'—*tsampa* (barley), meat, butter and tea—tea was the only traditional staple of Tibet that needed to be imported: it was grown, processed and controlled solely by China. Tibetans wanted it and needed it" (2014, 253). Thus, from an early point, as with opium in China, tea entered Tibet through China as a global commodity and became central to life.

Catholicism in Tibet and Northwest Yunnan

French and Swiss Catholic fathers first came to Northwest Yunnan and Tibet in the mid-nineteenth century.[2] In James Hilton's classic novel, the fictional Shangri-La is a mixed monastic community where Tibetan Buddhists, Chinese, and Western Catholics live peacefully in meditation together. This is largely the case in Cizhong Village today, although Catholicism historically faced a violent reception from some in the region while others openly welcomed it. Pope Gregory XVI first named Tibet as an apostolic locale in 1846 under the direction of the Missions Étrangères de Paris (MEP), with the society already assigned to manage missions in the neighboring areas of Yunnan and Sichuan. The MEP was (and still is today) a religious order and an association of priests devoted to bringing Catholicism to Asia (Bray 2011; Kilpatrick 2015; Loup 1956). They were not the first Catholic missionaries to enter Tibet at the direction of the Vatican. The Italian Jesuit Ippolito Desideri reached the Tibetan capital of Lhasa by way of India in the eighteenth century, staying from 1716 to 1721. The Vatican initially directed him to pursue setting up the first Catholic mission to Tibet; however, during his time there, conflicts emerged with another Italian missionary order, the Capuchins. Arguments ensued as to whom Tibet actually "belonged" as an apostolic region, and the Vatican ordered Desideri to return to Rome. During his years in Tibet, he developed a strong appreciation for the people and their religion, studying in monasteries and becoming so proficient in Tibetan language that he was able to author several books on Christianity in Tibetan. Desideri wrote one of the first in-depth European accounts of Tibetan society and geography (Desideri 1932, 2010; Pomplun 2010).

Other French Catholic missionaries also traveled to China and Tibet before the arrival of the MEP. The Lazarists, or Congregation of the Mission, another order based in Paris, worked in northern China. Two renowned Lazarist priests, Évariste-Régis Huc and Joseph Gabet, traveled extensively in Tibet and the neighboring areas of Qinghai and Gansu and reached Lhasa between 1844 and 1846. Huc wrote extensively about the region and its peoples, providing well-known accounts that are still cited today, although his writing favorably of Tibetan culture and traditions was somewhat frowned on by the Vatican. Conversely, Huc also spoke more distastefully about the Chinese. Despite their efforts and hopes to set up missions under the Lazarists in Tibet, Huc and Gabet completed their travels and were expelled from Lhasa when the region was granted to the MEP. The Capuchins had long since been expelled (Bray 1995, 2011; Huc 1928; Kilpatrick 2015; Reuse 2007).

Despite the successes over a century of Catholic missionaries reaching even as far as Lhasa, Tibetan converts were rare, and missionaries were never openly welcomed in Tibet in the ways that they wished. French Catholic fathers from the MEP who arrived in Northwest Yunnan and the neighboring areas of western Sichuan in the mid-nineteenth century viewed their work as a gateway to expanding their teachings across greater Tibet. Unable to reach far into the central areas of Tibet, often due to violent (in some cases lethal) resistance from local Buddhist lamas, the French eventually managed to set up churches and convert many Tibetan communities in Northwest Yunnan along the upper reaches of the Mekong and Salween Rivers. One of the difficulties at this time was that, administratively, the Sino-Tibetan borderlands occupied a liminal zone of fluctuating political power between Tibet and China. With the MEP fathers under the protection of treaties between France and China, their safety from local opposition relied on China's political power, which was often nonexistent in remote border regions. Secondarily, Tibet's acceptance of Chinese political influence and control in the border areas was reliant on the ideal that Tibet remained free religiously and under the power of the Dalai Lama (Bray 1995). This was seen as being violated, however, when the Chinese allowed the introduction of Christianity. Additionally, the mid-1880s were not a good time for proselytizing in Yunnan, which was in the midst of a nearly two-decade-long Muslim rebellion (Atwill 2005).

Nevertheless, the first of the MEP fathers, Père Charles Renou, a veteran in China, arrived in the region in 1852. Disguising himself as a Chinese merchant, he first arrived in the upper Yangzi, or Jinsha, valley, where he spent two years living at the Dongzhulin Monastery. There, Renou befriended the local lama and studied Tibetan language with him, despite not revealing his identity or intentions. Years later, when it was clear that Renou and his followers were missionaries, the lama, unlike most Tibetan Buddhist leaders, remained their supporter (Bray 1995; Davies 1909). Renou moved on to the neighboring Salween River valley in 1854 and established the first mission station just inside the Tibetan border with Yunnan in the small tributary valley of Bonga. From the beginning, the missionaries' presence was unstable, and they often faced threats on their lives. Indeed, Renou and the other priests who later joined him in Bonga saw their new church burned down and were expelled to Yunnan by local leaders after only a few years. Led to believe that the priests held a title to the land in Bonga and the right to be there, the MEP eventually managed to have their case heard in the highest-level district court in Chamdo, Tibet, and won. However, despite their success in court, their ability to maintain the original mission in Bonga remained politically difficult, and they permanently abandoned it by the 1860s. This was despite their great progress in converting over seven hundred local villagers in the Bonga region to Catholicism. The success of the missionaries in legal terms also made their endeavors more dangerous in the long run, as resentment toward their behavior and interference grew, and over the years many of the fathers were killed by lamas (Bray 1995; Gros 2001; Lim 2009).

The next missions were established in southern Tibet and today's Sichuan in the Mekong valley and neighboring areas around the upper Yangzi, with Kangding (formerly known as Daqianlu [Tatsienlou]) becoming the center of the diocese of Tibet. The first church and mission in the Mekong valley was built upstream from Cizhong (Tsechung) in today's Tibetan Autonomous Region at Yanjing (T: Yerkalo), by the fathers Félix Biet and Auguste Desgodins in 1865 (Loup 1956). Desgodins, an important figure in the history of the mission, and his elder brother C. H. Desgodins wrote several articles and journals chronicling their work and the people they encountered and also made and published many Tibetan translations of the Bible and Catholic texts. A missionary presence of priests was then firmly made in Cigu (Cikou), just downstream from Cizhong, in a few years' time (Bray 1995; Davies 1909; Moseley 2011). While Renou had been able to befriend local Tibetan lamas in the region, this peaceful coexistence did not last for those who followed him. Eventually, Tibetan lamas destroyed the churches and murdered priests in a major campaign carried out across the region in 1905. The British plant collector George Forrest, who had been staying at Cigu with the two priests stationed there, Pierre Bourdonnec and Jules Étienne Dubernard, described these events. The three of them, along with one of Forrest's Tibetan assistants, fled downstream, although both French priests were later killed (McLean 2009; Moseley 2011; Mueggler 2011). Forrest believed that Bourdonnec saved his life by sacrificing his own, leaving Forrest to crawl through the woods for several days, without food and water, before reaching safety. Bourdonnec had been stationed at Cigu for over a decade, and local people had been fond of him. He regularly provided medical services and medicine and never forced his faith on anyone. Rather, he viewed his mission more as providing hospice for both locals and the rare European explorer who traveled through the region (Kilpatrick 2015; Roux 1999).

Four years later, in 1909, the Tibetan converts who had remained faithful began construction on a new church along the river at Cizhong, just upstream of Cigu, where the French Catholics would also reestablish themselves. This community still exists today and has remained faithful to its Catholic beliefs; approximately 80 percent of village households are Catholic (Goodman 2001, 2010; Lim 2009; Moseley 2011). A group of Swiss missionaries, hailing from the Great Saint Bernard Hospice high in the Alps, joined the French in the 1930s. These fathers were famous for providing mountain rescues and services to Catholic pilgrims crossing the Alps en route to Rome. Their expertise in mountain travel and high-altitude living, including mountain viticulture, was crucial in helping to continue and eventually take over the work first begun by the French in Yunnan (Bonet 2006; Croidys 1949; Dickinson 2012; Loup 1956).

By 1930, the MEP felt it could no longer handle the work of the mission in Tibet and asked the pope for assistance. He then recommended the monks of the Great Saint Bernard Hospice. Fathers Marie Melly and Paul Coquoz undertook a fact-finding trip, departing from Switzerland on November 20, 1930, and arriving in Weixi, downstream from Cizhong, on February 15, 1931. Eventually, the French priest Francis Goré, who was in charge as vicar-general of Cizhong, met up with them. They explored the region for three months and chose the Lhotse (T) pass south of Cizhong and Cigu, at the crossroads of China, Myanmar, and Tibet and connecting the Mekong and Salween Rivers, as the location of their planned potential mountain hospice, modeled after the Saint Bernard Hospice in Switzerland. Melly and Coquoz then returned to Switzerland to report their findings. Their order unanimously agreed to take up the project and the missionary work. The first group of four, Melly, Coquoz, Louis Duc, and lay missionary Robert Chappelet, then left on January 13, 1933. Three years later, the second group of Maurice Tornay, Cyril Lattion, and Nestor Rouiller left on February 26, 1936. Throughout their years in Yunnan and Tibet, the Swiss fathers would keep their headquarters at Weixi, with priests stationed at several other locations, including Xiao Weixi, Cizhong, today's county capital of Deqin (formerly known as Atunze), Yanjing, and elsewhere along the Salween River (Bonet 2006; Croidys 1949; Loup

FIGURE 1. Interior of the Cizhong church
(built in 1909) during Christmas morning Mass, 2014.

FIGURE 2. Interior of the Cizhong church, early twentieth century.
Courtesy of Maison hospitalière du Grand-Saint-Bernard, Médiathèque Valais.

FIGURE 3. Exterior of the Cizhong church, early
twentieth century. Courtesy of Maison hospitalière du
Grand-Saint-Bernard, Médiathèque Valais.

1956). Basing themselves in Yunnan made more sense logistically, since
most of the missions were located there and the previous center of the
diocese, in Kangding, Sichuan, had never been easily reachable for the
fathers stationed in Yunnan's Tibetan areas. Given their activities around
Weixi and Xiao Weixi and along the Salween River, the fathers ended up
working with several other ethnic groups beyond Tibetans, in particular
Lisu, Naxi, and Nu.

Little has been published on the MEP's direct work in Yunnan and
Tibet beyond primary missionary sources written in French.[3] Two MEP

priests who wrote extensively about their time in the region were Auguste Desgodins and, later, Goré, who spent over forty years in the Sino-Tibetan borderlands stationed as vicar-general at Cizhong. Both published monographs detailing the history of the mission and their experiences, as well as contributed to Bible translations into Tibetan. Some of the fathers published accounts of geography and local culture in European journals, although little was included about their own involvement in agriculture and botany (C. H. Desgodins 1872; Goré 1939).[4] Much more, however, has been written about the later work of the Saint Bernard fathers, primarily due to their hospice-building project on caravan routes between the Mekong and the Salween in the Yunnan-Burma-Tibet border. These Swiss missionaries have also been made well known because of Tornay's murder by Tibetan lamas following his expulsion from Yanjing in the late 1940s and his attempt to travel to Lhasa to plead his case directly to the Dalai Lama. This was essentially a suicide mission, and Tornay's compatriots pleaded with him not to undertake the trip. For his martyrdom, Tornay was posthumously granted sainthood by Pope John Paul II in 1992 (Bonet 2006; Bray 2014; Croidys 1949; Dickinson 2012; Loup 1956).

Viticulture and Winemaking in Tibet

Local references to wine, whether among contemporary villagers in Cizhong, in a variety of tourism promotion materials, or in wine company advertising, suggest that the French introduced grapes and wine to Cizhong and other Catholic villages in the region. Material in the MEP and Saint Bernard Mission archives in Paris and Martigny, Switzerland, suggests that one French father, Emile Cyprien Monbeig, may have introduced viticulture on a very small scale in the early twentieth century. It was then practiced more widely during the 1930s and 1940s by the Saint Bernard priests ("Émile Monbeig, 1876–1942," n.d.). Although this crop and drink were not traditionally grown and consumed in this part of Tibet and China in large quantities, or used in ritual prior to Western introduction, other historical material suggests that grapes and wine existed on a small scale in the Sino-Tibetan borderlands before the French or Swiss arrived. Having thoroughly examined both Tibetan- and Chinese-language sources, the Tibetan historian Rolf Alfred Stein noted the following about grapes and wine in Tibet, with particular attention to the borderland region of Batang around Yunnan and Sichuan in the Kham region of Tibet and not far from the mission stations in Kangding and Yanjing:

> In the eighteenth century, white grapes were grown at Batang (along with pomegranates, peaches, plums, and nectarines), at Draya and Ngemda (where nuts were also to be had), and south of Lhasa at Chunggye (in addition to nuts and bamboos). The Jesuit missionaries who settled in Lhasa at the beginning of the eighteenth century used Dakpo grapes to make their sacramental wine. As early as 1374 the . . . Chaori district of Kham boasted 350 families whose long established profession was the production of wine from grapes. Tibetans nowadays only use the grape in raisin form, as a sweetmeat, their customary alcoholic drink being barley-beer (*chang*). But for the Bonpo ritual described in ancient manuscripts (ninth or tenth century), a fermentation of wheat was used, with another of grapes, a third of rice and a fourth of honey. The treasury of the eighth-century king Trhisong Detsen contained, according to a fairly old chronicle, an alcoholic beverage made of rice from the land of Mon (Himalayas) and another made of grapes from Tshawa(-rong). (1972, 25)

Perhaps at an earlier time grapes and grape wine had some level of use in Tibetan culture, even for ritual, although, as Stein suggests, these uses involved indigenous Bön (pre-Buddhist animistic religion), rather than Buddhist, rituals. What is known from oral histories collected in Cizhong today and the accounts of the French and Swiss fathers is that wild grapes in Tibet were supplemented with introduced varieties in wine production. This practice indeed melded well with earlier indigenous practices around Batang and Chaori in Kham, as described by Stein (1972). One missionary account from 1906 in the MEP archives observes this tradition in a village named Gunra, near Batang. Father Monbeig (1906) noted that wild grape vines were abundant and that families had actively cultivated these and made wine but had ceased the practice to focus on growing grain to fulfill tribute payments to local monasteries. Auguste Desgodins also observed wild grape cultivation and winemaking in this same region along the Mekong River in the mid-nineteenth century: "There are also various places where they make wine; we encountered vineyards a dozen-or-so days march south of Tcha-mou-to . . . above the Lancang River; the vine is never pruned and grows in trellises of large poles placed vertically and horizontally to support it" (C. H. Desgodins 1872, 291).

Monbeig (1906) translated the village name Gunra from Tibetan into French as "*enceinte de vigne*," literally "enclosure of vines." This is a rather liberal translation, however. *Gun* in Tibetan means "grape," and "Gunra" might more accurately be phrased as something like "Grape Garden," which matches oral histories I gathered in Cizhong with Liao, a devout Catholic and charismatic eighty-eight-year-old half-Han half-Tibetan man, who is a well-known local historian. A linguist working on Tibetan dialects in Northwest Yunnan has told me that, interestingly, the word *gun* seems to be a part of the indigenous vernacular only in places such as the Batang area, where grapes grow wild. In Northwest Yunnan, where the word was never part of local vernaculars, the term for grape, *putao*, has been borrowed from Chinese.

Catholic Missionary Agriculture and Local Landscape Impressions

The Catholic fathers engaged in viticulture, producing wine for the Eucharistic ritual and their own personal enjoyment. Liao, one of the few elders in Cizhong who remembers the French and Swiss, points out that, ironically, for all the interest in wine in Cizhong today, the fathers shared with villagers little of what they produced, drinking most of it themselves. Oral histories, archival materials, and my observations show that the Catholic fathers interacted extensively with the local agricultural landscape, introducing a variety of plants such as grape vines and also collecting

hundreds of plants and sending them back to Europe as herbarium spec-
imens. A Victorian infatuation with Chinese plants followed, prompting
European and American institutions to send professional "plant hunters,"
including Forrest and, perhaps most famously, Joseph F. Rock, to procure
plant material and seeds so that the plant varieties originally collected
by the French fathers could be introduced for gardening.[5] Although the
explorers and plant hunters have received much attention, the original
botanical work of the Catholic fathers was considerable, and yet these
men have gone largely unrecognized for their contribution (Kilpatrick
2015). A major exception was the Lazarist Père Armand David, who not
only made extensive botanical collections but was also the first Westerner
to "discover" the panda during his time as a professional plant and animal
specimen collector in the Tibetan areas of western Sichuan.

Viticulture was one of many agricultural and landscape-inspired activities in which the Swiss missionaries of Great Saint Bernard engaged.
Their recollections about the local environment, the geography, and the
feelings invoked by the landscape of Tibet were vivid and provide useful
ethnographic understanding of the region during their time (Kilpatrick
2015; Loup 1956). These men had already been mountain dwellers in the
Alps, where they were avid skiers and climbers, some perhaps even of
professional caliber; Pope Pius XI named Saint Bernard of Menthon the
patron saint of mountain climbing in 1923. Many of the men had grown
up in the mountainous Valais region of Switzerland in communities that,
like those in Yunnan and Tibet, were agropastoral. Valais is also perhaps
Switzerland's most famous and oldest region for wine and viticulture,
dating back into prehistory, with much of early winemaking conducted
by Catholic priests—a fitting place to learn the winemaking craft, given
the similar terrain and altitude of Yunnan (Wallace 2014; Zufferey-Perisset
2010).

The Valais native Louis Duc has been described as greatly enjoying his
time as a caravanner who traveled all around northwestern Yunnan and
oversaw the gardens and orchards planted in Weixi, along with caring for

domestic animals (Loup 1956, 93). Maurice Tornay and his compatriots viewed the agropastoral and mountain landscapes of Northwest Yunnan in deep wonder and adoration for their majesty and provision of religious solitude, perhaps reminiscent of the priests' homelands in Valais. Of their travels along the Mekong, he writes:

> The river roars like far-off thunder. Traces or outlines of villages seem to people this valley which the river has dug out between steep sides, without caring about men, as though it wanted to reserve this part of the earth for itself. The animals trot to the singing of the birds. Walnut trees furnish cool damp shade. You forget everything and expect nothing and would not be surprised if you saw the veil between God and us ripped apart. And you understand a little the well-being of souls in nirvana. (Loup 1956, 84–85)

Tornay continues in a letter home:

> The country is magnificent: limitlessly white unknown mountains, woods, little plains, slopes and crags, all unite to give an impression of unimaginable strength and beauty. It hardly ever rains here. The wind blows very hard. The fields produce barley and buckwheat; the gardens: potatoes, pear trees that bear dry fruit, and apple trees. (Loup 1956, 140)

In analyzing the works and writings of the Swiss fathers, Robert Loup notes their keen ethnographic and geographical observations:

> The Tsechung [Cizhong] region along the twenty-eighth parallel was an ethnic and climatic boundary. The people basically were Tibetans and Tibetanized Chinese. The climate was dry; the high massives of the Khwakarpo [T: Khawa Karpo] and the Pema [Ch: Baima] to the north held back the rains, and on the other hand, the strong winds kept the monsoons from driving the clouds that far. (1956, 140)

Father Tornay adds a few strokes to this picture:

Suddenly a flock of crows—very black crows—fly across the blue sky. You hear them before you see them. It seems that their cawing never leaves your ears because you will not hear anything else all day long. An antelope, a deer may go by; but they go by silently, without bothering anyone. That long straight line of trodden grass where you see pebbles and horseshoe marks is the trail, the main trail. . . . Tibet is solitude itself, a solitude that makes you afraid, for nothing else brings us so near to God. Can we approach God and not be afraid? (Loup 1956, 142)

Collecting plants and animals for the scientific endeavors of the West and writing about their interactions with the landscape and people were not the only ways the French and Swiss fathers interacted with the local landscape and environment. Though viticulture was of primary interest, the introduction of other food crops was also a major project. As early as the time of the MEP's first mission station in Bonga, Renou and his colleagues brought potatoes and cabbage, which persisted sixty years later, as observed by Goré (Bray 1995; Goré 1939; Lim 2009). Part of the Swiss missionaries' project involved active work on the high passes of the caravan routes between the Mekong and the Salween. In addition to building a hospice modeled after the Saint Bernard Hospice on a pass downstream from Cizhong, they improved trails and set up a small hut on the high pass directly above Cizhong leading to Catholic villages along the upper Salween. This stone structure, along with other religious markers, remains on the trekking route, with the hut affectionately called "the church" by local villagers. Even Rock (1947), who generally despised missionaries and their work, commended the MEP priest stationed in Baihanlo (formerly known as Bahang) on the Salween side of the pass, Père Georges André, for his work with the Saint Bernard fathers and villagers in improving and constructing a good trail leading from the pass down to the village. Rock also mentioned how many of the Swiss would regularly cross these high passes in the middle of winter (via skis), something few locals even today attempt.

FIGURE 4. Georges André working with villagers on trail improvement, circa 1930s.
Courtesy of Maison hospitalière du Grand-Saint-Bernard, Médiathèque Valais.

Local village elders in Cizhong and nearby areas who knew some of the French and Swiss fathers told me similar stories, indicating that both food crops and ornamental plants introduced by the missionaries were extensive. In Cizhong, Liao spoke of the impact the fathers had on the landscape and all the plants they introduced, including grapes, noting that many of the plants people in the community take for granted today came from the missionaries. Liao explained that the French fathers introduced grapes, apples, and eucalyptus, which was used for treating malaria. André planted two *mu* of grapes in Cizhong. According to Liao, missionaries planted grapes after they arrived in 1882 because they desired wine to use in their services. Liao also indicated that the French brought grapes overland from Vietnam and Tibet (via Yanjing). Archival sources confirm this interview-based information. It is also possible that grapes could have come from Vietnam via southern Yunnan, where the French built a railway connecting Vietnam with Kunming. This border area in southern Yunnan also included a strong MEP missionary presence (Michaud 2007). Grapes arrived in Yanjing, upstream in today's Tibetan Autonomous Region, before they did in Cigu and Cizhong, with missionaries who came from the north and then traveled down the Lancang (Mekong) River. Along this route they also discovered the village known as Gunra, or Grape Garden, where they found that Tibetans had historically grown grapes and made wine.

Today in Yanjing there is an active practice of winemaking based on the French and Swiss history, similar to what has emerged in Cizhong (Z. Li 2011). Rose Honey grapes, a varietal introduced by the French or the Swiss, or both, were first brought to Cigu and later to Cizhong, when the church there was rebuilt. The Catholic fathers also improved trails from Cizhong to Dimaluo (on the Salween) and from Yongzhi (upstream from Cizhong and where today a road is being built to replace the old trekking route) to Dimaluo. Liao also laments that today the church has no vineyard of its own. The original vineyard was a church asset, but after the government expelled the fathers in 1951, it took control of the vineyards. Today the government allows the church to own land, but this does not

FIGURE 5. The Cizhong church, 2013. The cabernet sauvignon vineyards were planted in recent years by the Deqin County agricultural bureau.

include any vineyards, which remain under the authority of the county forestry bureau. Villagers would like to get land back for the church so it can own its vineyards. Liao says passionately, "Wherever there is a cathedral, there is a vineyard."

With respect to agriculture in Cizhong more broadly, Liao explained that before "new China" (the communist era) and before the missionaries, only rice was grown in the paddy fields due to a local superstition about water leaking out if other crops were planted there. People did grow barley, corn, and buckwheat but not in the same fields as the rice. Today villagers use those fields for rice in the summer and other crops during the winter. Liao stated that in addition to grapes, the French fathers introduced eucalyptus trees, tomatoes, camphor trees, potatoes, and plantain lily (Ch: *yuzan hua*), a white flower "as pure as Christ." They also planted palms and banana trees in the churchyard.

Another elder, an eighty-five-year-old who interacted with the French and Swiss living in the downstream village of Badong, recalled about plants and landscape changes:

The fathers brought all sorts of seeds here to plant: corn, potatoes, ficus trees, grapes, pears, apples, and many kinds of flowers. The road from Cizhong to Dimaluo existed long before the fathers, but Father An [Georges André] repaired the road in the 1930s [approximately] to make it much better to travel. This father also helped to set zip lines and boat routes along the Nujiang [Salween], where he lived. When I was eighteen years old, I traveled over the road to the Nujiang together with a nineteen-year-old father, working as his assistant. The fathers here just planted grapes in the church grounds and kept them mostly for themselves, not really giving them out to villagers. The grapes were also lost when lamas burned and destroyed the churches. Even in Cizhong, the fathers did not really give away grape plants or teach about winemaking. Since I was an assistant to a father, I did, however, learn to make wine.

Missionary Records and Written Accounts of Viticulture and Winemaking

Other than the Desgodins brothers' (C. H. Desgodins 1872) and Emile Cyprien Monbeig's (1906) accounts about wild grapes and local Tibetan winemaking in Gunra, there are few written records by the MEP fathers on this practice or the introduction of grapes. An exception is Monbeig's biography in the MEP archives, which mentions that he introduced grape vines to Tibet from his family's French estate. Interestingly, Monbeig's brother, Théodore Jean Monbeig, who was also a MEP missionary in Tibet, oversaw the construction of the church at Cizhong in 1909 after the original church in Cigu was destroyed (Saint Macary, n.d.). Given that his brother introduced family wine grapes, perhaps he planted the first vines in Cizhong, although there is no proof of this. There are, however, extensive accounts—about both the introduction of Swiss grape varietals from the Valais winemaking region and actual winemaking among the Saint Bernard fathers in the 1930s and 1940s—in the Saint Bernard archives and in writings chronicling the work of these fathers. The historian Pierre Croidys described the following:

The "new" Fathers of the Tibetan marches were not just a little surprised to see that the grape vine they knew from home, the cep valaisan, could grow at their station! Father Coquoz was very proud of the results, and, in Siao-Weisi [Xiao Weixi], he was able to have his colleagues admire twelve grape bunches! But in Tsechung [Cizhong], Father Lovey encountered a little vineyard that was going to prosper so much that, in the following years, the harvest would permit the production of more than 600 liters of good wine. The Valais vine, too, had managed to settle on Tibetan soil. (1949, 153–54)

Another historian, André Bonet, provides a similar account based on archival work, noting the introduction of Valais grapes, their mixture with wild varietals, and again the role of the Valais, Father Coquoz, as the winemaker:

At the mission, the priests make wine. The wild grape vine grows everywhere. There are white grapes and red grapes, but most taste quite bitter. The vine grows at the bottom of the valleys, and wraps itself around birch, pine and ash trees that fill the landscape.

When they left the Grand-Saint-Bernard, they brought with them, in iron chests lined with damp moss, about fifty vine cuttings, each stuck into a potato so that they could survive the journey.

Father Coquoz, like a true son of a grape grower from the Valais, takes care of the plants. He mixes them with vines from inner Tibet and wild grape vines. Everything will prosper at it pleases, and in less than two years, he will harvest from the fruit of his "vineyard" about two hundred liters of wine, and he will save a small quantity for sacramental wine. (Bonet 2006, 161)

Materials in the Saint Bernard Mission archives shed further light on the fathers' practices of viticulture and winemaking in Tibet. One factual correction to Bonet's account seems to have been lost in translation: Coquoz did not mix the vines but rather grafted Valais varieties, brought from Switzerland in a shipment of potatoes, onto the root stock of the local wild vines or older vines, perhaps introduced by Monbeig, to make them more adaptable to the climate (Glarey 2009, 58). Father Marie Melly (1944, 1947), the on-site director of the order of priests, published two extensive articles on the successes and experience of growing grapes and making wine in Tibet, one for the mission's biannual review publication, *Grand-Saint-Bernard-Thibet* (later *Mission du Grand-Saint-Bernard*), and the other for the technical journal *Agricole Valais*. Several other mentions of viticulture and winemaking are scattered throughout the many letters written by the fathers chronicling their experiences and in shorter passages in articles in the mission review and other dispatches published by the priests before the official periodical began publication in 1946. One article from 1948 concerns making wine for Mass and lists the total production of wine for the year 1947 as 660 liters of 9.5 percent alcohol wine, with the individual amounts produced by each father and mission station:

Weixi (C. Lattion): 150 liters
Xiaoweixi (P. Coquoz): 250 liters
Cizhong (A. Lovey): 250 liters
Hualuoba (L. Duc): 10 liters

Preceding these figures are descriptions of the difficulties, successes, and necessities of producing wine for Mass at the time:

It is a big deal in these remote areas to have wine for Mass. The reserves we made before the war [World War II] are exhausted. With a lack of money, buying new wine is impossible. Besides, how to transport it? There are a thousand chances that the wine would spill out or turn into water. That is why the culture of the vine in the Tibetan marches is of paramount importance for missionaries. Thanks to the patience and tenacity of Father Coquoz and Friar Duc, the first vines have grown on the borders of Tibet, and the sacramental wine is henceforth assured.

FIGURE 6. Angelin Lovey working in the Cizhong vineyard, circa 1940s.
Courtesy of Maison hospitalière du Grand-Saint-Bernard, Mèdiathèque Valais.

Want to see the reports on the production of the Tibetan vineyards? Do not forget that for nearly three months, the rain has fallen
almost continuously. A veritable deluge. Despite this, we can say
that our wine growers could compete with the cooperative cellars.
("Les missionnaires vous donnent des nouvelles" 1948, 29)

These archives also include photos of Father Angelin Lovey (figure 6) working in the vineyards at Cizhong, which remain today in the
churchyard, and another of Friar Duc (figure 7), the gardener whom
Loup (1956) described, working in the vineyards at Weixi. In one of his
letters, Duc wrote about the care that must be taken in growing grapes:
"Certainly the wine will not be as good as the Fendant of 1945, but you
must be content with both the quality and quantity when making wine"
(Glarey 2009, 58). In articles written for a column published in each issue
of the review, Vicar-General Goré (1946a, 1946b) provided dispatches

FIGURE 7. Louis Duc working in the Weixi vineyards, circa 1940s. Courtesy of Maison hospitalière du Grand-Saint-Bernard, Médiathèque Valais.

from Cizhong, noting how Lovey, his assistant at the time, was success-fully producing good grapes (in spite of the grapes' fragility, caused by the sometimes cold climate) and how much the two of them enjoyed drinking kegs of this wine together, which he aptly named Le Clos Lovey after its maker.

Earlier in Lovey's own winemaking years, in a 1942 letter home to his parents in the agricultural community of Orsières, he described the suc-cess of Coquoz's viticulture and winemaking. He mentioned how Coquoz had recently provided him with some of his own vines to grow in Cizhong and that they had begun to fair well. To his amazement, Coquoz's wine was already comparable to some of the best back home in Valais:

> About Mr. Coquoz, I forgot to tell you something extraordinary: it is that he is becoming the country's largest vine merchant. As he planted the vines, he could not be sure what would happen or if he'd be fortunate due to the environment.... But, it would seem that the vines are promising this year, and in the small vineyard in Xiao Weixi, the father produces no fewer than 20 bottles! ... After an old missionary passed through and left some plants, which have grown wild in Xiao Weixi, Coquoz began to work with this kind of varietal, and each of the past four years has been unprecedented. It is easy to see that in 10 years, ORSAT [one of Valais's oldest and most famous wine families] himself can no longer fight against Coquoz & Co. cellars.... Father Coquoz, however, is not jealous with his secret! One year ago, he sent me some vines, which have grown nearly 3 meters in height since that time. The vitality of this plant is extraordinary, and the grapes are much less subject to disease than the plants brought from Switzerland. Old Valais winemakers, brace yourselves! (Lovey 1942)

Goré (1943) wrote, regarding growing grapes in Cizhong: "With his ex-tensive experience, Father Coquoz has given full winemaking instruction to Father Lovey, who became a brilliant emulator and is now becoming a formidable competitor."

It is difficult to tell from these passages, though, whether Coquoz grafted Valais grapes onto wild varieties or perhaps onto a variety introduced earlier by Monbeig of the MEP. Indeed, Lovey suggests that Monbeig was the source of the vines that are found in Cizhong today ("Analyse de vin, Cépè de Bacot" 1999). In the photo of Duc working in the vineyards (figure 7), the large leaves on the vines differ from those of most wine grapes, such as cabernet sauvignon, and match those of the Rose Honey varietal grown in Cizhong today. These accounts reveal that, contrary to recollections of elders today, the Swiss fathers produced wine for more than distribution in small quantities as a sacrament in Catholic Mass, although how much was shared with locals is unknown. This conforms with Loup's (1956) depictions of these fathers' devotion to their cause as well as their enjoyment of limited comforts, which included drinking mission wine and also smoking tobacco pipes (figure 9). With respect to sacramental wine, on display in the treasury of the Saint Bernard Hospice today are a gold chalice and matching paten with Tibetan artwork and calligraphy (figure 10), commissioned by the fathers from a local Tibetan artist in Yunnan as a gift for their newly named head of congregation, Provost Nestor Adam, in 1939 (Voutaz and Rouyer 2014a, 2014b).

Today in Cizhong, where the 1909 church still stands, a Han priest from Inner Mongolia, sent by the Patriotic Catholic Association of China, leads in prayer village households that have maintained their Catholic beliefs.[6] Before 2008, the village had no priest, and no formal Masses took place after 1952, when the government expelled the remaining French and Swiss Christians. Villagers nonetheless practiced their religion and began to pray openly in the 1980s. In addition to Catholicism, the grape vines the French and Swiss fathers planted within the walled churchyard persisted, despite neglect and no active cultivation. These grapes, introduced by the fathers, found in the churchyard, and now growing in the fields of some

FIGURE 8. Rose Honey grapes and vines. The leaves are larger than those of the cabernet sauvignon and other varieties more typically grown in the region.

FIGURE 9. Swiss priests drinking and smoking pipes, circa 1930s or 1940s. Courtesy of Maison hospitalière du Grand-Saint-Bernard, Médiathèque Valais.

FIGURE 10. Tibetan chalice and paten from 1939 in the Saint
Bernard Hospice Treasury. The decorative motifs are Tibetan
in style like those commonly found in both religious and
nonreligious Tibetan paintings and sculptures.

Cizhong households, are the varietal today called Rose Honey. This hardy
and disease-resistant *Vitis* cultivar is thought to contain at least some
DNA from the wine species *vinifera* hybridized with *labrusca*, though its
definitive origin is still unknown (Dangl 2011; Mustacich 2015). Assumed
to be of missionary introduction and previously grown in Europe, it was
wiped out, various experts suggest, in the mid-nineteenth century in

Europe by an infestation of phylloxera (an aphid-like insect) introduced from the United States and is thus extinct in Europe. By a twist of fate, it still exists in Yunnan.

Much of what is known about Rose Honey and its origins is speculation and guesswork. Gerald Dangl (2011), a grape DNA expert, emphasizes that it is difficult to verify where this plant came from and when. Further complicating the question is that the most definitive writings about the French or Swiss introducing grapes to Tibet and Yunnan date to the 1930s, long after the phylloxera crisis decimated Europe's vineyards. Another opinion, suggested to me by a contemporary Swiss Valais winemaker with his own boutique vineyards and winery in Yunnan, is that this grape found in Cizhong today is not from Switzerland or Europe at all, but perhaps was brought by missionaries from Korea or Japan. We also know that the Saint Bernard fathers grafted Valais vines onto local wild rootstock or earlier French-introduced rootstock, which would further complicate DNA identification. The exact timeline or origin of Rose Honey and its introduction remains undetermined. Local tales among both villagers and wineries continue to trace this grape back to French origin and as being extinct in France, despite evidence to the contrary. This is largely because such a story lends itself well to mythmaking and creating a unique terroir for Cizhong wines.

Adding further intrigue to the story of the Rose Honey grapes supposedly introduced by the missionaries and found in the churchyard is a document in the Saint Bernard archives that was written by Father Lovey during the 1990s, when he was serving as the provost of the order of priests. The document describes how a younger priest who visited Cizhong collected a sample of grape vines, took the sample to Taiwan, and from there sent it back to Lovey in Switzerland. Lovey then sent the sample to a viticulture lab in Italy, which described the vine's usefulness for making wine as good. In this document, which includes the order form sent by Lovey to the lab, he mentions that the vine came from Cizhong, and specifically from a vine first introduced to Tibet by Monbeig. This is surprising given that Lovey and his fellow priests brought many vines from Switzerland to Tibet themselves. One wonders what led Lovey to believe this was an older vine introduced by Monbeig to Cizhong ("Analyse de vin, Cépè de Bacot" 1999).

When I described the characteristics of Rose Honey vines to a priest at the Saint Bernard archives, who was himself a viticulture expert, winemaker, and relative of Tornay, he indicated that the vine almost definitely sounded like a Valais varietal introduced to Tibet and hybridized with a North American species of grape to make it resistant against phylloxera. A final suggestion and guess, from a contemporary Chinese viticulturist working with a French winery near Cizhong and experimenting with Rose Honey, is that it arose from the cultivar Baco Noir. Baco Noir fits the description from the priest in Martigny of the vine being something hybridized to withstand phylloxera. It was developed in 1894 in southwestern France by François Baco, who hybridized *Vitis vinifera* with the North American species *Vitis riparia* to make it more resistant to phylloxera from North America (Wine-Searcher 2022). Today, for many Cizhong villagers, Rose Honey grapes and vines provide a seeming connection to the community's missionary Catholic past and a means of reconnecting with this history. But is Rose Honey the "true" grape left behind by the Swiss and perhaps the French before them? I do not have a definitive answer, but within the larger context of Shangri-La, the sense of localized Tibetan Catholic identity that these grapes provide to Cizhong people is quite strong.

Transitioning to Wine and Vineyards in Cizhong Today

For the missionaries, at least initially for the French in Cizhong, wine was essential for conducting Catholic Mass. Later, for the Swiss, the functions of wine seem to have changed, in some ways providing a foundation for the role it plays in life in Cizhong Village today. For the Swiss, including Coquoz and Lovey, growing grapes and making wine seems to have become more of a recreational activity that produced large enough quantities for personal enjoyment and consumption in addition to sacramental use. Cizhong villagers today draw on the history of these Swiss missionaries in their winemaking practices, marketing, and production. Many elders maintain that wine's first and most important role is for ritual or Catholic Mass, but younger generations highlight the role of winemaking as an economic activity and wine drinking as recreational and cultural—in taste appreciation and terroir making.

CHAPTER 2

Landscape Change, Tibetan Identity, and Terroir in Cizhong Village

Between the river and the mountain slope extended a narrow platform along which a few huts were scattered from Tsu-kou [Cigu] to Tsu-chung [Cizhong]. Below Tsu-chung rice is cultivated, this being the last village on the Mekong where it is known, for immediately to the north the climate changes abruptly. With the climate and the want of rice the people change also; there are no more Mosos or Lissus now, only Tibetans, and such Chinese merchants as have settled at the big trading centres.

The platform just referred to however, which is only a few hundred yards wide, does not represent all the cultivation, for the slopes of the first hill range have to a large extent been cleared of their open pine woods and rhododendron scrub, and here are raised crops of wheat and barley. It is wonderful to see the Tibetans ploughing these hill sides with bullocks drawing the wooden plough, which is so light that the man picks it up at the end of the day's work and walks home with it.

Frank Kingdon Ward, on the landscape of Cizhong in 1911

Driving south through the Mekong River valley from the county seat of Deqin, one sees the dry shrubbery of the canyon walls that tower up into alpine mountains and forests miles above. Along either side of the river, Tibetan hamlets clutch the hillsides with homes and vineyards carved out of the mountains, leaving one to wonder how and why anyone ever chose to live so precariously, eking out an existence on the side of precipitous cliffs in this narrow, dry landscape. Living here must not be easy, I sensed the first time I saw this place. An hour or so downstream, the view and environment suddenly change. The canyon widens out, and across the river from the main highway sits the large table of land described by Ward in 1911. The environment also changes, from brown, arid, almost desert-looking vegetation to green forested hillsides along either side of the river. On the plateau across and several hundred feet above the river sit over two hundred houses built in a style melding the whitewashed walls of Tibetan homes upstream with the arched roofs found in Naxi and Lisu homes to the south. In the middle of all these houses and rising above the rest of the village is a church built in a Chinese style, with a bell tower and two palm trees. Encircling the church are large eucalyptus and camphor trees, and surrounding the entire community are verdant rice paddies unlike the fields in any other Tibetan community I have visited. Interspersed within the paddy fields and upslope of the village plateau are rows of vineyards.

When I first came to Cizhong Village in the summer of 2013, I arrived across the Mekong River and was taken by my local driver down a bumpy, dusty dirt road to the riverbank, where one needed to drive across a metal suspension bridge before climbing up the opposite bank to the village plateau. That day, the local Chinese anthropologist friend who had accompanied me told our driver to drop us off at a large community building by the riverside. As we stepped out of our minivan after the long rough ride down the mountains and along the river, a Tibetan elder wearing a blue Mao cap stepped forward to greet us. My friend introduced him as Wu Gongdi, and he shook my hand. He explained that the community had gathered for the funeral of a friend of his who had lived there by the river. He invited us to join and observe as well as share in the meal that would be served to everyone. As we entered the building, the villagers were chanting a song softly in Tibetan language, with lyrics and intonation unlike anything I had ever heard before. I would later learn that the chants, which sound like Gregorian chants, were Tibetan translations of European Catholic songs and rosaries, used for events such as the funeral that day as well as during regular Sunday Masses in the church. After a delicious lunch of several meat and vegetable dishes served alongside steamed rice, we walked with Wu Gongdi and his adult son, Hong Xing, further along the road and up the mountainside, past the bridge, to their home. This place would become a regular residence for me over the next several years as I learned about the family's and the community's history, winemaking, and other agricultural practices.

Cizhong Life and Winemaking Today

In Cizhong, villagers are reworking the agricultural landscape and life with widespread household grape growing and winemaking, a newly emergent industry that relates to the village's Catholicism and history. Although elders such as Liao, introduced in chapter 1, indicate that the original vines were mostly restricted to the churchyards, and winemaking knowledge was never passed on to a large number of villagers, this past has not prevented a reworking of local agricultural practices and identities. Villagers describe the practice of growing grapes and making wine as both historically important and even expected as part of being a Tibetan person living in Cizhong Village, applying to not only Catholic households but Buddhist ones as well.

According to most accounts, the contemporary interest of villagers and the community in growing grapes and making wine was first initiated by Wu Gongdi in 1998.[1] This was one reason why my anthropologist friend brought me to meet him and arranged for me to stay in his home. Wu Gongdi told me that what inspired him to take cuttings from Rose Honey vines in the churchyard to plant his own vineyards and then make his own wine was that, before, wherever there was a missionary, there was a vineyard, and to have a proper Catholic Mass one needs to have wine. For him, especially as the director of the church management association and, at that time, a lay spiritual leader, not having wine meant that religiously and culturally, life in Cizhong was incomplete. Additionally, with a burgeoning tourist interest in Cizhong, coupled with the beginning years of tourism promotion across greater Shangri-La, making wine to serve to tourists as a way of sharing local history seemed to him a good idea.

Wu Gongdi explains in two documentaries made in the early 2000s (one filmed by him and his son with the assistance of Yunnan academics) that his interest in producing wine is also connected with rising concerns over health and naturalness in China. As an alternative to hard grain liquor (*baijiu*), people in China are increasingly turning to grape wine for its healthful qualities and, in the case of Wu Gongdi's wine, because it is organic. In a memorable vignette from *Christmas Eve in Cizhong, Cizhong Red Wine* (Cizhong shengdan ye, Cizhong hong jiu), the documentary Wu Gongdi and Hong Xing co-produced with another villager, father and son perform a drinking song about the health and religious benefits of their wine (Liu 2002). Before the song is sung, the entire family discusses their potential future economic gains from the grapes they have begun to grow and the wine they are making, and they also toast with the family's grandmother, wishing her a long life from drinking their new healthy grape wine. After I transcribed this song from the film for a publication and showed its performance in a lecture, I was told by two other Tibetan studies scholars that the song is in fact a traditional Tibetan drinking song reworked with a Catholic theme. The lyrics' edits represent the melding of Catholicism with Tibetan identity and folk custom and illustrate the role that wine and winemaking has played in this process and transformation.

Ah, wine! Beautiful fragrant wine!
Ah, wine! Sweet dew that makes men happy!
Plant a grapevine in the lands of Cizhong,
Present the first glass of sweet grape wine to Almighty God,

Take the last glass of clear and fragrant grape wine for ourselves and play a game.

To ensure that the production of his wine used the traditional methods employed by the missionaries, Wu Gongdi traveled upstream to Yanjing in 1997 to learn about winemaking from his grandmother's sister, who was a Catholic nun. He insists these methods are limited to his family, though other villagers in Cizhong often say he boasts too much and that everyone now uses these winemaking methods. Following Wu Gongdi's lead, by around 2002–4, most families in Cizhong had begun planting grapes and making wine using Rose Honey cuttings, seeing the potential market and success that selling wine as a historical product from Cizhong's landscape could provide. Compared to corporate and state-based wine projects, winemaking in Cizhong is a grassroots, individual agentive response to modern economies and markets that draws on the community's history and identity as Tibetan Catholic people within the larger landscape of Shangri-La. Cizhong people have created a unique niche for themselves within Shangri-La, indigenizing and adapting to modernity.

Villagers in Cizhong have developed an identity based on their wine and vineyard landscape and on the place they are believed to occupy within Shangri-La as Catholics fitting into the myth that Hilton's *Lost Horizon* created of Tibetan Buddhists and Catholics living side by side. Some people in Cizhong, including Wu Gongdi, are familiar with the novel through readily available Chinese translations and apply it to their lives in turn. Buddhist and Catholic households for the most part live peacefully together, participating in each other's festivals, often intermarrying, and both taking part in viticulture, despite occasional conflicts and misunderstandings. There is no doubt that grapes and wine are a foreign introduction, and most villagers themselves freely admit this, but Catholic villagers, when asked, often assert that wine is cultural and a ritual item for them as Catholic Tibetan people and also because of Cizhong's history and religious ritual practices, coupled with new Shangri-La tourism. As Wu Gongdi and other villagers have remarked:

Wine is important to local culture because it is needed for Catholic Mass, and this ritual can't take place without wine. Wherever there

is a cathedral, there is a vineyard. Wine is not for play—it is for ritual. (Liao)

Cizhong is a big name in local Tibetan culture and lore. Before,
wine and grapes were not part of Tibetan culture, but now they are
because everyone knows about our winemaking. (Village farmer)

After the Chinese government kicked out the Catholic fathers,
there was no more wine, but there were still grapes here. In 1997, I
traveled to Yanjing to visit a relative of mine who is a nun to learn
about making wine. She learned from the Catholic fathers. I think
Catholic culture is part of Tibetan culture, so wine is also part of
Tibetan culture. But you also can't talk about wine without talking
about Catholic Mass. The fathers who were here even learned to
speak Tibetan, and I think this also makes wine part of Tibetan
identity here. (Wu Gongdi)

These comments suggest that wine and vineyards are a part of Tibetan
culture and identity in Cizhong for three reasons: history, religion, and,
now with the development of Shangri-La and tourism, a reputation and
expectation among visitors and villagers that Cizhong's landscape includes
the original French church and accompanying vineyards. Consequently,
according to many villagers, every household should also have homemade
"French technique" (*Faguo gongyi*) wine to serve to visitors. Without
that, they are not proper hosts, nor are they fulfilling their identities as
Cizhong people, even though the vineyards and winemaking were never
as extensive in the past as they are today. The sociologist Francis Khek Gee
Lim, who conducted ethnographic work in Cizhong, comments on local
villagers' new identities as a result of wine in the context of exoticizing
Shangri-La: "In an interesting way, the increasing commercialization of
wine production has discursively facilitated the inscription of a 'foreign
religion' into the local tradition of the Catholic Tibetan areas, through an
advertising narrative that connects the legacy of the French missionaries
with the exoticism of an earthly paradise in China" (2009, 93).

This discussion helps form a way of thinking about Cizhong, landscape, and identity through terroir, along with other recent forays into rural commodities and value. As Lim explains, Cizhong villagers have taken on the idea that they fulfill a role within the mythmaking surrounding Shangri-La as a touristic "paradise," in that their Catholic religion lends itself well to Hilton's story of Catholics living in Tibet. Creating a unique terroir and story built around the history of the French and Swiss missionaries and their wine provides an avenue through which to directly engage in state "shangrilazation" (Yeh and Coggins 2014a) while simultaneously forming a unique identity as Tibetan Catholic winemakers. In discussing matsutake mushrooms (also found in Yunnan and Deqin), Anna Tsing (2015b) suggests that rural commodities can confer different forms of meaning and value on both those who produce and those who consume them and that more research is necessary on how such value among producers is created. People who collect matsutake and those who consume them or give them as gifts each develop special connections with the commodity and the landscapes in which it grows. For many matsutake collectors the search for the mushroom itself, just as for village winemakers in Cizhong the tending of their grape vines and transforming grapes into wine, becomes a process of self-identification within a larger landscape and system of diversified capitalist commodity chains. For Cizhong people living within the larger landscape of Shangri-La and Tibetan commodification, producing wine as a special commodity with a Catholic historical past confers a unique niche identity on winemakers and the agricultural landscape of vineyards in Cizhong.

In discussing rural vintners and terroir in Burgundy, France, the anthropologist Marion Demossier (2011, 2018) describes terroir making as a twofold process that has evolved into a localized discourse. A similar process is occurring among Cizhong Tibetans. While having previously been used as a legal protection of the geological and geographical uniqueness of French wine on a national scale, terroir, according to Demossier, has been recontextualized by rural vintners today as a process of historical and cultural differentiation within the global economy; terroir provides farmers with a means by which to make themselves distinct even within and among their fellow Burgundians. Through terroir, small-scale local farmers directly identify themselves with their wine through connections to landscape, family histories, and particular methods of production.

As Demossier (2011, 685) explains, the entry into terroir studies by ethnographically focused anthropologists has brought to light new details on production, consumption, and social actors involved in winemaking. Anthropologists ask how wine is given meaning and value by those who make it, referring to terroir as a special ecological and cultural process that brings together actors, their histories, and agricultural practices (686). Burgundian histories reveal ways that terroir can be used to discuss how old histories and landscapes of winemaking are made new and what the roles of history and local agency are in these processes. "Winegrowers," as Demossier refers to them, and people who work in the vineyards in Burgundy are today viewed as "translating" the terroir of the wines they produce into taste and an identity for themselves (697).

A similar process of creation and re-creation of history and producers' identities is taking place with wine in Cizhong. Cizhong wine and household vineyards are designated with terroir-like language (though this is not explicit), with terminology such as "traditional," "natural," "handmade," and "French technique." In fact, while most villagers market their wine as produced using traditional French techniques taught to them by the Catholic fathers, Wu Gongdi's story about how he first learned to make wine from a nun in 1997, along with other oral history accounts, suggests that these marketing claims are slightly inaccurate. Still, the methods of production according to Cizhong villagers are special on historical grounds. The use of Rose Honey grapes gives Cizhong wine a special terroir. Each of these factors helps to tell a good story, which is why the terroir-style packaging and naming of Cizhong wine is so effective at creating attachment and interest in the wine among visitors. Villagers who grow these vines and produce these wines play a role in creating its culturally and regionally defined terroir.

Chinese and foreign tourists who visit Cizhong and purchase wine do so primarily because of the history of colonial Catholicism embedded within the landscape of Cizhong, an inherently "temporal landscape" that brings together village homes, the church and its associated rituals, and history (Ingold 1993, 2000). The creation of a landscape of "dwelling places," as Tim Ingold (2000) calls them, and the commodity of wine that villagers work to meld into it, is inherently historical, formed over two eras. The first was during the nineteenth and early twentieth centuries, when missionaries and villagers built the church still standing today and when missionaries planted the first vineyards. The second began in the early 2000s, when villagers converted large swaths of household farmlands into vineyards.

By planting vineyards and invoking Cizhong's colonial Catholic history, villagers have extended terroir to encompass not only soil, geology, and geography but also cultural and ethnic elements and particular productive practices originally learned from the French and Swiss. In doing so, they are not simply becoming subjects in the state's "mapping of Shangri-La" (Yeh and Coggins 2014a) or its "imagining" of contemporary Tibet's landscape (Smyer Yü 2015). Rather, they play active roles in these state processes of landscape creation while shaping their own image as Cizhong Tibetan people. They create new kinds of localized Tibetan identities through the terroir of their wines and through articulations with new capitalist dynamics surrounding tourism—in particular, touristic imagery associated with their Catholicism and its ties to the Catholicism in Hilton's novel about Shangri-La. Elsewhere in Deqin County, wine and viticulture are primarily state, commercial, and entrepreneurial projects. The state, corporations, and private individuals make wines part of Shangri-La and attempt to give them terroir while relying on the land and labor of village households. In Cizhong, although the state promotes tourism because of the village's Catholic history, the endeavor of making and promoting wine as part of this tourism scheme and simultaneously promoting it as "Tibetan" or "Franco-Tibetan" made has been a village-based undertaking, beginning with Wu Gongdi's efforts in 1997. This is not to say that Tibetan villagers elsewhere lack agency with respect to the state and its viticulture projects. Agency in designing the local economy around grape growing and wine or beer making exists in earnest, but only in Cizhong does this agency involve villagers working to create their own terroir.

Ethnic Minorities and Civilizing

While villagers engage in these efforts largely in response to the "shangri-lazation" occurring around them, they seek to take part in this process on their own terms, through wine production. Liao compares serving visitors butter tea (the ubiquitous Tibetan drink offered throughout the region) to serving them wine: "People like the wine here for its unique history. The French fathers brought wine here, and wine is more civilized than butter tea, and it is getting more and more popular in China. Through wine we can provide a civilized way to welcome tourists into Tibetan culture and to experience it and the region."

"Civilizing" in the context of ethnic minorities and their identities in contemporary China has been a focal point of discussion among anthropologists, and Liao's particular background and history informs his use of this term to describe and think about wine. For hundreds of years through multiple dynasties, China's border regions or "ethnic frontiers" have been contextualized as areas of "difference," in comparison to central Chinese society (Harrell 1996). Minority ethnic groups have historically been contextualized as barbarians, with their status as such often differentiated as "cooked" or "raw" depending on their perceived level of social development or civilized Confucian ethic (Fiskesjö 1999, 2002).

Managing the ethnic groups of these regions has involved the Chinese government's use of what Stevan Harrell (1996) has called "civilizing projects." Harrell groups these into three types: (1) the Confucian project, before 1949, to bring the values of Chinese society, including governance and pragmatism, into the folds of ethnic minority life; (2) Christian projects, also before 1949, in which the Western values of Christianity were introduced; and (3) the communist project of classification of ethnic groups (*minzu*) after 1949. The first two projects assumed the superiority of Chinese or Western values over those of "barbarians." The communist project, which was based lightly on Soviet ideas of social development and the potential of all peoples to obtain the highest level of civilization, was not as explicitly discriminatory. This view conveniently placed the Han majority in the highest level of social and evolutionary development, above other ethnic groups. During the Cultural Revolution (1966–76), however, the communist project took on a more violent and discriminatory tone, especially for ethnic minorities who had historically been associated with foreigners, such as Liao. Since this early contextualization of ethnic minorities and civilizing projects, Harrell (2001) reformulated his analysis to frame all three projects more as "literalizing" or bringing different ethnic groups into the fold of communication with a larger, morally higher world of the Han majority or Western ideals. However, his earlier term "civilizing" has continued to be used more prominently by other scholars. It was also often directly referenced in the Chinese state's vernacular toward managing ethnic minorities, especially during the communist era, likely explaining Liao's use of the term.

Liao experienced two civilizing projects that had a direct impact on his life to a great degree, which, I suggest, has led him to contextualize serving and drinking wine using this form of language and terminology. As a young man, he was very close with the French and Swiss fathers before 1952, working as an assistant in the church, learning to speak both Latin and French, and memorizing various forms of liturgy and hymns. His first round of civilizing at the hands of the Catholic missionaries led to more extreme civilizing during the Cultural Revolution, when he was sent to a labor camp and imprisoned, during which time he was particularly ridiculed for his association with the "evil" foreign missionaries. Given the strength and persistence of his Catholic faith today, it appears that the first civilizing project affected him deeply, although both are perhaps reflected in how he views wine. To him, wine is or becomes the blood of Christ through the sacrament of the Eucharist, and it is this ritual use for wine that remains the most important. However, wine also represents something different from butter tea, and in a communist/socialist development framework that views wine as more civilized, butter tea is associated with a more backward (Tibetan minority) lifestyle. Liao is clear in expressing that he is half-Tibetan and half-Chinese, and his civilizing by the Chinese state may also prompt him to downplay being Tibetan when it comes to wine and butter tea.

Winemaking and Distinction

This idea that wine allows Cizhong villagers to provide a more civilized experience to tourists than other villages in the area can is also an important cue toward distinction in winemaking. Villagers emphasize the unique, authentically "ethnic Tibetan," and rural-household-produced aspects of Cizhong wines. As Wu Gongdi explains: "All the bars and hotels in places like Zhongdian and Lijiang sell fake Rose Honey wine. It's not real. My family has actually received a certificate from the quality bureau of Deqin County stating that our Rose Honey is authentic. People especially also like wine made in Shangri-La because it says minority and homemade. This makes Chinese people more curious and interested in the wine."

"Authentic" (in this case, validated by the state), "organic," and "household made" all contextualize Cizhong wine as having a village terroir. Rose Honey grapes are special historically, due to their stated French (likely Swiss) introduction and preservation within the churchyard, and villagers in Cizhong actively promote their wine as organic and made from Rose Honey grapes. This wine project differs from those of the large corporations taking over village fields throughout the rest of Deqin, where recently introduced cultivars, primarily cabernet sauvignon, are grown, usually with heavy chemical use. Recognizing the difference, Cizhong villagers utilize terroir-style markers of authenticity to define themselves through their wine and the planting of vineyards. In doing so, they highlight what makes them not just Shangri-La Tibetans, but also "religio-ethnic" Catholic Tibetans (Lim 2009). Wine confers on people in Cizhong a newly emergent form of regional ethnic identity within the larger Shangri-La landscape, moderated by economic distinction as winemakers situated within the new dynamics of global capitalism.

For most Tibetan farmers in Shangri-La who sell grapes to wineries, grapes are nothing more than a cash crop and provide a decent income. Similarly, Tibetan winemakers outside of Cizhong produce their wines based predominantly on taste and aesthetics. While taste has become more important in Cizhong to compete with other wineries, Cizhong people believe that their understanding and internalization of their own Catholic history, its blending with Tibetan traditions, and its ties with European winemaking and vineyard care are what distinguish them from other winemakers. As in the sociologist Pierre Bourdieu's (1984) original framing of distinction, this particular form of economic or taste appreciation is developed and cultivated over time. In this case, though, it is distinction based not on learned behavior or taste but rather on unique forms of religion and "being ethnic" (Harrell 2001) within the context of larger state-supported ethnic expression and expansion across Shangri-La.

Sociocultural anthropologists and cultural geographers have produced abundant studies on ethnic identity and cultural diversity in Southwest China. In places such as Yunnan, state-sponsored tourism thrives on minority cultures, along with a variety of other global influences, and has generated ways for ethnic groups to observe and practice their cultural identities within larger China.[2] Certainly, state-promoted tourism has not been entirely beneficial to ethnic minorities, but especially following the reform and opening-up period of the 1980s and 1990s, ethnic groups have located a variety of modes for self-expression within the context of tourism. Land ownership and agricultural relationships and beliefs are also some of the many ways of "being ethnic" (Harrell 2001). Many groups, including Yunnan Tibetans, have also found ways to differentiate themselves among other communities of the same ethnicity, often through tourism. For small ethnic groups who have been classified with other Tibetans, this has allowed them to formulate unique ethnic identities that make them simultaneously Chinese, Tibetan (or another ethnic minority), and indigenous to individual regions, based on specific cultural traits (Jinba 2014).

In the case of Cizhong, such regionally indigenous or ethnic identities form through the production of cultural commodity products. Cizhong wine producers fulfill an ethnic niche with their identity as Yunnan and Shangri-La Tibetans. In Cizhong, producing wine articulates a locally indigenous identity for villagers such as Wu Gongdi (Clifford 2001; T. Li 2000). This articulation differentiates Cizhong people from other Tibetans due both to their Catholicism and to their distinction from those who grow grapes for state and corporate wineries. These processes reconfigure the agricultural livelihoods of all Tibetan villagers in the region, but in Cizhong (and in Bu and Hada Villages, discussed in chapter 3), villagers engage with tourism and economic development–related projects to reformulate them in their own images.

Although Cizhong Tibetanness does not arise solely through producing wine, without their household wine production based on "traditional French techniques" and Rose Honey grapes, Cizhong people could be viewed as largely no different from any other Tibetan agricultural community in Deqin County or Diqing Prefecture. Wine (and their associated Catholicism) articulates their distinctiveness. Almost all Catholics in Cizhong, and to an extent Buddhists in the village, will say that part of being a Cizhong Tibetan person is also being a grape grower and winemaker. The two have become inseparable today, and every household in the village, including Tibetan Buddhist families, grows grapes and produces wine. As the mother of one of Hong Xing's close friends explained: "We drink a little bit of wine ourselves. Because Cizhong is famous for wine and grapes, we think grapes and wine are necessary when visitors come here because they ask about these things. If we didn't have them, then we'd be ashamed. We are also able to be proud when we go to other Tibetan villages that grow grapes but don't know how to make wine, because we do. So, I do think they are important and even necessary for Tibetan identity for us and make us special."

While "indigeneity" (*yuan zhumin* or *bendi*) is not part of the vernacular in Chinese or Tibetan in Northwest Yunnan, there is a phrase best translated as "identity" (*shenfen rentong*) that villagers in Cizhong utilize when discussing how they represent themselves through Catholicism and wine. Outside of Cizhong, if one were to ask a Tibetan person whether grapes or wine have anything to do with their *shenfen rentong*, the most likely answer would be no. Buddhists in Cizhong often suggest that their *shenfen rentong* (with respect to wine) is connected more to touristic income over any cultural ideal or aspiration, but they still indicate that their livelihood is place-based and tied to the church and the community's history with wine. For those Buddhists who intermarry with Catholics, such ideas can become even further pronounced. For Catholics, though, wine and viticulture are certainly a method of "indigenous articulation" tied to *shenfen rentong* (Clifford 2001; T. Li 2000, built off Hall 1996, 1997). In Cizhong, this articulation takes place within the larger state inscription of the landscape and region as Shangri-La and the thinking among Shangri-La Tibetans and within the Tibetan vernacular that indigeneity is often place-based and localized, as opposed to indigeneity relating to broader questions regarding sovereignty or territory (Mortensen 2019; Yeh 2007a).

Village Wine Drinking

Wine's role in ritual is also important given its history in Cizhong as a sacrament for Catholic Mass. However, drinking in Cizhong today is primarily a social act, except during Catholic Mass.[3] Rarely does one drink alone, although Wu Gongdi often sips a small glass of his home-distilled barley liquor (*qingkejiu*). He will typically consume larger amounts only in the company of others with whom he can toast and be merry. Hong Xing is part of a relatively large group of men his age who meet several nights a week to socialize and drink, primarily cheap Chinese beer. For someone who makes good-tasting wine, he rarely drinks it himself. In the years since my fieldwork, his choice to drink beer over his own wine has been due mainly to the increasing value and quality of his wine as an economic asset. He and his friends, whom I often joined, meet late in the evening, after eating dinner at home and after dark, usually at the house of one man who has a large sitting and dining area for tourist guests, right next to the church. These men will sit for several hours drinking beer, playing cards, engaging in singing competitions, and toasting each other, usually with the typical Chinese "Ganbei!" (Bottoms up!), requiring one to drink an entire shot glass or can of beer. While most of these men are in their thirties and forties, they will occasionally be joined by an older man, who seems to find more company and enjoyment drinking with his son's friends than with men his own age. His contemporaries cannot keep up with his drinking, as this man holds his liquor extremely well, usually opting to drink Chinese store-bought *baijiu* while others drink beer. This man, who most affectionately call Da Ge, "Big Brother," always has something fun to say. For instance, once when I asked him if wine and winemaking were important for him as a Cizhong Tibetan, he—a Buddhist, not a Catholic—replied sarcastically and exaggeratedly (and already quite drunk), though with a hint of truth, "Growing grapes and making wine is the most important thing to being a Tibetan person."

While daily social drinking tends to be limited to cheap Chinese beer and *baijiu*, wine has made entries into village festivals and weddings in both Cizhong and Bu Villages. Wedding season occurs between December and February in Deqin's villages due to the slowdown in agricultural activity and the availability of more free time. Typical weddings in Cizhong involve many toasts among the guests and the bride and the groom, with a variety of spirits served to guests with a pre-dinner snack and during the ceremony and the dinner and dancing that follow. Beer, *baijiu*, and red wine are available, as are soda and juice for those who choose not to drink alcohol. Usually, women drink fewer of the alcoholic options, though some women do drink as much, if not more, than men; some elder men choose not to drink, unlike the younger men, who all drink. I attended several weddings from 2014 through 2015, and when I asked Hong Xing about the serving of wine with other spirits, he explained that this practice began recently, when many households in both Cizhong and Cigu started producing large quantities of wine, and that some villagers, particularly elders, seem to enjoy drinking wine more than traditional or Chinese spirits.

With an assortment of beverages served, guests often find themselves debating what to drink, as I did while attending one wedding and engaging in the singing and performance game that took place at the encouragement of Da Ge, with whom I sat. As somewhat of a connoisseur of beer and wine, I had grown tired of drinking warm and rather sour Chinese beer and tried to avoid it. On this occasion, I chose wine, whereas most villagers chose *baijiu, mijiu* (rice wine), or beer.

One exception to the addition of wine is local festivals. Christmas is by far the largest and most important festival celebrated each year in Cizhong by Catholic and Buddhist families alike and brings many visitors—both foreign and Chinese.[4] Most, if not all, villagers associate wine with hospitality and consider it a necessary drink to serve to visitors and tourists. However, during the 2014 Christmas festival, I was surprised when wine was not served as part of the post-Christmas morning Mass lunch feast. Instead, options included beer, barley liquor mixed with meat, and locally made *mijiu* mixed with egg. Nobody could explain why villagers had not served wine, though it seemed that quantity may have been an issue due to the sheer size of the crowd in attendance. Or perhaps in other years they do serve wine, and 2014 was just an oddity in this regard.

Despite limiting how much of their own grape wine they will drink, beyond special occasions villagers will drink it and share it with the tourists who visit Cizhong, as happened on multiple occasions when tourists arrived while I was visiting homes in the village and when I was living with Wu Gongdi's family. Villagers will also share and drink wine with government officials when they come calling. In many ways, wine becomes an intermediary between the local state and villagers, who work to demonstrate their hospitality and Tibetan Catholic culture through serving wine. These activities exemplify an ideal of extending the lives of the producer to the consumer expressed in scholarship on terroir (Gudeman 2001; Manning 2012). Over the past few years, more and more people in Cizhong are also beginning to highlight specific tastes, such as Rose Honey, as they improve their winemaking. In Hong Xing's descriptions of the flavor profile of his 2017 vintage, which he advertises on the social media platform WeChat, he makes specific references to the fruity sweet flavor of Rose Honey.

During one wine-sharing event on a Sunday in 2013, county and provincial forestry bureau officers came together to visit the church, observe the Mass, and look at the local county-planted vineyards around the church. After these morning activities, villagers served lunch to the twenty or so officials in one of the larger and nicer family guesthouses next to the church. The lunch included a multitude of grape wine poured and served from decorative clay jars. Normally, many families serve wine out of plastic jugs. Hong Xing, who happened to be helping host these officials, invited me to join as well. This was the first and probably only time I ever drank grape wine as a shot drink in the Chinese *ganbei* style. It took a lot of effort due to the strength and sweetness of the wine, but my being a foreigner who was there studying the community gave perceived social capital to Hong Xing and the other village hosts in welcoming these men.

In the traditional Chinese circles of gift giving for favors, and in the cultivation of *guanxi*, that is, relationships with government officials and other figures of importance (Osburg 2013a; M. M. Yang 1994), village wine has also come to play a role, much as luxury wines from France have in affluent eastern China (Mustacich 2015; Ross and Roach 2013). Whenever Hong Xing travels to the township or county seat to meet with government officials about funding to support his village projects, he always takes bottles of wine as gifts. He will do the same when people of importance, often foreigners whom he perceives as possessing some social capital, visit his guesthouse, whether they are customers or not. He gives them wine to show his appreciation and potentially build some *guanxi* with them.

In discussions about wine and grapes, the original Rose Honey and government-planted cabernet vineyards around the church are a popular topic among certain Catholic villagers and the resident Chinese priest. They often insist on taking tourists and other visitors to view these vineyards and learn about them. Images of vineyards side by side with the Cizhong church also adorn the bottles of many village wines and the promotional material of other wineries in the region. Villagers such as Wu Gongdi and Hong Xing have never been prevented from taking cuttings from the original Rose Honey vines planted by the French and Swiss, but the vines remain closed to the public, in a walled-off and locked area, the key for which is kept by the county government. This remains a point of contention among Catholic households who believe that these vineyards would be managed better under their care. The county agricultural office neglects the vineyards, allowing them to become overgrown, less sightly, and less productive. To promote Cizhong culture and create idyllic imagery for wine throughout Diqing and Shangri-La, the township planted additional vineyards of cabernet throughout the traditional garden areas of the church (except for the walled-off Rose Honey vineyards), but it rents these out for harvest and winemaking to Buddhist families who reside in the area immediately surrounding the church. Return of the land and these vineyards to the village's church management association and to the Catholics is still often discussed. While Buddhists and Catholics in Cizhong typically experience few disagreements, possession of the vineyards surrounding the church causes some disfunction because their ownership is tied to Catholic identity and history.

Agricultural Life in Cizhong

In Cizhong, managing vineyards and wine production is one of many agricultural activities, unlike elsewhere in Deqin where grapes have become the only abundant crop grown. Cizhong's special niche as a Tibetan community producing paddy rice creates a more diversified agricultural calendar and pattern of life. In other communities upstream, seasonal agropastoralism is fading away as vineyards become monocultures and families sell off their yak herds. In Cizhong, only a few families practice seasonal agropastoralism and keep large numbers of yaks. Most simply keep one to three cows in their households for milk and butter production. This also makes the community unique because many households produce daily butter tea with milk from cows rather than yaks. Villagers plant flatland paddy fields with rice in the summer and wheat and barley in the winter. Cizhong remains one of only a few places in Deqin County where large quantities of these grains are still grown. After rice seedling beds are sown in May and June, and then the fields are planted out for the summer, there is little work until rice harvesting in October. Villagers leave the fields fallow for a month or so and then plant both wheat and several varieties of barley in December for harvest in April.

Villagers care for and manage their vineyards, which they plant mostly upslope of the paddy fields, throughout the year. In December and January, after the vines have lost their leaves for the winter, families prune each vine, removing all the previous year's stalks and leaving only the vine's woody base. In March and April, just as the vines are beginning to resprout, families plow all the vineyards by hand with hoes, turning over all the soil between each row of vines. Villagers then load baskets full of mulch and manure from the livestock pens outside their homes and carry these on their backs to the vineyards, where they apply a layer to the newly overturned soil. They then plow the vineyards' rows once again to mix in the manure. As the vines grow out later in the spring and summer, families prune and train them, tying the new stalks to the trellises built along each row. People also regularly return to their vineyards to remove unwanted small and stubby stems and especially the tendrils. Harvesting of the grapes takes place beginning in late August or September for Rose Honey and in October for cabernet. According to my own survey data, all households in Cizhong are engaged in growing grapes in vineyards on household land, making wine, and maintaining small wine cellars in their homes. Nowhere else in the region does every single household throughout one community make wine with the grapes they grow. Cizhong wine is mostly handmade, though some families, including Wu Gongdi's, use a machine to crush the grapes.

Wu Gongdi and Hong Xing's Story

The role of wine and winemaking as a marker of identity and distinction is well illustrated in the lives of Wu Gongdi, his son Hong Xing, and their family, a family of especially zealous winemakers. Wu Gongdi has passed winemaking on to Hong Xing and his daughter-in-law, Azu (the wife of his other son, Hong Bao). More than any other family in Cizhong, they put an incredible amount of care into both tending their vineyards and producing their wine. They practice the special method taught to Wu Gongdi in 1997 by his nun relative upstream in Yanjing and have documented it in a variety of ethnographic media (Liu 2002; *The Way to Tibet* 2004).

As with many Tibetans in Yunnan (Hillman 2010), much of Wu Gongdi's success as a communist leader, lay catechist, and political influencer among local government leaders has come from his embrace of the local Communist Party, in which is he is an active member. This role has enabled him to obtain funds for various village development projects and the preservation of the Cizhong church. One of Wu Gongdi's projects has been the establishment of a grape and viticulture cooperative. For this program, he received ¥30,000 (US$4,219) from the county government to conduct training courses on grape growing for villagers in nearby areas. For these training sessions, he prepares handouts about good vine care. Wu Gongdi maintains a bit of pride and a small income by working to pass on his self-developed knowledge of vineyard management and by working to build the wine industry of Cizhong and the surrounding villages.

Wu Gongdi's family currently plants eight *mu* of vineyards, terraced along slopes below the forested mountains next to his house. This plot is larger than most other households', though there are a few others who also plant this much. From 1998 to 2024, Wu Gongdi's family produced an average of two thousand kilos of wine per year, one of the largest annual household wine outputs in Cizhong. Domestic and foreign visitors have suggested that the alcohol content is between 10 and 20 percent, and an alcohol company with which the family has begun working measured the alcohol content of Wu Gongdi's wine at 15 percent in 2014. The wine fluctuates in taste and quality. In addition to making his grape wine, Wu Gongdi has also been testing the production of ice wine (a dessert wine), grape liquor distilled from leftover grape skins and seeds, and Rose Honey grape jam. To produce the grape liquor, the same method used to distill barley liquor is employed. Families have produced this liquor since long before 1998, when grape wine production began. The process involves filling a metal cylinder with barley or grape skins and seeds and placing it on top of a pan of boiling water. A pot of cold water is placed on top of the cylinder to promote the condensation of liquor, which flows out of the cylinder through a small spout and into a second pot or kettle. All openings and connections in the cylinder are sealed with clay.

The Process of Making Red Wine

Winemaking begins by harvesting the grapes, which villagers carry home in bamboo or plastic baskets on their backs. All members of Wu Gongdi's family actively join in the harvesting; even his young granddaughter and grandson copy the others' actions. After all the harvested grapes are piled in the households' courtyards, people crush the grapes by hand in large plastic or metal basins or sometimes by using a machine. Some seniors recall that before the 1950s, locals used a large wooden stick to crush grapes in wooden barrels. People no longer use wooden basins due to weight considerations and because plastic ones are readily available. After the grapes are crushed, the stems are picked out of the basins, leaving the juice and the skin and seed sediments, which are then poured into large plastic buckets. Most villagers, including Wu Gongdi, add sugar when they crush the grapes, as local people in Cizhong prefer a sweeter-tasting wine.

Villagers leave the grape juice to ferment for three to ten days, depending on the maturity and sweetness of the grapes, and they then filter or sieve the wine through bamboo baskets and cheesecloth. To filter the wine, they use a plastic tube to siphon it from larger buckets into small basins or barrels. Although, after sieving, few other households reserve leftover grape skins and seeds in a plastic bucket for later grape liquor distillation, Wu Gongdi does so. The filtered wine is then poured back into the buckets and tightly sealed with plastic film to ferment. Villagers repeat the filtration and sieving process several times, until the wine becomes a pure liquid, free of sediment.

The liquid eventually becomes the final wine product after six months to one year and is kept in clay jars for storage, sale, and display. In 2014, Wu Gongdi's family began experimenting for the first time with storing and fermenting wine in oak and stainless steel barrels. Most households use only plastic and clay containers, while Wu Gongdi and Hong Xing stress that they are trying to move away from using plastic because it results in lower-quality wine. One kilo of raw grapes makes half a liter of finished product.

Marketing, production, and distribution vary between one family and another. Some simply sell wine by the glass to tourists and other visitors, while others sell larger quantities in plastic jugs. Hong Xing and Wu Gongdi were the only family I observed in 2016 that had begun to bottle their wine. Hong Xing now sells his bottles at a rather high price of ¥180 (US$23). Several families note that they sell wine outside of Cizhong to restaurants and government officials in places including the towns of Deqin, Shangri-La, and Lijiang. In both Deqin and Shangri-La, I have seen Cizhong wine for sale in restaurants, usually displayed in either clay jars or plastic jugs. In these situations, the venues selling the wine promote it as from Cizhong, giving it a special history and identity. The marketing in such restaurants makes references to Cizhong's Catholicism and the introduction of wine by French missionaries.

Family Wine Culture and Business

Wu Gongdi and his family's pursuit of viticulture and winemaking continues to expand as an industry and remains by far their highest source of annual household income. Their wine-based income comes both from selling wine to tourists who visit their guesthouse and through making wine for a large conglomerate from Anhui Province that is involved in producing and selling other alcohol and spirits and has offices in Kunming, the provincial capital of Yunnan. Well known in Cizhong and around Deqin County for their winemaking, this company first approached Wu Gongdi and his family in 2014, hiring them to produce wine annually using cabernet grapes purchased in another village upstream. The family also continues to produce and sell their own wine using the Rose Honey grapes they grow. The company has provided them with two oak barrels and two large stainless-steel barrels to ferment the company's wine. The family previously had used only plastic and ceramic barrels.

After Wu Gongdi's family made the company's wine in fall 2014, the company returned in December and January and worked together with

FIGURE 11. Wu Gongdi filtering fermenting wine, 2014.

the family to fill hundreds of mini-keg dispensers. Everyone then boxed up and packaged the kegs for shipping to Kunming. The company sold each keg for the lofty price of ¥695 (over US$100). They branded each dispenser keg with the mark "Cizhong Jiu Zhuang" (Cizhong Château), using a custom-made wood-burning engraving tool. In working as hired winemakers with this company, the family is now making an additional ¥40,000 (US$5,528) per year from winemaking alone. At the time I was staying with the family in fall 2014, when they first became engaged in this new venture, I recorded the following in my field notes: "This project puts Wu Gongdi and the family's winemaking practices, not just their wine itself, into a place of distinction. They have become recognized and sought out for their winemaking skills."

These skills and the family's promotion of organic Rose Honey grapes and wine, juxtaposed against nonorganic cabernet, are another facet of what Wu Gongdi, his son Hong Xing, and his daughter-in-law, Azu, describe as making them special as a Tibetan winemaking household and family. Hong Xing has spent the past several years developing his own winemaking and expanding his own vineyards, replacing all government-introduced cabernet with organic Rose Honey grapes, which he actively promotes. Hong Xing has developed his own small bottling operation with custom-made "Cizhong Wine" labels and brochures, which he produced with the help of my fieldwork assistant, his good friend, and with money from a local NGO. Hong Xing promotes his winemaking hand in hand with his small trekking business. He takes people across the high pass over to the Salween River valley, where he has built a lodge along the same path that was improved on by the Swiss fathers. Today this route is a popular hiking trail among more intrepid travelers. For Hong Xing, wine, Cizhong's history, and the area's scenic beauty are all important to producing a good livelihood.

Beginning in 2017, Hong Xing also greatly expanded his own personal winemaking business and endeavors. He purchased a small storefront space right next to the Cizhong church, with windows that look out at the original Rose Honey vineyards. Here, he stores all his wine in large barrels, with glasses for tasting, and sells bottles to the almost daily Chinese and foreign tourists who arrive to visit the church. His shop has many photos on its walls of Cizhong's landscape and descriptions of the winemaking process and the history of the place, along with captions in both Chinese and English. With his storefront space and increased advertising exposure, Hong Xing has also expanded his winemaking capacity and skills and now has burgeoning online wine sales. His 2017 vintage wines were particularly refined and rival many produced by the region's larger wineries due to assistance he received from French experts involved with a boutique winery downstream in Cigu.

For Hong Xing, wine and winemaking do not have the same direct links to ritual and Catholicism that they do for his father, but rather relate to cultural and religious changes in Cizhong over time:

> Grapes are important to me, my family, and other people in Cizhong, but I can't say they are important to Tibetan culture directly. We participate in this because of our background and history with the church. In the traditional annual living cycle, we grew grains and grass and raised animals for meat and butter, and they ate the grass and gave us fertilizer. I think butter and barley are thus more classically important to Tibetan culture. But with our story here in Cizhong, we have changed with grapes and wine, and they have become a part of who we are. Actually, Tibetans living in Tibet are less farmers and known more for grazing animals, while other minorities here in Yunnan, such as the Naxi and the Bai are known for barley and wheat like us, but we are still Tibetan like those living in Tibet.

Both Hong Xing and Wu Gongdi take their winemaking and vineyard care very seriously and equate doing so with being a Tibetan in one form or another. During the annual winemaking in September 2014, the entire family participated, including the two young children. At one point, while we were all crushing grapes by hand in the courtyard of the family's home, Azu dressed her two children up in contemporary Tibetan festival clothing to take photos during the grape crushing. When I inquired whether this

FIGURE 12. Wu Gongdi's grandchildren during grape crushing, 2014.

posing for photos was merely for my benefit, Azu insisted that it was not
and that in fact they did this each year while making wine. Indeed, there
are photos on the walls of the family's home showing both Wu Gongdi
and Azu dressed in their traditional clothing and working in the vineyards
and in the courtyard crushing grapes. For this family, annual winemaking
has become a miniature festival of sorts when they enjoy their Catholic
Tibetan identity. The family's Tibetan festival clothing, though, which
is bought in local stores, perhaps also says something about modernity
and capitalism and how people in Cizhong articulate them through their
winemaking. These outfits are not typically associated with being "traditional," but exemplify a more modern palette, further reflecting the ways
in which, as Hong Xing explains, Tibetanness continues to evolve over
time in conjunction with new capitalist dynamics.

For Azu, though, seeing wine and winemaking as cultural is less definitive. A Buddhist who married into the family, she has become the manager
of all the household finances and has embraced the family's integration of

culture into this practice along with Catholicism. Still, when the family makes their wine each year, while taste is important, profit becomes her number one concern. In many ways, she is not unlike most villagers in other areas of Deqin for whom growing grapes and making wine is purely economic. In 2015, Wu Gongdi and Hong Xing were placed in a bit of a bind over favoring quality or quantity in their wine. They are the only family in Cizhong with an extensive quantity of Rose Honey vines, since most plant a combination of Rose Honey and cabernet. Because the family own so many Rose Honey vines, they were approached in spring 2015 by a Frenchman and a Swiss winemaker who were developing their own small boutique winery at the site of the original mission just downstream in Cigu; the two men wished to manage the family's vineyards in exchange for purchasing the grapes at a good price.

Initially, I helped to arrange the introduction and the meetings at the request of Hong Xing, who sought to improve his winemaking skills. The goal of these businessmen was to try their hand at producing a quality wine from Rose Honey, rather than from the cabernet grapes now planted throughout the area. In exchange, they would train the family in new and more sophisticated viticulture and winemaking techniques—something Wu Gongdi and Hong Xing both wanted to learn. However, Azu was clear during the negotiations that the way these men would manage the vineyards, reducing the grape crop overall to improve the quality and sugar content in the grapes, was not acceptable. In Azu's mind, the quantity of grapes and wine produced from year to year is more important than the quality of the wine. Removed from these affairs on an everyday basis, Wu Gongdi deferred to Azu despite his own interest in learning more about winemaking. Hong Xing was eager to learn from these men but lacked a large enough quantity of Rose Honey grapes to offer them, and the agreement never materialized in 2015. But by 2017, Hong Xing developed enough of his own vineyards and had quantities that allowed him to work together with the same French winemakers from this nearby venture to produce what, judging by taste, I considered his best wine yet, and the first made by "traditional" means without added sugar.

This vignette about a new foreign wine venture in Cizhong alongside Wu Gongdi and Hong Xing's undertakings illustrates an important dynamic that is occurring with wine production across China and in other countries transitioning in post-socialist economies. Until recently, wine was not viewed in China as a high-quality item. It was produced in mass and had what anthropologists Adam Walker and Paul Manning (2013), in referring to wine in Georgia, have called "socialist quantity" versus "post-socialist quality." This has changed drastically in China today, with the state actively promoting grape wine production and consumption as a healthy alternative to grain spirits and hard alcohol, the middle- and upper-class consumer base growing, and awareness of global trends increasing. In a sense, there has been a move toward global cosmopolitanism with disposable income versus mere economic pragmatism, which existed more immediately after the reform and opening-up policy was adopted in 1978. Rural farmers such as those in Deqin, outside of Cizhong, who primarily grow grapes for larger wine producers, face a significant challenge, however. For those supplying grapes to the wineries, and who still live near the bottom of the social pyramid, quality has not entered the vernacular in the way that it has for those consuming wines at the top. This is something many wine producers in China have discussed, as they attempt to train farmers to manage vineyards for optimal grape quality. Even if profits seem lower, increased quality will mean increased profits. Yet this is not the view of the mostly village farmers who are growing the grapes (Luo, Andreas, and Li 2017; Mustacich 2015; Ruffle 2015). For over thirty years, quantity alone has dictated farmers' agricultural profits, so changing this way of thinking overnight is not easy.

This dilemma confronts families such as Wu Gongdi's. Wu Gongdi clearly wants to make wine that gives him and his family distinction, but with increasing competition from corporate and other small business interests in Deqin and Shangri-La, the task is becoming more and more difficult, given the family's limited capacity and capital. Indeed, Hong Xing, probably more than anyone, can see the long-term gains in this new approach in his marketing and production. His shop opened in 2017, and its daily profits from wine alone are now anywhere from ¥200 to ¥800 (US$26–$103). Will small household operations be able to continue to play a role in meeting these new demands among China's emerging wine consumers, or will people like Wu Gongdi and Hong Xing all eventually be pushed out of the market and end up producing for larger state and corporate interests?

Reflections on Agricultural Life and the Ideal of Terroir

Throughout my time in the field while working in the vineyards and while making wine, I often found myself thinking about how the wine landscape and the people themselves were being invoked as actors. In going back over my field notes, I began to see a thread and called it "Distinction and Shangri-La," to refer to how, at the time, I felt that wine production was providing villagers with some sort of economic distinction. In many ways, this also exemplifies what the state might be wishing to invoke when it uses Shangri-La as an advertising hook for wine and the greater landscape. It is obviously pure marketing, but even for someone like me, with an open mind and an understanding of local agency and the people, the concept clearly works when one spends time in the region and observes how villagers and the landscape interact. As one villager even said: "I do actually think it is good how the government and the company promote their wine as Tibetan. There's no pollution here, and we have a very clean, beautiful environment."

Working in the vineyards, I often sensed there really was something idyllic about agricultural work in this setting of mountains along the river, listening to Hong Xing and the women sing in Tibetan while we worked. One day in Bu Village, as I was helping my host Zhouma water and irrigate her vineyards, I sat down by the irrigation canal and listened to the water flow, felt a light breeze, and looked down at the Mekong River and up at the glacier and snowy mountain above. At the time, I thought about how there in the vineyard, in that setting, an incredible story was occurring. Taking in the beauty and power of the place and the warmhearted nature of the people, I thought to myself that this was, ironically, a Shangri-La of sorts. As I watched and worked with her, Zhouma exemplified the distinction I saw in the winemakers of the region. Tibetan grape farmers and winemakers carry a deep connection with the lands they have been cultivating for generations, regardless of how the crops change. These attachments are more than economic.

I clearly remember a similar experience years earlier, in Meilishi Village upstream in 2011, walking around the vineyards with another host father of mine, Adong, who described how he cared for and managed his vines like children, even though his grapes would just be sold in bulk to the government-sponsored Shangri-La Winery. Returning to the present moment, as I watched her, Zhouma was attentive to the cultivation of her grapes and all the different grape varieties, often asking me to share with her what I had learned in Cizhong about the varieties. She was also very interested in how I perceived her wine and how it tasted. I thought at the time that there is a "taste of place" in this wine through the people, even if it does not conform to traditional notions of terroir. Zhouma, Wu Gongdi, and Hong Xing recognize which of their wines are better and which need further work. Wu Gongdi similarly feels great pride in his family's wine and its history in Cizhong and believes that his family's wine is unique. Zhouma insists that her wine is organic and free of chemicals, unlike the company wine; this gives it distinction. For Wu Gongdi, wine is a ritual drink that has become enmeshed in his family's culture and religion in an inseparable way, and producing wine for outsiders allows them to share a piece of their family and this culture.

The lives of Cizhong people as winemakers connect with who they are as Tibetans, Catholics, and citizens of Shangri-La today. Oral histories and the individual story of Wu Gongdi and his family illustrate these ideas, but much of what these actors have shown is true for villagers throughout the community, perhaps in a more limited way, especially among solely Buddhist households. Villagers' deep and temporal connection with the landscape intersects with the tourists and wine consumers who visit the village and come to understand an ideal of Tibetan terroir. Cizhong wine and identities are thus an embodiment of both history and modernity through villagers' understanding of French and Swiss colonial history and contemporary state efforts to meld them into the fold of Shangri-La and to benefit from this form of state landscape inscription and naming. Wine has been a prominent mode of indigenizing modernity for Cizhong's villagers for over two decades.

So, what is the terroir of wine produced in Cizhong? Is it more than just marketing? For some, creating a local terroir is exemplified through the process of vinting wines that share flavors without additives. Villagers and small-scale foreign investors alike evoke a strong link to locale, history, and productive practices and contrast these against corporate wines in Shangri-La. In the eyes of Cizhong villagers, corporate wines are not authentic because they do not represent the history that household wines do. In contrast, Wu Gongdi and Hong Xing claim there is a place-based flavor in their wines produced in Cizhong that makes them distinct.

Cizhong household wine production provides a more sustainable example than does wine originating elsewhere in Deqin, where villagers grow grapes for the Shangri-La Wine Company under heavy agrochemical use. The state views things in Cizhong differently. While it actively promotes Cizhong as a unique locale in Shangri-La tourism materials, it also views household wine production as lacking in the quality standards that corporate brands can provide. Still, this has not stopped Cizhong households from entering the wine market in Deqin on their own terms. Unlike other villagers, Cizhong people persist as actors in commodity and landscape production, using their own history and the state's promotional framework of Shangri-La to their benefit, both economically and culturally.

CHAPTER 3

Producing "Tibetan" Wine and Altering Landscapes and Livelihoods

He calls himself a man of Jin,
Who cultivates grapes like jade,
Makes it into delicious wine,
For which men can never slake their thirst,
Take a cup of this wine,
Go and gain Liangzhou's rule and power.

"The Song of the Grape," by Liu Yuxi (772–842 CE)

Late May 2007. It was pouring rain. Our group huddled around a campfire under a tarp suspended high above, trying to stay warm and dry in a subalpine meadow. As we snacked on peanuts and sunflower seeds, we listened to a lecture on China's Sloping Land Conversion policy by an instructor in our environmental and cultural field studies program, which focused on the Yunnan borderlands and upland Southeast Asia. The final part of the program was to have been a sixteen-day *kora*, or circumambulation, around the sacred Tibetan mountain Khawa Karpo, but nonstop spring storms had dumped too much snow on the high mountain passes. Our dozen or so local Tibetan guides and horse wranglers had managed to put together two weeks of trekking in and around their villages and alpine grazing areas, all on the Mekong side of Khawa Karpo, since we could not cross over to the neighboring Salween River canyon. After giving a lecture about Grain for Green, a national upland crop replacement and reforestation program that had been widely implemented among local communities in this region after 1998, our instructor invited three of the local guides to share stories about their experiences farming alternative crops.

Two of the men, Gege and Aba, told how their families had given up growing wheat, barley, and corn on mountain slopes and planted walnut trees and buckwheat instead. Those crops would contribute better to reforestation and preventing landslides and erosion. In exchange, the government provided the families with both tree seedlings and ongoing annual subsidy payments to offset the loss of grain crops until the new trees began producing nuts to harvest and market.

The third man, Sonam, talked about how the government has been giving his family grape vines to make wine. This caught everyone a bit off guard. From where we sat at the moment, and what we had observed over several weeks, the local environment did not appear to be ideal for growing grapes or making wine. Sonam's chance remark opened my eyes to the forms of livelihood and landscape alterations that were occurring with wine in the region. I would learn that other villagers had been told that viticultural development programs were part of the Sloping Land Conversion Program, introduced alongside a national logging ban in upstream areas of the Yangzi River watershed after major flooding down-stream in 1998. It seemed that the local government had initiated a scheme to co-opt funds from this national development program to help promote Shangri-La and tourism through wine production. The impact of grapes and wine on Northwest Yunnan's capitalistic and transnationally driven agrarian change and shangrilazation is significant.

How do people and landscapes come together to create new identities and commodities? Beyond Cizhong Village, how have Diqing Prefecture and Deqin County become a significant wine region with the development of contemporary vineyard landscapes by the state, corporations, village cooperatives, and private individuals? Shangri-La Winery represents perhaps the most extreme version of state-initiated agriculture and capitalism compared to other winery projects that straddle corporatism and regional or entrepreneurial identity creation through wine and terroir. With Shangri-La Winery as an example of a state project and form of economic and agricultural "development," I suggest that vineyards and the wine they produce are an "agriculture of inclusion" within state-based landscape transformation. Such state projects are meant to bring rural farmers into the fold of national and global capitalism, in contrast to traditional shifting forms of agriculture in Yunnan, which have been framed by scholars as agricultures of state avoidance or escape (Scott 2009). Viticulture is a sedentary form of monocropping, unlike seasonal agropastoralism, which involves communities moving up and down the mountains with their yaks and cattle. Different corporate, state, and private approaches to making and marketing wine in Diqing also illustrate a Chinese hybrid model of capitalism that mixes state-led markets and individual entrepreneurialism (Osburg 2013b). Each of these projects seeks to exemplify and promote the terroir of its wines. However, while for household winemakers in Cizhong the deployment of terroir serves as an agentive response to modernity, it remains more of a marketing tool for "shangrilazation" in state-conceived wine production and is more conventionally tied by private and foreign winemakers to soil quality, geography, and climate.

With a diversity of approaches to vinting wine as a commodity, the global capitalism that shapes the wine economy is not an all-encompassing and homogenizing force but in fact one of great diversity and character, like that described by Anna Tsing involving matsutake mushrooms (2009, 2015a). However, while Tsing argues that such diversity manifests through the creation and diversification of global commodity chains for matsutake across locales, and through the salvage of ruined landscapes of industrial nineteenth- and twentieth-century capitalism, I suggest a different view of wine and commodities in a single locale, Diqing. Wine production and landscapes take many forms in Diqing, including individual household production, state-promoted household grape growing, private corporate vineyards managed with villager labor, small-scale foreign-owned and operated wineries, and village collective corporations. Each of these forms of production stems from historical and contemporary global connections among Diqing, other regions of China, and Europe. The agricultural and village landscape involved in the production of wine is not one of salvage but rather of indigenizing modernity among the state and the region's peoples to fit the mold of emerging markets and historical contingencies. Wine production as a state-based project has certainly caused negative ecological and social impacts; capitalism as a project in producing Shangri-La as a wine region is not all beneficial. However, as Tsing (2015a) argues, we should move away from conceptions of capitalisms as being all-encompassing and homogenizing projects.

Corporate- and State-Driven Wine Landscapes in Diqing

Throughout the valleys of the Mekong and Yangzi Rivers in Deqin County and in other areas of Diqing Prefecture, vineyards and wine have transformed village landscapes and household farming since the early 2000s. Unlike in Cizhong, these changes do not involve grassroots household developments of winemaking but rather are connected to the development interests of the state, corporations, private individuals, and village administrators. The wine industry developing across Deqin, and more recently in neighboring Weixi County, has grown increasingly complex. With more than ten separate wineries now operating in the region, this industry has brought changes to village agricultural landscapes.

Wine promotion and production is big business today and has become a major local policy initiative for rural economic development, with the government monopolizing most of the grape and wine production. The Diqing prefectural government directs most village grapes for sale to the Shangri-La Wine Company, which has been granted a monopoly on household grape crops. However, there are exceptions to this monopoly. Shangri-La Winery was not the first to enter the market. A smaller company, Sunspirit, which focuses on high-quality ice wines, was the first to pursue winemaking in the region.

Sunspirit Meri Ice Wine in Bu Village

Sunspirit is owned by an independent businessman, Liu Jiaqiang, who is described by his winery manager in Deqin as a real "lover of wine."[1] Sometime between 1997 and 2000, around the time that Wu Gongdi was beginning to plant vineyards and make wine in Cizhong, Liu began working in the mining business in Deqin. Previously, he had been an executive at Yunnan Red Wine in central Yunnan, two hours from Kunming. With his experience in producing and marketing wine, Liu believed that Shangri-La had potential for producing wine. Two locations and features that captured Liu's attention were Cizhong, with its French history, and nearby Khawa Karpo, the tallest peak in Yunnan and one of the most sacred mountains in all of Tibetan Buddhism (Coggins and Yeh 2014; Da Col 2007; Litzinger 2004). Coupled with the idea of Shangri-La, Cizhong and Khawa Karpo provided advertising potential, so Liu sought to develop an industry.

To test his ideas for growing suitable grapes in the region, Liu worked with the Deqin County agricultural bureau, planting sixty *mu* of cabernet sauvignon grapes in Bu Village, several miles upstream from Cizhong, near Khawa Karpo. Bu was the home of a local county agricultural worker named Wang, who worked closely with Liu to make his village one of the test sites. Bu Village became the eventual site of Liu's Sunspirit winery and lodge, with construction and wine production beginning in 2008, according to the facility manager. However, some of Bu's households began planting vineyards and making money as part of the pilot project in 2002. After 2008, every Bu household converted its fields to vineyards, abandoning the growing of wheat and barley as well as the practice of seasonal agropastoralism. From this point forward, each family kept two to three yaks or cows (rather than its previous herd of twenty to thirty) and fed them with small amounts of chaff from grain intercropped in the vineyards. Before 2008, much higher quantities of grain were grown to feed the animals during the winters, when they were not grazing in the high mountains.

Sunspirit's investment and experimentation in Bu, along with its own vineyards surrounding its lodge and winery just up the road from the village, were meant to produce a high-quality cabernet product, Meri Ice Wine. Meri is a rendition of Meili (part of the Chinese name for the mountain) or of Menri, an alternate Tibetan name for Khawa Karpo. The bottles sell for hefty amounts, ¥500–¥600 (US$64–$77) for the cheapest varietal and over ¥1,000 (US$129) for the more expensive ones, and feature a picture of the mountain on the label. On the basis of critical acclaim and my own tasting during a winery tour, the wine is worth the price. Indeed, since entering production in 2008, Sunspirit has won multiple awards in international competitions (Salick and Moseley 2012).

Part of the success of this investment, according to company officials and the villager Wang who introduced Liu to the area, is Bu's location. Wang explained: "The land in Bu is very unique. We have a small microclimate here because of the proximity to Khawa Karpo and Mingyong glacier. Sunspirit has hired a lot of experts to come here to study the climate and region." According to wine experts in China, Bu is an ideal place for ice wine given the combination of its dry arid climate and the water that comes directly from snowmelt year-round. In fact, Sunspirit pumps all its water across the Mekong River directly from Khawa Karpo's glacier. Though this may be a bit of a terroir/marketing ploy, bringing experts to Bu to study the terroir and conditions for producing ice wine was indeed a major component of Liu's investment. The resulting research not only led to the creation of a successful product but was also published in an academic paper (M. Yang et al. 2007). Ice wine has been considered ideal for cold mountain climates due to its production process, which requires leaving grapes on the vine (and covering them with mesh bags to prevent animals from eating them) long after the normal harvesting season. Grapes are harvested after the first deep freeze or snow in the early winter, which leads to increased and concentrated sugars, ideal for producing a sweet drink.

Wine development has transformed the agricultural landscape of Bu Village in a much different way than has occurred in Cizhong. Bu is the only village working with and selling its grapes to Sunspirit. Other than

Cizhong, Bu is probably the only other community with an extensive household winemaking industry, which developed around 2002 as vineyards started taking over all household land. Winemaking is not religious or historical in Bu, but it has entered daily life and household economies. Many households now produce their own wine, which they sell to the tourists passing through the village on their way to Khawa Karpo National Park. In fact, an interpretive sign the park management installed on the road above Bu Village, in the style of other signs identifying the local ecosystems and cultural features, describes how Bu's climate and landscape have made it a center of ice wine making. A few villagers now exclusively make their own wine with the grapes they produce and no longer sell any to Sunspirit. They can make more money this way, some even shipping their wine to buyers as far away as Beijing.

As villagers have explained to me, their knowledge of winemaking and ability to produce a quality product came directly from Liu and Wang. Wang, who now owns his own small winery and lodge in the center of the village, trained in central Yunnan at Liu's former company, Yunnan Red Wine. He brought his skills back to the village and, along with some of the winemakers from Sunspirit, taught others. By contrast, Shangri-La Winery has not engaged villagers in Deqin in any sort of vocational training, the consequences of which have led to significant problems in economic stability and food security, with concerns from year to year about whether the company will even come to purchase grapes. For those who have no knowledge of winemaking, selling grapes to Shangri-La Winery is the only option for providing an annual household income.[2]

While not inherently religious or cultural, wine drinking has become an everyday practice in Bu, with villagers actively drinking and discussing their wines in the evenings. Dry grape wine and ice wine have become regular items of consumption during weddings and New Year's festivals. I happened to spend the evening of the Chinese Mid-Autumn Festival (also known as the Harvest or Mooncake Festival) with my host family in Bu. Wine was the drink preferred by Zhouma, the mother, and her young adult daughter. Zhouma explained their choice as twofold. First, as she has continued to refine her own winemaking over several years, she has also come to enjoy drinking it as a significant part of this process to work on improving taste and quality. Second, she also finds the taste considerably better than that of either beer or *baijiu*. During the New Year's festival each year, which the whole village takes part in, everyone drinks wine. On the evening we spoke, however, Zhouma's husband stuck with drinking beer and *baijiu*, which seem to remain the drinks of choice for most men in the village.

In Bu, evening social drinking typically involves wine for women and beer or *baijiu* for men. Such drinking usually occurs on weekends, when certain family members, particularly men, return home, including Zhouma's husband and brother, who work for various government agencies around the county. These gatherings also involve toasting and singing competitions like those in Cizhong. Zhouma, her husband, friends, and relatives—all middle-aged—seem to enjoy these weekend evenings when everyone is at home together. During this time, they sit around talking, singing, and making many "*tashi delek*" toasts (a general greeting used for cheers in Tibetan) with beer shots or sips of *baijiu* or wine, though Zhouma's brother often easily finishes at least three full wine glasses of *baijiu* by the end of the evening.

A difference in exposure to tourists and foreign visitors in Bu and Cizhong affects social drinking activities. Many families in Cizhong keep guesthouses and are accustomed to having guests join in family activities. In Cizhong, winemaking and grape crushing are seasonal activities and many tourists are invited to participate. Bu is different. The village is located on the main road to the Khawa Karpo National Park, where thousands of tourists come each year to hike and trek, but these visits simply involve driving through Bu to reach the hiking areas and "scenic" villages on the other side of the Mekong River. Most families make wine to sell to visitors who might stop along the way, and that is the extent of their tourism interactions. Social drinking in Bu thus remains primarily a community activity that the occasional visitor may join rather than an everyday tourist practice as in Cizhong.

Shangri-La Winery

The Diqing prefectural government caught on to the idea of viticulture and wine production a few years after Sunspirit, following the success of this first venture.[3] Unlike in Cizhong, where there is at least some limited history of growing grapes and winemaking, villagers who never engaged in grape agriculture (or in wine production) on their own have now done so only at the urging of the prefectural and county governments. In this project, the state collaborated with Shangri-La Winery. The winery was approached by the government to begin producing wine from grapes grown by Deqin's villagers as part of a Shangri-La promotion scheme and a method of improving household incomes. Shangri-La Winery today produces a mixture of pure cabernets and red blends. In early years, these wines were drinkable to a "Western" palate but a bit lacking in taste and quality. Since around 2015, some wines in its Altit, or Altitude, series and new stand-alone labels have been outstanding and have placed well in international competitions. These wines were previously on the expensive side, costing over ¥300 (US$39), but can now be found for as little as ¥175 (US$23). Shangri-La Winery also produces some white wines, but these are not heavily marketed or available, no doubt due to the scarcity of white grape vineyards in Diqing, except in Weixi County. Shangri-La Winery is also known for its unusual "Tibetan dry" wines fermented using a mixture of grapes and local highland barley, creating a uniquely strong flavor. Given China's love of red wines for their auspicious color, the focus on reds throughout Deqin is not surprising.

Some contextualization of how the Shangri-La Winery has been set up in reference to larger agricultural transformation schemes in rural China is worth noting. One of the most common processes observed in rural agricultural transformation in China since the 1990s has been the arrival of what are called "dragon head" enterprises or agribusinesses. These are large corporate agricultural firms backed by local states that mass-produce agricultural products (including wine) using raw materials, in this case grapes, grown by local smallholder farmers who have been encouraged,

FIGURE 13. Ice wine tasting with the manager of Sunspirit Winery, 2014.

FIGURE 14. National park interpretive sign (in Chinese, Tibetan, and English) at the foot of Khawa Karpo describing Bu Village as an ideal location for producing ice wine, 2014. The English text, at times grammatically unsound, reads: "Bucun is a village located at the foot of Kawagebo Peak. Theoretically, the geography and climate of Bucun tallies with the typical production area of ice wine. In practice, in here it has proved that the high quality ice red wine can be produced by using Cabernet Sauvignon, the world famous wine grape. The snow mountain ice wine produced by Shangri-La Sun Soul Wine Company sold at home and abroad and is very popular in consumers all over the world. It is one of the types of the top ice wine in Asia."

induced, or even coerced by government agents into solely producing these crops and abandoning others in the belief that industry will nurture rural agriculture.[4] Earlier forms of these dragon head corporations that existed in the post-1978 reform periods involved primarily local state-owned agricultural enterprises operating within a model of "local state corporatism" and played a similar role in converting smallholder farms into production bases for these agricultural enterprises (Li and Tilt 2007; Oi 1995, 1999). In many cases, this process has moved rural agricultural communities away from subsistence agriculture, leading to a variety of concerns over sustainability due to increased use of chemical fertilizers and pesticides, long-term soil vitality, and issues of food insecurity when subsistence comes to depend on the sales of crops with uncertain futures and markets (Galipeau 2015; Li and Tilt 2007; Tilt 2008).

Historically, the institutions governing market risk from growing cash crops and risk with respect to subsistence have gone through various stages of transformation in rural China. Under the collective system of socialist China, risk was basically subsumed by the state and collectives, and there existed a strong level of built-in risk of crop failure. Agriculture was a form of subsistence that was prone to failure due to state mismanagement. The entrance of large agribusiness firms and long-term lease transfers of land alongside labor agreements instituted within the context of the Household Responsibility System represented a new stage. After 1978, risk was transferred to households, which were then able to choose between balancing subsistence needs and growing crops for the open market. However, in the 1990s and 2000s, "local state corporatism" (Oi 1995) and dragon head enterprises began to create more volatile situations for household farmers as local governments and state-owned corporations induced them to invest in single crops to feed local industries. Many communities abandoned subsistence altogether, assuming great risk.

Shangri-La Winery is a private corporation that operates within the model of these dragon head enterprises, combined with local state corporatism. The winery and the Deqin County and Diqing Prefecture governments have transformed virtually all the lowland agricultural fields in Deqin County into vineyards as part of a massive household income improvement strategy tied to further inscribing an image of Shangri-La on the landscape. Shangri-La as a marketing tool for wine is quite effective, especially when the quality of wine is linked to landscapes and geography. Shangri-La is framed as a pristine Himalayan paradise coupled with the French and Catholic history of Cizhong, which Shangri-La Winery actively employs in its marketing. Cizhong villagers do not take this lightly, explaining that Shangri-La Winery's wines are in no way authentic with respect to the craftsmanship of winemaking learned from the missionaries, and, furthermore, they are not made with Rose Honey grapes.

One can observe the semiotic constructions by the Shangri-La Winery brand in the company's ad in figure 15. This advertisement does not include the French history of Cizhong, though this narrative is found on many of the winery's bottles. This ad focuses on the Tibetan landscape, displaying a bottle of Shangri-La Winery's premium Sacred Land label with the sacred snow- and glacier-covered Tibetan mountain Khawa Karpo in the background and the Chinese phrase "Find sanctuary of heart." It is important to recognize that the semiotics of the advertisement are entirely authentic. The image of the mountain accurately depicts the region where Shangri-La Winery grapes are grown. However, the non-Catholic, predominantly Buddhist communities that surround this mountain and grow grapes for the winery as a cash crop possess no investment or interest in the final wine product. The company uses the idyllic imagery of their homelands to market a product they are not connected with.

My initial research in 2011 focused mostly on the direct experiences of village farmers due to my lack of access to government and company officials (Galipeau 2015). In 2014, I was able to conduct more interviews and retell the story of Shangri-La Winery and village development, drawing on an interview with a public official named Litsing Gerong, who was working in the Deqin County biological resource office.[5] According to Gerong, government and corporate interest in grapes and wine first began with the pilot project by Sunspirit and the government in 2000 in Bu Village. This involved not simply promoting the growing of Rose

FIGURE 15. Advertisement for Shangri-La Winery's Sacred Land premium label, 2024. In recent years, this top-quality wine has won international awards.

Honey grapes but introducing cabernet varieties across the region, including in Cizhong, to sell to wineries as a new means of income. This venture failed in Cizhong, with most cabernet grapes often becoming too diseased without the heavy use of fertilizer and pesticides. Many villagers in Cizhong have since abandoned the state-promoted growing of cabernet for Shangri-La Winery and produce their own wines to sell to tourists.

According to Gerong, the original pilot project with Sunspirit involved over 200 *mu* of land, but Wang contradicts him, saying only 120 *mu* were planted across two villages. Shangri-La Winery began business in 2002 following the initial observed successes of the Sunspirit project. In 1999, the government collaborated with Huaze, a barley liquor company located near Shangri-La City, to form Shangri-La Wine Company under the umbrella of the large liquor conglomerate VATS Group. By 2013, there were 130,000 *mu* of vineyards planted in village fields in the region. Gerong also explained that his own wine and grape expertise has been exaggerated in press reports, including a *China Daily* article that credited him with the introduction and success of this industry (Xiao and Li 2012). He began working in 2003 for the county biological resources office, where his superiors instructed him to learn about grapes and wine. In September 2013, he and others visited wineries, restaurants, and châteaus in California to learn more about the industry. By introducing grapes as a new form of village agriculture, Gerong suggested that the local government significantly increased household incomes across the region. My own survey research (Galipeau 2015) confirms this information. As the organizer of the program at the village level, Gerong comes across as possessing a genuine interest in the well-being of villagers. He provides every villager with his cell phone number and prides himself on his direct and personal connection with all the rural people in the region, telling them to call him whenever they have any problems with their vineyards or need assistance.

Observations on the Shangri-La Winery project, however, raise several concerns. These include heavy use of chemical fertilizers and pesticides in most villages that sell their grapes to the winery, a lack of support for household wine production in places such as Cizhong, and the overall instability of the industry in terms of future outlook and food security (Galipeau 2015). These worrying trends have all occurred with little to no remaining subsistence grain production. Villagers are also uneasy about being able to sell grapes to Shangri-La Winery in the long term. Gerong responded to these concerns, offering some keen insight. He admitted that buckwheat, a traditional Tibetan staple and culturally significant crop, has become expensive in Deqin after being replaced by grapes and that this is a problem because local people still enjoy eating it. He claimed that for grape growing, fewer pesticides and fertilizers are used in Deqin than in other parts of China, owing to the vines being well adapted to the dry, arid climate and mildew not being an issue. He also explained that in the villages where the grapes are farmed, more organic manure from yaks, cows, and pigs is available for use as fertilizer. I could not confirm his statement that in wine regions in northern China many more chemicals are used, and I did see a lot of chemical use in Deqin, where only a few environmentally active villagers seem to care about its impact.[6] Concerning individual villagers' ability to promote their wine as organic, as villagers in Cizhong do, Gerong explained that the government does not encourage household winemaking and marketing because it makes meeting and upholding health, hygiene, and quality standards much harder. While perhaps a valid concern, it seems not to have prevented virtually all of

Cizhong's villagers from making their own wine, something that might be beneficial for income diversification in other villages in Deqin. Due to the annual instability of selling grapes to Shangri-La Winery, whose purchasers often show up late in the season to buy grapes after they have begun to rot, concerns over income and thus food security are prevalent; having alternative outlets for grape sales, perhaps through households producing their own wine, as in Cizhong and Bu, is important (Galipeau 2015).

During my last visit to the region, in 2018, grape sales had become more diversified, with additional private wineries popping up in the market, though this is not widespread. Wang, the former county agricultural worker in Bu Village who first introduced Sunspirit, reiterated these problems, rather bitterly: "Litsing took my idea and takes credit for my work with grapes and wine, especially here in Bu, where I am the one who engaged with the community, not him.... He really made a planned economy rather than an open market by arranging for all the villagers to sell to Shangri-La. What he worked to put in place is not really an open capitalist market, be-cause the Shangri-La monopoly controls most of the market." At the time of my primary fieldwork and when I first observed the wine economy in 2011, these issues were of great concern. For many years, the economic market surrounding grapes that were sold to Shangri-La Winery, with its monopoly over the purchase of these grapes, was worrying to many village farmers since they lacked contracts guaranteeing the purchase of their grapes. With a more diversified market through the introduction of more wineries and a recent soft lifting of Shangri-La Winery's monopoly, along with new land lease agreements for some communities, economic stability has improved.

Moët Hennessy

The French firm Moët Hennessy is another prominent wine corporation in Deqin County, having operated there since 2012 as part of the luxury conglomerate LVMH (Louis Vuitton Moët Hennessy). This project in-volves a large transnational French firm with different motivations and perspectives from those of the Chinese state or of domestic agricultural companies. Moët has wine estates around the world, including in France, the United States (California), Australia, and Argentina. By 2012, Moët had already begun a sparkling wine operation under its Chandon brand in Ningxia, in northwestern China, the country's fastest-growing wine province. There, several Chinese winemakers are producing excellent wines and winning international top prizes in Europe. Despite settling on Ningxia as the location for its sparkling wine, Moët's experts were convinced, based on climate, soil, and terroir studies, that if they could overcome the logistics of working in remote Shangri-La, this region might be able to produce the best red wine in China. They believed this would be possible through a combination of recouping some of Shangri-La Winery's vineyards and also planting new ones. Indeed, China's top viticulture and enology experts in Beijing confirmed Moët's ideas about Shangri-La, assuming the question of logistics was taken out of the equation.

Moët collaborates in a joint venture, required for foreign firms in China, in which it holds the majority stake with Shangri-La Winery. Its first 2014 vintage of organic (uncertified) and premium-priced wine known as Ao Yun (or Proud Cloud, a wordplay on the Chinese term *yun*, meaning "cloud," and Yunnan) appeared on the international market in fall 2016 at a price of US$300, after many delays.[7] Moët's project began with a growing desire among the French wine industry to move operations into China itself, as both the world's fastest-growing wine market and the largest consumer of top-level Bordeaux wines by import. However, the opportunity to break into the rapidly emerging industry of fine wines in China was not Moët's alone, as the famous Château Lafitte had also begun its own vineyards and winery in Shandong Province in the northeast, one of China's largest wine regions beyond Ningxia.

According to Gerong, Moët rents seven hundred to eight hundred *mu* of land in four villages in Adong, a tributary valley with eight villages just upstream from the Mekong in northern Deqin. While Moët's winery and many vineyards are in Adong, it also maintains vineyards directly along the Mekong in Xidang and Sinong Villages and in the higher mountain community of Shouri, where Liu Jiaqiang also experimented with viticulture. Some of Moët's winemakers suggest Shouri has perhaps the best climate and terroir. Working in four distinct villages and microclimates, using terroir in the traditional geographical and climatic sense, Moët explains that it is producing grapes with four very distinct and unique "Tibetan" terroirs. While its initial vintages were a red blend of 90 percent cabernet sauvignon and 10 percent cabernet franc, Moët has begun growing and harvesting many more varietals. These include merlot, petit verdot, and chardonnay, now being marketed based on specific village names, reflecting a micro-regional terroir, also especially prominent in Burgundy, France, where wines are tied to specific village names and locales.

I learned additional information about Moët from interviews with individuals working at Moët in Deqin (who asked to remain anonymous) and with villagers who have leased their land to the company and work for it in the vineyards on a per day basis. One significant difference between Moët's and Shangri-La Winery's operations is that Moët's project involves a long-term, fifty-year lease with villagers for their land, whereas Shangri-La Winery purchases grapes from villagers each year with no guaranteed contract beyond verbal government assurances that the company will show up.

The overall landscape transformation that has come with Moët's project is the same as elsewhere, with most households choosing to grow fewer subsistence grains such as wheat and barley and to abandon seasonal agropastoralism by selling off large numbers of yaks and cattle. However, in Adong, Xidang, Sinong, and Shouri, where long-term lease agreements have been made with Moët, there is far less insecurity in annual income than in villages that sell their grapes to Shangri-La Winery. Moët guarantees households an income of ¥2,000 (US$275) per *mu* of unplanted land per year and ¥2,200 (US$304) per *mu* of vineyard land. Even if the vineyards fail to produce or the company is unsuccessful, Moët still guarantees income for fifty years. Additionally, villagers can choose to work in the vineyards, making ¥120 (US$17) per day. Everyone I have talked to in Adong is pleased with this arrangement compared to the previous situation of growing and selling grapes to Shangri-La Winery. In fact, many say that they have not only good income security this way, but also the opportunity to work in the vineyards for pay, which means that they can remain at home in the village with their families instead of needing to hike up into the mountains to collect caterpillar fungus and matsutake or seek out wage labor elsewhere. This is not to say that changes in people's attitudes are all positive or that they easily accept working as wage laborers or "plantation" workers on their own land, producing crops for someone else. This type of somewhat regulated wage-based income is new to many. Despite higher incomes, some still choose to escape or avoid it at times.[8]

The comments of one person who works for Moët and also works with villagers are enlightening, especially when juxtaposed with the experience of most villagers in Deqin who work with Shangri-La Winery. When asked about the timing of harvests and company purchases, this individual said that farmers will always complain and do not always understand ripeness, quality, and sugar content for winemaking. This stands in contrast to villagers' complaints that Shangri-La Winery purchases grapes after they rot. However, most of this person's insights about his company's project differ from observations of viticulture elsewhere in Deqin. Although Moët has a joint venture with Shangri-La Winery, this is mostly out of necessity, since every foreign company requires a local partner in China. The two companies do not actually work closely together. As the individual from Moët described:

> With Shangri-La's program they are probably getting about 900,000 kilos of wine per *mu* of grapes since they focus on quantity and not on quality overall. Shangri-La honestly has big problems with quality in my mind. The system currently in place is not good, since there is no open market; Shangri-La has a monopoly, so the long-term outlook isn't good. The system is, however, good for the farmers and good for the Shangri-La Winery since they don't care about quality. With a quality system in place, there would be less income and food for the farmers because they would not be able to sell all their grapes at a flat rate or at all due to poor quality. We at Moët are going all or-

ganic unlike Shangri-La, but also spending lots of money doing this. This comes from respect for the farmers, land, and environment. With more time and money, you can make organic wine anywhere, but it takes a lot of effort. The reason everyone in the region has chosen to grow cabernet is because it's a very easy cultivar to establish and is very adaptable. It will easily become localized and distinct within a specific region. This is part of why cabernet has been chosen here. We are starting with cabernet in Adong but will also add merlots and other varietals over time.

Villagers in the Shangri-La Winery project experience more income insecurity than do villagers who have long-term lease agreements with Moët for their land in Adong and nearby areas. This can lead to food insecurity. However, based on the Moët employee's perceptions, while there are problems with Shangri-La Winery's virtual monopoly, the project can still function as a method of income improvement and economic "development" because quality is less of a concern. If the company were to focus on quality, the situation would be different. A focus on quantity by Shangri-La Winery has also led to heavy chemical intensification and environmental degradation. The cases of Cizhong and Adong prove that this is not necessary and, in fact, would be avoidable if the state and Shangri-La Winery were to develop a more sustainable long-term approach to the viticulture in Deqin.

Some differences between Moët's vineyard operations and individual households growing grapes for Shangri-La Winery became apparent to me one afternoon as I walked around the vineyards and chatted with villagers in Adong, including a twenty-eight-year-old Chinese viticulture and wine expert who provided me with more insight into Moët's project. Originally from Chuxiong Prefecture, a mountainous area near Kunming, he had studied viticulture and winemaking at Xian Agriculture University, China's top institution in these fields. On this day, he was doing his weekly survey of the vineyards for a database that tracks every plot. He looks at the grape bundles for their fruit percentage and checks for diseases and mildew. In one newly planted section of seedlings, he also dug a hole to check the soil moisture. In addition to managing the vineyards, he assists the French with winemaking. Each week after surveying all the vineyards, he enters the information in the database and sends copies to his French supervisor. As he finished his surveying, I asked him about organics and the local practice of intercropping vineyards with corn and other crops, since in most villages the grapes sold to Shangri-La Winery are still grown this way. He reiterated that with Moët, everything is completely organic and that it imports its fertilizers from Europe. He also explained that from a viticulture standpoint, intercropping is not good. Tall crops like corn can shade vines and interfere with their growth, for example, by limiting the availability of water and nutrients. Moët believes it manages its vineyards much better than can individual households tending vineyards themselves and selling their grapes as an annual cash crop.

Xiaoling Estate and Château Roduit

Alongside local villagers, I first encountered the two French and Swiss boutique wineries operating in Cizhong and Cigu when they approached Wu Gongdi and Hong Xing about managing the family's vineyards and purchasing Rose Honey grapes. The first of these wineries, Xiaoling Estate, was originally part of a French Catholic development NGO. Now registered as a for-profit company in Hong Kong, it is under direct supervision by a French investor from Burgundy who is based in Shanghai and had provided previous financial support. Originally, another Frenchman, who had spent many years working in Northwest Yunnan on various projects, led the winery. Most recently, he was involved in Yunnan's lucrative Pu'er tea business. With a deep-seated interest in the history and background of the MEP and the Saint Bernard fathers in the region, he began a wine project in the early 2010s, collaborating with a Burgundy-trained Swiss Valais winemaker from Martigny, where the headquarters of the Saint Bernard priests and archives are located. In 2015, the third year of their

FIGURE 16. Adong villagers planting vines, with Moët winery
and lodge atop the hill in the background, 2014.

project, they began to sell their wine, at least initially, to the French and
other Europeans in larger eastern cities, including Shanghai. In their first
year producing wine, they purchased cabernet sauvignon grapes from
local villagers in Cigu but planned to secure land to manage their own
vineyards as well, much in the same manner as Moët, though on a much
smaller scale.

   After spending an afternoon with the men from Xiaoling and learning
about vine care and management, I better understood the necessities of
these practices when I visited their small winery, next to Cigu's church,
and tasted the wine. They were pouring the previous year's wine into three
oak barrels they had just purchased. This involved siphoning it out of a
large stainless steel fermenting tank upstairs and into the barrels on the
lower level. They also had many Chinese-style clay barrels, traditionally
used for liquor production, with which they were experimenting. When I
tasted their wine in 2015, after it had been fermenting for one year in clay

jars and had just entered oak barrels for further aging, I found it quite good. It tasted like what I would expect and desire from a more expensive cabernet. The winemaker said that the alcohol content, at only 12 percent, was a bit too low and should have been 14 percent. He explained that the villagers they bought their grapes from harvested too early and had not managed the vineyards in an ideal way—hence the need to own and manage vineyards to produce optimal grapes.

When I returned in spring 2016 to visit the Swiss Valais winemaker, to see how their business and wine were coming along, I was even more impressed. The wines this time were excellent—by far the best I have had in Shangri-La. The winemaker had glasses set out for assemblage, and he was tasting and testing the alcohol and sugar content in all the clay barrels, which they were now using with Swiss-made pressure-regulated seals. In a professional and sophisticated manner, he wrote down the fermentation and sugar content on each barrel. He explained that they had organized formal tastings in Shangri-La with the French owners of the Flying Tigers Café, a French and Tibetan fusion restaurant in Old Town, in the popular tourist destination of Dali, as well as in Kunming. They were also preparing for a formal presentation of wine in Shanghai with representatives from the prominent magazine *Decanter*. Later, in summer 2016, I learned that they had won a gold medal for their 2014 vintage in one of China's largest annual wine competitions and a bronze medal in *Decanter*'s regional Asia Wine Awards. Reviews from *Decanter* describe the wine as follows: "Lovely black fruit aroma with hints of toasty oak. To taste, it boasts plenty of bright black fruit, a fine structure and texture, and a liquorice-driven finish" (Decanter Asia Wine Awards 2016).

During my visit to the winery, the winemaker expressed his desire to create for the first time a good wine for China with a true local Tibetan terroir. He felt that Moët had a different focus and that was to sell more of its wine overseas. His thinking behind creating a Tibetan terroir is that most of the excellent wine in China is trying to replicate Bordeaux wines rather than develop something new in terms of character and capture the purest flavors of local grapes. Coming from a professional European winemaker, this framing of Cizhong as having a terroir, or the ability to develop one based on the missionary history of the region and Tibetan culture, was well expressed. The Xiaoling company statement posted on its website in December 2016 makes a lyrical assertion:

> Himalaya Development Group [a former parent company of Xiaoling] finds its inspiration in the beauty of the Himalayas and their surrounding regions, their people, their rich and diverse cultures, as well as their ecological resources. We are convinced that those unique assets could be valorized a lot more than they have been until now. Our purpose is to develop high-end productions that will be deeply rooted in this very fertile environment, and serve the global market.
>
> Our most significant venture is located in the northern part of Yunnan, one of the most promising emerging wine-producing regions in China. The vineyard finds its origins in the French missionaries who planted there the first vines in 1850, and today is producing one of Asia's finest wines. . . .
>
> It is there, on the legendary Mekong River, surrounded by unviolated mountains, that the unique encounter between the French wine-making tradition and the Tibetan culture has slowly evolved into a great terroir. Himalaya Development Group is proud to give Xiaoling everything it needs to maintain its excellence, and be promoted to the level it deserves to the world of demanding wine connoisseurs. (Himalaya Development Group 2016)

From what I tasted, observed, and believed, Xiaoling Estate was shaping up to be an amazing operation in 2015 and 2016, but when I returned in 2018 things had changed significantly. The Valais winemaker remained in the region but had moved on to begin his own operation and winery and had been replaced by the French director from Shanghai with Chinese staff and a quite renowned seasonal French expert from Burgundy. The French expert recommended the new Chinese winemaker, who had trained and worked in Burgundy. This expert had worked closely with

Hong Xing in fall 2017 to produce his first truly outstanding wine, which continues to earn Hong Xing great praise from visitors. Xiaoling's wine continues to impress foreign and domestic critics, garnering praise in top-ten global wine lists. Its 2023 chardonnay, Hongpo (named after the village from which the grapes were harvested), was named China's best wine of the year by reviewers representing the prominent global wine critic James Suckling. Like Moët, Xiaoling has begun to experiment with village-specific wines to highlight individual flavorings like those found in Burgundy. Working closely with village growers in Cigu and Cizhong and now further afield, Xiaoling has begun planting and vinting wines from chardonnay and new red varietals, including producing a refreshing rosé from Rose Honey, which it has determined to be Bacot Noir.

Having become friends with the Valais winemaker formerly of Xiaoling and being impressed with his award-winning work, I was happy to learn in 2018 that he had started his own venture. His Château Roduit had been developing wine in the region, selecting grapes from a variety of locales along the upper Mekong and Yangzi Rivers. He had developed his own vineyards with local villagers and was creating one-of-a-kind blends and aging the wines in clay barrels at high elevation, over 10,000 feet, in Shangri-La City. His first vintage appeared in 2018. Both Xiaoling Estate and Château Roduit have continued to receive major accolades as some of the best wines being produced in China today. To maintain the pure flavor of the region's grapes and to give Shangri-La wines their own terroir, Château Roduit is insisting on using only clay jars, rather than oak barrels, for aging. This method has worked well. Château Roduit has also become a localized family business, as the Swiss winemaker married a local Tibetan woman from Badong Village, a Catholic community downstream from Cizhong, and he now collaborates with her in all the winery's affairs and business promotions. I regularly see photos of them on WeChat hosting tastings and exhibitions in places such as Beijing, Shanghai, Hainan, and Hong Kong, along with photos of similar events hosted by Xiaoling.

Hada Village White Wines

I had been hearing about new ice wine projects and wineries in neighboring Weixi County by word of mouth and in various media publications for a few years. After reading in 2016 about an ice wine festival the
government hosted in Weixi in late 2015 with experts and winemakers
from Canada and Germany (F. Yang 2015), I decided to visit and find out
more about these projects. As I would come to learn, one of the wineries
in Weixi represents a middle ground in terms of village and household
entrepreneurialism, with local people finding ways to indigenize modernity through a collaborative and shared corporate framework, blending
the individual cottage wine industries seen in Cizhong with large-scale
corporate ones such as Shangri-La Winery, Moët, and Sunspirit. Quite
fortunately, when I returned to Shangri-La from Cizhong for a few days
in April 2016 to meet a colleague, he introduced me to a local Naxi government official who was involved in a white ice wine project in Weixi.
In this man's home village, a winery was producing both white ice wines
and dry wines. After I received this introduction and tasted some of the
dry wines in Shangri-La City, the official offered to host me in his village
and help me learn more about the project.

The winery is located in Hada Village, in the scenic district of Tacheng
in Weixi County. The village is situated in a subtropical tributary valley of
the Yangzi, which is lush with palm trees and bamboo, compared to the
arid central Mekong valley of Deqin and the Yangzi proper, where most
viticulture is located. While the valley is green and warm in the springtime,
snowcapped peaks ring the area. In this region, paddy rice fields are the
primary form of agriculture, unlike in most of Diqing Prefecture, which
for such crops is either too high in elevation or too dry. While minority
Naxi people inhabit Hada Village, Tibetan communities surround the area.
Larger Weixi County is a Lisu autonomous region, with Lisu being the
largest ethnic group and making up the government administration. Of
the three counties in Diqing, only Weixi is not inhabited by a majority of
Tibetans. Unlike in most Naxi areas, such as those to the south in Lijiang,

the general center of Naxi culture, in Hada most people follow Tibetan Buddhism rather than the Naxi shamanistic religion known as Dongba.

In Hada, winemaking and viticulture are one of three industries developed as part of a larger village agricultural cooperative company. It is corporate in structure, but not state-based or private, so village households share ownership, profits, and management responsibilities. The other two products produced are local Yunnan ham (some of the best I have ever tasted) and wild organic honey (sold at lucrative prices, close to ¥800 [US$112] per jar). Before viticulture began in 2009, the only crop grown in fields at elevations higher than the paddy areas was corn, which did not create good profits. Seeing the benefits of viticulture elsewhere in Diqing, the Shangri-La official from Hada worked to start the village winery corporation. Under guidance from a New Zealand–based winemaker and consultant who had worked extensively in Ningxia, and given the abundance of red grapes, he decided to focus on white varietals. The grape cultivar chosen and still exclusively planted is Vidal, a complex hybrid developed in Europe but grown in the largest numbers in Canada for ice wines. This varietal is well suited to cold climates, with high sugar content and tannins or acidity. There have been discussions about planting Rieslings as well, but instead the village has used available investment funds for the construction of a new winery in Hada. Rieslings will likely be added later.

Winemaking in Hada first began in 2011, two years after the planting of grapes, and production has taken place several hours to the south using Shangri-La Winery's facilities and equipment. The village-based viticultural assistant whom I spent time with often travels to Tiger Leaping Gorge Town to the south to check on the production of the wines on a regular basis. By harvest time in 2016, the village had planned to complete its new on-site winery. It built the winery at the edge of a forest up above the village, with splendid views looking out across the valley. Before 2016, the company had not sold or marketed the wines directly. It wanted to perfect them. However, it has distributed the wines privately and made some available to tourists locally in a boutique lodge known as Songtsam, which has locations throughout Diqing, including in Hada and Cizhong.

On the day I arrived, we sampled the ice wine, which was superb, light and sweet with a honey flavor and, for me, a bit easier on the palate than Sunspirit's red cabernet sauvignon ice wines. The dry white wine also produced using Vidal grapes is similarly splendid, though a bit drier and sharper than something like a chardonnay, due to the high acidity of the grapes. The villagers and company grow the grapes for these two wines in different locations. Dry grapes are grown in the valley in Hada Village, while ice wine grapes are grown in a much colder area higher up the mountain, above the valley, in the snow and frost needed before harvesting. In addition, while the company itself manages many vineyards cooperatively using its own methods, every household also maintains its own vineyards and sells grapes to Shangri-La Winery individually. Hada is one of the few locales from which the winery buys white grapes. A major difference in Weixi County is that Shangri-La Winery has never held a monopoly on the production and purchase of grapes, so villagers can create their own winery. The monopoly established in the early 2000s over vineyard land exists in Deqin County only.[9]

One can also observe a difference between the two types of vineyards in Hada: those of the company and those managed by households. The company manages its vineyards strictly for producing the best wine, and these vineyards look much like those owned and operated by Moët and Sunspirit. The spacing between the vines is much larger, allowing more sunlight, and there is no intercropping of corn or other crops to interfere with irrigation and nutrient needs. Households plant vines closer together and with various intercropping. A viticultural assistant from southern Yunnan, who trained at Yunnan Agriculture University under an expert from Xian Agriculture University, the location of China's most prominent viticulture program, manages the company vineyards. He also continues to work with and receive guidance from the New Zealand consultant, who returns most years around the harvest and winemaking period.

In addition to the Hada winery project, one other ice wine operation, called Pabala, produces whites further west, closer to the center of Weixi County and its capital town above the Mekong valley. The story of winemaking in Hada Village and Weixi City today is linked with earlier stories of the Saint Bernard fathers. All the archival materials indicate that winemaking at the mission stations in Weixi City and nearby Xiao Weixi was extensive, likely more so than in Cizhong. The more recent development of viticulture and winemaking in the Weixi region is something of a transnational renewal of these earlier activities among the Swiss.

Terroir Making among Shangri-La's Wineries

Drinking specific wines and spirits can be framed as a practice of linking producers with consumers through meaning and materiality. This is enlightening with respect to terroir making and the motivations of the various wine producers throughout the regions. Drinks tend to differ from other consumables (aside from food) in that they represent "embodied material culture," and their meaning is completed by their human embodiment through the practice of drinking (Manning 2012, 2).

Colonial histories are often linked to drink production. For example, drinks such as a gin and tonic, and in particular such gins as Bombay Sapphire and Old Raj, are meant to invoke a feeling of returning to some sort of exotic lost colonial empire (Manning 2012, 2). Drinking gin, for instance, was an afternoon ritual among colonial outpost residents, as exemplified in George Orwell's 1934 novel *Burmese Days*. In much the same way, drinking a Singapore Sling could bring someone back to the Raffles Hotel in colonial-era Singapore (Manning 2012, 18–20). The embodiment of Shangri-La through wine and marketing now comes from Western-owned Moët, whose marketing of its Shangri-La wines to the West is indicative of these sorts of semiotic constructions. As Paul Manning summarizes this trend: "Drinks thus construct elsewheres within space and time, imaginative geographies that make their consumption meaningful in a way that transcends here and now" (20).

For Chinese drinkers and consumers, wine has become a physical embodiment of Western culture and cosmopolitanism. As Tim Tse, president of a private club in Shanghai says: "Wine now is the new Silk Road.

It is one of the intermediaries, to connect China to the rest of the world. I mean, you look at China now, they're all dressed in a shirt and tie, like me. It's part of the Westernization—they wear it on top of their skin. Now you're talking about wine, that they swallow it . . . inside their body. I mean, now they swallow the Western civilization inside their body, in their bloodstream" (Ross and Roach 2013).

This "new Silk Road" is thus a vehicle for globalization and transnationalism. Given the development of Shangri-La and the Sino-Tibetan borderlands as a new wine region intended to meet China's growing demand, and as a Tibetan region of touristic consumption, Northwest Yunnan has returned to its historical roots as a region of intermediation between Tibet and China through the embodiment of wine by villagers and visitors alike. This region was long a link between China and Tibet as part of the tea trade, with brick tea and other goods transported from southern Yunnan to Tibet. Wine consumption and production has taken up a role that tea once played to bring this region into the fold of a globalizing China. Indeed, if one looks at the development of Moët's winery in Adong Village, Xiaoling Estate, and Château Roduit, consumption and embodiment of the wine produced there broadens the order and magnitude of exchange for the region with wine sold to Western consumers abroad as part of "Shangri-La."

Wine constructs a bridge along this "new Silk Road" between the Sino-Tibetan borderlands, affluent Han China, and the West. Among Cizhong winemakers such as Wu Gongdi and Hong Xing, wine possesses meaning in relation to family histories, connections to ritual and the church, and economic success. With the help of experts from Xiaoling Estate, Hong Xing has also further infused meaning through perfecting his wines to create a particular taste profile in connection to Rose Honey grapes. These are all components of what gives at least Cizhong wines a unique terroir.

Wine from Shangri-La Winery, Moët, Xiaoling, and others translates meaning from producers to consumers in a different manner but is still linked with locality through terroir, branding imagery, or taste profiles created by these locales. For Shangri-La Winery, having been initiated by the state, wine is meant to play a direct role in "shangrilazation," taking a consumable Tibetan commodity from the landscape and the local people and translating it into a form that can be consumed by predominantly Han people interested in Tibet and Shangri-La. A secondary goal has been to use winemaking and viticulture as a form of poverty alleviation for local people, but for many, they have no direct role in creating a terroir for these wines. Yet, these functions for wine change between the village grape growers, winemakers, and consumers across space and time.

The predominantly foreign wineries (Moët, Xiaoling, Roduit) are each working to create singular and new terroirs, which can be tasted by consumers on the basis of characteristics such as soil and climate. They work toward featuring these traits using different methods, including abstaining from aging their wines in oak barrels to show off the flavor of the grapes as dictated directly by the local ecology, a traditional construction of wine terroir. Simultaneously, though, they play up the Tibetanness of the region, using local villagers in marketing and displaying them as direct actors in the processes of managing vineyards, harvesting grapes, and making wine, although the involvement of local Tibetans is in fact still heavily regulated and managed by these foreign actors.

Wine for Chinese Tourists and Consumers

How is wine across this "new Silk Road" perceived? For many people in Cizhong and Bu, winemaking has become an important part of culture and livelihood. Most local people have their own perceptions of what makes wine important or good in quality, which are not necessarily informed by consumer ideals. However, in conducting interviews with villagers in Cizhong, Bu, and Adong, where Moët's winery is located, whenever I asked about why Han people like wine from Cizhong, Deqin, and, in general, Shangri-La, certain themes percolated. By far the most common response from Cizhong villagers was that their wine is well known because of the French history, in this case by urban-dwelling Han tourists. Being marked as French makes sense, given the perception among many Chinese consumers that French wine is the best in the world. Another common theme expressed by villagers throughout Deqin was that outsiders like the wine because it is pure, organic, and has no chemicals. This assertion was often juxtaposed against the factory wines made by Shangri-La Winery, which according to villagers are not organic. In fact, Shangri-La Winery now markets some of its wine as organic, though among the villages that sell it grapes I have yet to find one that does not use chemical pesticides and fertilizers, so this marketing remains suspect. Villagers also said that tourists as well as consumers throughout China enjoy the region's wine because it comes from Tibet and is a product of Tibetan culture, which is an expression of a "pure" environment, without the pollution found in China's large cities. Tibetan villagers seem to be fully aware of Han outsiders' fascination with them as an "other," an allure they feel is passed on to the consumer through the wine made there.

Experiencing this "Franco-Tibetan" countryside and visiting village guesthouses in Cizhong and elsewhere to eat local food and partake in local farming life is also a tourism trend in China. With a growing middle class situated in urban centers, some Chinese have begun to experience a disconnect with their agricultural and rural roots, and tourism in places like Yunnan and even to countryside villages outside Beijing for a local organic lunch has become popular (Hessler 2010; Klein 2014). Organics in and of themselves in China have garnered much scholarly attention in recent years. What brings Chinese consumers to places like Yunnan and Cizhong is a combination of history, religion, and the ideal of what the food anthropologist Jakob A. Klein (2014) calls "connecting with the countryside," a form of healthy eating and a way to avoid the increasingly common food scares with factory food in China. The chance to take part in novel agricultural activities, such as grape crushing for making wine, is also a completely novel experience for China's new traveling middle class. The fact that Shangri-La wine is branded as being from an ethnic minority makes people more curious. Consumers can believe the wine is healthier because minorities, especially Tibetans, are often stereotyped as being more "green." It is not surprising, then, that brands such as Shangri-La Winery and Sunspirit use Tibetan culture as a marketing tool, given the curiosity and the desire to consume Tibetan and minority cultures along with their association with being natural, healthy, and free of chemicals.

The development of viticulture and wine production in Northwest Yunnan has followed many paths. In Cizhong Village, individual producer identities, religion, culture, and history are all tied up together with wine and winemaking. Elsewhere, the state (represented by Shangri-La Winery), Chinese corporations, transnational corporations, private individuals (Tibetan, foreign, and Chinese), and entire villages are becoming entwined within the larger national Chinese and global economy, "shangrilazation," and consumption of Tibet.

These projects have all changed local villagers' livelihoods and agriculture. Grapes have become the crop grown in most abundance in river valley villages, often forming a virtual monocrop of vineyards. Villagers still intercrop the grape vineyards with corn, which they mostly use for animal feed. Many explain that they may occasionally also grow small amounts of wheat and barley within the vineyards, but much less than previously grown for subsistence and cultural/ritual purposes, before the introduction of grapes. These grains were once the staple crops in the region. Over time, villagers have replaced the traditional grains grown and consumed in Tibetan society with corn and grapes now in the fields and purchased rice on household tables (although in this region of Tibet, rice was consumed through trade for many generations and grown in areas to the south such as Cizhong and Weixi). In thinking about ethnicity and minority identities in China, I have tried to avoid using the terminologies "Sinicization" or "Hanification" in reference to assimilation of minorities into Han culture and society. However, these terms work well to explain the primarily Chinese state-based development that has come with the promotion of Shangri-La Winery (and to a lesser extent with Sunspirit in Bu and Moët in Adong) and the transformation of Deqin's agricultural landscape.

I view the development and promotion of grape growing as a household form of agricultural inclusion in wider economies, as opposed to traditional agropastoralism, which could be characterized by avoidance or escape (Scott 2009). These changes also represent a state methodology by which to enhance "shangrilazation" (Yeh and Coggins 2014a), as a primarily state-based, top-down form of development and landscape alteration framed in the context of what Emily T. Yeh (2013b) calls ambiguous "development as a gift." Yeh discusses how state territorialization and landscape transformation in central Tibet around Lhasa has followed three paths: urbanization, vegetable farming first by local household labor and then by migrant workers, and village and countryside modernization.

Within these three examples, Yeh frames development ambiguously because it does not always benefit rural Tibetan households. Two key points from her analysis are pertinent to the case of wine and landscape change in Deqin. First, tracing agency and power in the production of material landscapes illuminates how development produces contradictory subjects and complex subject positions. Second, development and landscape transformation are central to the processes of state territorialization in Tibet. In the case of the first point, while agency may seem nonexistent among some villagers growing and producing grapes for Shangri-La Winery, and many are trapped in a monopolized market with no other option for selling their crops, some have found ways to agentively create and market their own wines beyond the confines of the state and corporate interests, as in Cizhong, Bu, and Hada. By tying their wines back to the Tibetan landscape, its soils, its geography, and their own cultural identities, as Tibetan, or in the case of Hada, as Naxi, many families have found ways to circumvent the state's monopoly on winemaking to benefit from it on their own terms, indigenizing modernity and crafting wines with their own terroirs.

However, indigenizing modernity and defining the terroir of wine on one's own terms is not universal. While the changes to agriculture have significantly raised household incomes across the region (Galipeau 2015), they have also led to alterations in the cultural identities of agricultural landscapes and even cultural practices such as agropastoralism. This connects with the idea of landscape change and viticulture in Deqin as an agriculture of economic inclusion, in reference to Yeh's (2013b) point about landscape transformation being central to the process of state territorialization. The growing of a virtual monocrop of wine grapes among Tibetans in Deqin proceeds as a form of state inclusion. State-supported viticulture in the form of Shangri-La Winery works to bring household economies into the fold of greater China, moving families away from subsistence and into the production of not just a consumable crop, which contributes to national economic growth and markets, but in this case also a luxury commodity for China's emerging middle and upper consumer classes.[10]

Wine as a commodity is then not only marketed as wine but also sold as being Tibetan, from Shangri-La, following recent trends among urban Han who seek to "consume" Tibet (Osburg 2013a, 2020; Smyer Yü 2012, 2015). Moët Hennessy exoticizes its wine further by using the Chinese name Ao Yun (Proud Cloud), alluding to the inclusion of *yun* in the provincial name Yunnan (South of the Clouds), alongside imagery of Khawa Karpo, to sell its products. Moët in fact first exported this wine for its Himalayan terroir to Europe and the United States before the company introduced it to Chinese markets. Moët is re-creating wine as a transnational connection between China, Tibet, and Europe, which began with the French and Swiss missionaries.

Most villagers do not complain about new sedentary lifestyles, indicating that being able to remain at home more and have a higher annual income from growing and selling grapes is preferred. However, this raises questions about state economic incorporation at the expense of cultural preservation, especially when this incorporation is marketed at the consumer end of the commodity chain as being distinctly "Tibetan." Not surprisingly, when asked about wine and Tibetan culture, and why Shangri-La Winery and Sunspirit wines are being marketed as Tibetan, virtually all villagers outside of Cizhong say that the wine is not Tibetan but foreign and that calling it Tibetan is purely for advertising. A few concerned individuals have even suggested to me that wine and grapes are destroying the landscape and the local Tibetan culture associated with it due to the chemical intensification of viticulture.

In summary, many different situations exist in Diqing concerning its wine economy and the changes this has brought to the landscape. In Cizhong, a grassroots revival of winemaking, vineyards, and history exists. Elsewhere, we see a mixture of corporate ideals in the case of Sunspirit and Bu Village, village-level entrepreneurialism and indigenizing modernity in Hada, top-down state-led "development" and incorporation into capitalism with Shangri-La Winery, corporate but socially and environmentally conscious viticulture in the case of Moët Hennessy, and foreign entrepreneurialism more directly connected with local communities through family ties or other means with Xiaoling Estate and Château Roduit. The wine landscape of Diqing today is transnational and historical, in both literal and imaginative ways. Past French and Swiss histories are invoked to create a dynamic new image of the people who live there, along with the state crafting the landscape as a place with unique local and colonial characteristics. Contemporary transnationalism stems from the presence of multiple French and Swiss corporate and individual entrepreneurial wineries and actors. This landscape is a dynamic assemblage of multiple actors (Tsing 2015a). However, for some, landscape alterations through wine and viticulture have come at the expense of cultural practices, livelihood pathways, food security, sustainability, and a variety of other concerns.

CHAPTER 4

Free in the Mountains
or Home in the Vineyard

If barmaid never dies,
Beer will never run out
Young man's Lasting Refuge
In it I'll surely trust.

Tsangyang Gyatso, the Sixth Dalai Lama (1683–1706 CE)

"Sometimes I really miss having all my yaks," Adong said to me one afternoon after we had hiked an hour or so up the mountain from his village to retrieve a yak, one of the few that he still owned, from a small pasture with some wooden herders' cabins.[1] As we sat down to eat some bread and drink butter tea, made for us by another villager who had been staying up there with his yaks, Adong continued:

> We used to come up here to the mountain or higher up in the caterpillar fungus area and stay for several months at a time in the summer with all the yaks. They were kind of like kids we cared for. We make a lot more money selling grapes, but the first few years were hard, never knowing if the company would come to buy them, and we still worry about this every fall. When all the families in the village raised yaks, we made less money, but at least it was a stable

standard of living. With yaks, I came up here to the mountains and was able to search for other resources like wild fruit and matsutake. Since we started growing grapes and sold most of the yaks, we rarely come to the mountains now except when we look for caterpillar fungus. This is not really a problem for my children since they've moved out of the village and attend university. I don't expect them to herd yaks or collect caterpillar fungus, but for me and my friends, we all look forward to coming back each year to look for the fungus.

After this conversation and our simple lunch, Adong excitedly suggested that before heading back down to the village with his yak we hike up the mountain a bit further to look for some wild red fruit, seemingly related to cherries, which he knew grew in the area. We proceeded upward, and in no more than fifteen minutes, he started to shimmy up the trunk of a tree to reach the small red berrylike fruit high in the branches. I always enjoy watching Adong, a small, diminutive man, as he works and nimbly climbs up things, including walnut trees during harvest season. Upon reaching the fruit, Adong pulled on a large branch until it broke off the tree and crashed down to where I was standing. He then climbed back down, and we enjoyed snacking on the sweet spoils of our afternoon escape up the mountainside from the dry Mekong gorge below.

Finding continuity with the past within the present and keeping connections with the mountains is important in the face of global and national changes that are reconfiguring Tibetan and ethnic minority livelihoods across China. The state favors people with sedentary lifestyles who are economically integrated into China's national and global economy, and with wine and viticulture the local state in Shangri-La has mobilized the population in this way as opposed to encouraging people to maintain mobile agropastoral lifestyles. But at least for Adong's generation, such a transition is not easy. In nearby Adong Village, where Moët has further transformed livelihoods into corporate labor, the transition has been even more fraught with complexities and ambiguity despite enhanced economic productivity and security. As villagers explain:

It is also better here than other villages in Deqin. This is the best village because we have the high mountain with lots of resources, and if we work hard, we can make lots of money from the mountains.

We're all pretty satisfied here with the leasing price and deal. Certainly, under this plan we have a better guarantee: there is no risk even if the grapes are diseased, no need to purchase chemicals, less work on other crops or individually owned vineyards, and no need to spend as much time in the mountains collecting caterpillar fungus.

These comments seem to suggest both that collecting mountain resources, including the prized caterpillar fungus, is a favorable activity and that it is good that such collection is no longer a necessity because of the new land lease agreements received though the government-brokered program with Moët's winery. However, many still choose to collect caterpillar fungus. How do villagers in Adong and neighboring communities differentiate between working as contracted day laborers on the vineyard land they have leased to Moët and choosing to collect caterpillar fungus and other valuable mushrooms in the mountains? When collecting fungi, villagers do so on their own schedules, without the scrutiny of vineyard overseers, and on community-managed land with specific access rights and responsibilities. This provides a more cohesive, freer, and more family/community-oriented way to indigenize modernity (like growing grapes or other crops for subsistence or for cash under one's own management), compared to working as contracted labor on leased land. To be clear, many still take part in both activities, given that fungi collection is seasonal and still involves producing a capitalist commodity through collection, though not in the same manner that making wine does. However, given the income and social security that long-term land leases from Moët provide, fungi collection, as many villagers point out, is no longer necessary to maintain a good livelihood, and they can easily remain home in the village for the entire year without having to seek wage-paying jobs outside the village or to trek up the mountain to herd animals or collect fungi.

Why, then, does much of the community, beyond children and the elderly, still choose to partake in such activities that take them further away from home? How do villagers differentiate between working as agricultural contractors and taking part in the unregulated "freedom" (Tsing 2015b, 75–76) of fungi collection in the mountains? The answers to these questions illuminate a key difference between earlier forms of state-promoted agriculture with Shangri-La Winery and new transnational corporate forms as seen with Moët and show how global capitalism is reconfiguring the institutions of land management and the landscapes and identities surrounding agricultural transformation in rural China, Tibet, and abroad. While significant scholarship on agrarian change within China exists, the global and transnational implications of these transformations remain understudied and the scholarship that does examine foreign transnational agribusiness firms in China has tended to focus more on retail and food service sectors than on the production side of the equation (Schneider 2017). Life in Adong illustrates the different ways that rural farmers adapt to and indigenize modernity while working as contracted labor in vineyards on their leased household lands. New transnational forms of land and labor management in rural China and Tibet, different from previous state and domestic corporate forms of marketized agricultural production seen with Shangri-La Winery, are leading to two significant changes in livelihoods, with mixed benefits for rural farming communities.

First, new long-term foreign leases over household land provide better guaranteed income security and social safety nets and buffer rural farming communities against year-to-year market changes and volatilities. All market risk is assumed by the foreign firm. This has led to a paradigm shift in the earlier state- and domestic corporate-led income improvement and poverty-reduction schemes seen with Shangri-La Winery, which forced entire villages to rely on single crops with uncertain futures. Specifically, in the past two decades, under the Household Responsibility System introduced during the 1980s, local governments and Chinese corporations have induced and coerced communities to produce specific cash crops for niche markets, which often have failed and left households with little recourse for recovery after long-term investments in single crops (Gali-peau 2015; Li and Tilt 2007).

Second, despite improved incomes and livelihoods and decreases in agrochemicals use and their potential impacts on soil and local environments, villagers in Adong have become alienated from agricultural production. The option of becoming a regulated workforce on land now managed by foreign and Chinese companies leaves many Tibetan farmers with a desire to escape to other work and locations where they can revive a sense of cultural and community identity that allows them the freedom to create their own work schedules and forms of livelihood continuity. These findings point to a complicated and contradictory picture for rural farming populations in terms of the nascent impacts and benefits of transnational corporate agriculture developing in China. Such impacts are further compounded by the deployment of agricultural development projects in minority regions such as Tibet, where ethnic relations are a contributing factor. Class and ethnic issues cannot be separated from agrarian studies and rural politics in China, yet they remain missing from much of this scholarship. This reinforces misunderstanding of the resistance strategies of these minority groups (Yeh 2013a). An examination of the contradictory ways in which villagers in Adong as a minority Tibetan community have engaged with various forms of agrarian change will help bridge this gap.

Contemporary Agrarian Change in Rural China and Northwest Yunnan

China has seen rapid urbanization in recent years and the overtaking in size of urban populations over rural agricultural ones. With social and cultural forces at play in transforming rural China's agrarian countryside, these regions are not disappearing, but experiencing significant and transformative social, political, and ecological processes (Yeh, O'Brien, and Ye 2013; see also Chen, Zinda, and Yeh 2017). Household farmers, including those in Tibetan regions such as Shangri-La (which have not featured significantly in discussions on agrarian change), continue to experience drastic changes themselves, most particularly at the hands of both the local and national states, which see a need to corporatize and bring the country's farmers/peasants (*nongmin*, a term increasingly decried as backward) into the folds of larger capitalism and the global economy. Household farmers or smallholders (perhaps the least loaded term without the historical class-based connotation of peasant) are cast as a problem in political discourse over food production in contemporary China due to their small-scale production capabilities, despite their long history of sustainable practices.[2] I will continue to refer to the people in Adong simply as farmers or villagers, although these smallholders are unique in that their roles have been split into those of dual contract workers and land rentiers.

This transformation conforms to the process that Mindi Schneider (2014), a sociologist of rural China, suggests is occurring across the country to push *nongmin* off their land to create large-scale industrialized agriculture that removes smallholding and farmers as a problem for food production. In earlier contract farming systems, such as those that existed previously in Adong and still do elsewhere with Shangri-La Winery, despite coercion and enticement to engage in new forms of cash cropping, village farmers in most cases maintained control over their own lands and property. Of course, in a community in which all of one's neighbors are engaging in viticulture or other cash cropping, it would be difficult not to follow suit. Nonetheless, some households occasionally chose not to for various reasons (see Galipeau 2015).

The primary pattern in the corporatizing of rural household agriculture in China since the 2000s has mainly involved domestic agribusiness firms attempting to scale up their production to create a larger global reach for Chinese agriculture. In most cases, foreign firms are left out of the picture or intentionally kept out of Chinese agribusiness to promote the global rise of China (Schneider 2017). The case of Moët's winery in Adong remains unique in this regard in that a foreign wine and spirits firm has been openly welcomed as part of the larger local state project to open up and transnationalize the Sino-Tibetan borderlands through "shangrilazation" (Yeh and Coggins 2014a; Hathaway 2014). In Adong, the impacts have been particularly unusual and contradictory for villagers, who benefit economically while simultaneously being alienated from their own methods of agricultural production and traditional patterns of household and community life. This second change did not happen with Shangri-La Winery, and while villagers verbally indicate that these livelihood alterations do not bother them, their actions speak otherwise. These nascent changes perhaps foretell a future trend toward abolition of rural collective land ownership, with consequences yet unseen and unfathomed.

New Labor, Land Regimes, and Livelihood Strategies

Since the arrival of Moët in Adong in 2012, representatives from most households in the village still choose to travel to the mountains and away from home for extended periods for fungi collection, despite arguing that it is not a necessity anymore. This juxtaposition is useful for analysis because of the profound difference in the forms of labor and land tenure that produce two primarily luxury commodities—wine and caterpillar fungus—in Adong. Caterpillar fungus has a long history as an item of Tibetan and Chinese medicinal use and consumption and more recently has entered Chinese markets as an item of luxury, desire, and gift giving, whereas wine is completely new and foreign, with most in Adong insisting wine has nothing to do with Tibetan culture, identity, or ethnicity.

By returning as a community to the mountains every year, where land is also managed as a community to protect the availability of natural resources equally for all members, Adong's people have found their own way of indigenizing modernity through caterpillar fungus collection and sales to engage with new market economies while maintaining social and community cohesion. There is also a form of livelihood continuity at play and a desire to maintain a connection with the mountains that has existed for generations but is slowly disappearing with the removal of yaks and seasonal agropastoralism from household livelihoods as villagers transition to sedentary monoculture. This form of indigenization is different from that occurring in other villages in Deqin County, especially in Cizhong, where villagers directly use grapes and winemaking to adapt to modernity through the government's Shangri-La Winery incentives and coerced market integration. In Adong, working in the French vineyards, villagers must adhere to a strict work schedule and follow the directions of predominantly Han vineyard managers and high-ranking village officials tasked with oversight by Moët. Whereas the introduction of leasing household land and the introduction of grapes and viticulture for Shangri-La Winery as a cash crop can both be viewed as ambiguous "development as a gift" (Yeh 2013b) with reference to the Chinese state's attempts to develop Tibetan areas through new agricultural techniques and technologies, in the context of managing mountain land where caterpillar fungus is collected, land tenure and management is a community endeavor, as is collection. For villagers in Adong, fungi collection is not "alienated" capitalist labor, but rather an act of envisioned or imagined "freedom" as an economic livelihood strategy in the mountains (Tsing 2015b, 75–76); it is a method of resisting or avoiding being forced to work and follow specific rules and regulations, a form of everyday resistance to being viewed as a capitalist labor force (Scott 1987, 29–30).

This type of freedom from capitalist work that fungi collection brings parallels that explored in Anna Tsing's (2015b) work on Southeast Asian mushroom collectors in the US Pacific Northwest, where matsutake, like the caterpillar fungus, serve as "trophies of freedom" that become transformed into capitalist commodities (62). Contrarily, Moët's wine grapes are purely capitalist commodities from the first stage of their production, grown with paid village labor. The way villagers spend time collecting caterpillar fungus as a social and community-based activity contrasts with working as day laborers in the vineyards for Moët and resembles the freedom that Tsing describes: "Th[e] mushroomers' freedom is irregular and outside rationalization; it is performative, communally varied, and effervescent. It has something to do with the rowdy cosmopolitanism of the place; freedom emerges from open-ended cultural interplay" (76). Among villagers in Adong and their neighboring families and communities, caterpillar fungus collection proceeds in much the same manner. Everyone travels up the mountain together at the beginning of the season, singing songs as they hike, playing music on their phones, sharing meals, along with other activities that express an exuberance and delight at being up in the mountains with one's family and community.

In a similar vein, Tsing juxtaposes mushroom collection with capitalist work: "Picking is also not labor—or even 'work.' Sai, a Lao picker, explained that 'work means obeying your boss, doing what he tells you to.' In contrast, matsutake picking is 'searching.' It is looking for your fortune, not doing your job" (2015b, 77). And like caterpillar fungus collection in Adong Village, collecting mushrooms provides a sort of vacation or escape of sorts from this capitalistic work: "[Lao-Su] and his wife look forward to joining the vibrant Mien community in Open Ticket [in Oregon] every year. They consider it a vacation; on weekends, their children and grandchildren sometimes come up to join them in picking" (78).

Villagers make more money working for the French winery in Adong, but this is managed capitalist work, of a type to which they are unaccustomed and which makes them feel uncomfortable. One day while planting new vines for Moët, a middle-aged woman complained to me:

The French and Chinese vineyard managers say we can only take two thirty-minute breaks and one hour for lunch each day. Why is this important and why do they care when and how much we work as long as we finish the job? When we farm ourselves, we always do a good job and finish our work. So, they should stop bossing us, and let us grow these grapes for them like we always have. The Tibetan assistant for that French guy even says the French boss really respects us and likes how we care about the land and our plants. So why doesn't he treat us like he respects us and our farming? They pay us well, but I don't like it when they tell us what to do all the time.

Unlike previous smallholder farming activities or fungi collection, which I think of here as a livelihood continuity of these self-instructed agricultural practices, working for Moët is new and can be described differently, as capitalist labor versus work, because it explicitly involves working in a position of subordination for someone else. Value, like that found in gathering caterpillar fungus and other fungi, however, can be produced in or through other forms of work that are different from explicit capitalist labor (Standing 2014). Tsing (2015b, 126–27) suggests that mushrooms, when they are initially picked by those seeking freedom and first exchange hands with middlemen, represent value but not capital or capitalism, since the early stages of the matsutake commodity chain (as with caterpillar fungus in Adong as well) are all cash businesses with no accumulation of capital.

Working as laborers for Moët can be frustrating when vineyard company representatives instruct villagers on how to properly farm land they have been cultivating successfully for generations with grain, and with grapes (albeit with heavy chemical use) for the past two decades. This was clear one afternoon when a Han manager derided villagers for doing something incorrectly as I was working with them. After the man left, they shrugged off his stern instructions. I also remember once noticing a social media post from the father of my host family in Adong in which he complained about being stuck working in the fields one day until 6:00 p.m., unable to leave because he was working on the winery's schedule. Previously, individual households grew grapes and other cash crops, and people created their own work schedules. Villagers' responses illustrate some of the impacts of global capitalism and foreign investment on local livelihoods and household decision-making. Moët and other foreign firms rely on Han "experts" and high-ranking village and government officials in managing investments while simultaneously marketing their wines and products as being from a distinctly ethnic region and environment (in this case Tibetan). This raises a host of issues related to class and ethnicity that have been given little attention previously.

Class differentiation has become further substantiated within the community by Moët's new labor and land lease agreements. Lease contracts were negotiated by county and prefectural government officials alongside village leaders without direct consultation with individual village households. Today, village leaders and predominantly Han vineyard managers work under the direction of French company representatives to instruct and direct villagers in agricultural labor, while previously farming and decision making were conducted at the household level with regular labor sharing between families. The arrival of new land lease and labor agreements with Moët has thus also further substantiated and magnified class differentiation within the community between everyday household farmers and village and government leaders.

Work in the Vineyards

In Adong, I spent much of my time working in the French vineyards each day with villagers and conversing with them about their experiences engaging in this new form of wage labor, along with their thoughts on the lease agreement with Moët for their household land. I also traveled with my host family in Adong to Meilishi upstream to hike with the entire village up the mountain to camp out and take part in the annual caterpillar fungus collection in May 2015. I had conducted research in Meilishi earlier, in 2011, on the political ecology and economic vulnerabilities involved in viticulture commodification and caterpillar fungus collection (Galipeau 2014, 2015).

A consistent finding in my research in Adong was that everyone was extremely happy with the land lease agreement that had been negotiated with Moët for their vineyards. As one household father stated: "This is the best income we've ever had, and our quality of life has improved so much since the French winery arrived and started paying us to use our land." I never met anyone in Adong who expressed any ill feelings toward the arrival of Moët or the leasing of their land to the winery. In most cases, the general infrastructural development that has been brought to the community has been welcome, including the paving of the one access road, which Moët paid for.

One day early on in my time in Adong, while working to plant new grape vines with a group of younger and middle-aged women, I asked them about any linkages between wine and Tibetan culture and identity. After some time discussing with a few of them why they thought tourists and Chinese liked the wine from Shangri-La and Deqin so much, one boisterous middle-aged woman exclaimed loudly to everyone that Chinese men drink grape wine because they think it will give them big penises. After that, for the next hour or so before breaking for lunch, the mood among the group remained jovial, with continuing jokes along the same line of thinking.

This interaction about Chinese versus Tibetan perceptions of wine consumption and use reveals a tension between Tibetan workers and Han managers for Moët who supervise villagers' work. For villagers in Adong, the production of wine has no history or meaning. The state and Moët are using Tibetan villagers, their land, labor, and identities, and the "Tibetan" landscape to engage in a method of "shangrilazation" (Yeh and Coggins 2014a) and "internal orientalism" (Smyer Yü 2015). This form of landscape development and wine promotion brands wine as a local product produced by local people, even though it is not. Perhaps in a way, before Moët arrived, villagers did produce Shangri-La Winery wines with a certain level of local accomplishment and recognition since individual households were responsible for the quality of their grapes. With the arrival of Moët and contracts for villager land and labor, there is now more alienation from land and labor and increased ethnic, power, and spatial divisions reflected by differences between production, distribution, and consumption of wine. Since Moët's wine is sold in Europe and the United States, it could not be further removed from Adong's people, although they are featured by Moët in advertising imagery overseas.

For Adong people, grapes and wine are primarily economic, unlike in other Tibetan village locales in Deqin County where they possess more social or cultural value. Nobody in Adong believes that wine has anything to do with being a Tibetan or the Tibetan environment. However, because wine produced in Tibetan areas comes from a clean and beautiful moun-

tain place, my young host mother and her older aunt speculated on why
Chinese like the wine from Adong and associate it with Tibet:

> Grape aren't really part of Tibetan culture, they come from outside
> and are foreign. . . . As a young person, actually I don't really like
> being here because it's too boring, but it's beautiful and there's no
> pollution, so I can see why tourists like it. I think they must have
> a similar feeling buying and drinking the wine from here.
>
> There's no Tibetan culture with the wine. Caterpillar fungus
> has importance for us as Tibetans as a traditional medicine and is
> really important economically. I eat caterpillar fungus and it's good
> for the body and has really helped my high blood pressure. I have
> also heard that wine is good for your body. Maybe this is why the
> Chinese like it, especially because we live in such a pure and healthy
> place. I do actually think it's good how the company promotes
> their wine as Tibetan. There's no pollution here, and we have a
> very clean, beautiful environment.

A typical day working for Moët in the vineyards begins at eight or
nine o'clock in the morning. At noon, everyone returns home for lunch,
and an hour or so later, they take up work in the vineyards again, working
until around six o'clock in the evening. The freedom of working at one's
own pace, which comes with household-based agriculture and collecting
caterpillar fungus, is different from what Tibetan villagers in Adong experience working for Moët, although they attempt to subvert this system
by avoiding interaction with and ignoring instructions from company
managers when they are out in the fields. On multiple occasions, the
troop of women with whom I was working took long breaks when they
were technically on the clock working for Moët. Moët pays villagers ¥120
(US$17) per day, not by the hour, so the long breaks may not really be an
issue. Villagers told me that sometimes the village leader (one of them,
but of higher class and with closer connections to the company) or a Han
vineyard manager from Moët would come and check in on them while
they were working, but that most days work was relaxed. When I walked

around with the Chinese vineyard manager one day, we stopped so he could instruct a group of women to water the newly planted seedlings well due to the hot weather, and he mentioned to me that the villagers can sometimes be hard to manage. In turn, they complained to him about wishing to quit work at five o'clock instead of six.

Villagers in Adong are already making far more money than ever before by leasing their land to Moët, and their working in the vineyards provides them with an additional bonus. Contrary to earlier forms of household-based agriculture and collecting caterpillar fungus, there is no investment or return from working for Moët other than a daily salary. Villagers often say that since the company does not seem to watch them closely, there is no need to work too hard when they will still make the same amount of money each day. Additionally, days in the dry valleys of the upper Mekong can be extremely hot, well over 90 degrees Fahrenheit. In most situations and locations, villagers in the area do not typically carry out agricultural work in the middle of the afternoon due to the heat, and instead rest or perform other activities at home for several hours after working in the morning and breaking for lunch. The freedom to create one's own schedule to allow this flexibility is then lost for workers who spend the entire time out in the vineyards. To subvert such obligations, one can relax while in the fields and not work the entire time, or one can escape to the mountains for one to two months each year to collect caterpillar fungus, with other shorter trips later in the summer for also collecting matsutake and other valuable mushrooms. In these situations, villagers work entirely for themselves on their own time, while also taking part in a large social and community-wide event and activity. The French manager of Moët's winery has even commented on the difficulty of recruiting villagers to work in the vineyards during the summer season (Robinson and Lander 2014). Villagers carry an advantage in their relations with Moët given the isolation and remoteness of the village and the winery, and part of the lease agreement the local government brokered states that Adong people, not outsiders, get to work in the vineyards. They are the only available workforce, so they have the luxury of leaving for the mountains for one or two months without fear of reprisal or of losing their jobs.

Collecting Caterpillar Fungus

Caterpillar fungus has many names and a complex life cycle. In Chinese, it is called *dong chong xia cao* (winter worm, summer grass) or simply *chong cao* (worm grass). In Tibetan, it is called *yartsa gunbu* (summer grass, winter worm) or simply *bu* (worm). Among villagers in Deqin, it is referred to by its short Chinese name, *chong cao*. As described by Daniel Winkler (2005, 2008), human use of caterpillar fungus has spanned hundreds of years in both China and Tibet, with its earliest known existence in Tibet, despite its modern-day explosion as a consumer item in China. Outside Tibet and China, caterpillar fungus is found in surrounding regions in Nepal, India, and Bhutan, in areas inhabited predominantly by Tibetans (Winkler 2010). Historically, it has existed as a traditional form of medicine in both Tibet and China, used as a tonic and stamina booster and an aphrodisiac (Winkler 2008).

The biology of caterpillar fungus is strange and complex, and its literal name in English is an accurate description. It is about the size of a matchstick. The fungus, which is collected from the body of a caterpillar, is associated with ghost moths that have been parasitized by the fungus *Ophiocordyceps sinensis*, formerly *Cordyceps sinensis* (Boesi 2003; Winkler 2008, 2010). In the autumn each year, the caterpillars, which live in the high grasslands above fourteen thousand feet, eat the fungal spores released by the previous year's fungi and then burrow under the ground for the winter to pupate. The body of the caterpillar becomes completely parasitized and killed by the fungus, leaving behind only the exoskeleton. In the late spring and early summer, the fruiting body of the fungus emerges from the ground as it grows out of the former head of the caterpillar. This is the object that the local Tibetans and other collectors look for each year as they crawl across the grasslands. When the fungi are sold by village collectors, they can fetch anywhere from ¥90 (US$12) to ¥120 (US$17) per pair.[3] In the larger cities of eastern China, they are worth roughly the same value as gold, based on their weight.

In 2015, when I traveled with my host family in Adong to Meilishi, just upstream on the Mekong, where the father was originally born, we hiked with the entire village up the mountain to camp out and collect caterpillar fungus. I chose to take part in this activity in Meilishi mostly because I wanted to develop contacts with the community and renew long-term relationships there, especially with a family who in 2007 had welcomed me to camp out, cook, and collect with them for several days.

My decision to accompany my host family ended up working out well, since Meilishi's annual collection activities included relatives from Adong. On the day chosen for travel up the mountain to the collecting area, we departed at 6:30 a.m. with most of the village (minus children and elders) and a long train of pack mules carrying food and other supplies. A sense of community was formed immediately, and when we stopped to eat lunch halfway up the mountain, people listened to Tibetan music playing on a cell phone and joked around. We arrived at the collecting site at 4:30 p.m. and set up camp in small huts already constructed on-site. After a break for steamed bread and butter tea, at 6:00 p.m. everyone headed out to an area near the camp where collection would begin. The primary collecting area, to which we would go on subsequent days, was about an hour's hike further up the mountain.

The whole village rendezvoused by one of the huts, and the village head provided instructions. After discussing how they would split up and where people would go, everyone ran off. Immediately, around the camp only a small amount of caterpillar fungus was found, but villagers still wished to try to find some more that first evening. Within a minute, a woman in the group I was following found one. A few minutes later, an eighteen-year-old man, whom I had talked with a lot that day, found one too and, as many others would, let out a loud excited yell to the mountains. He then demonstrated how one must get down close to the ground to see the fungi. This man was the best collector in the small group I followed, and he had already found two fungi before others had any. As it was getting dark, the village leader called everyone to a meeting. He explained that the next day they would travel over one of the nearby mountains to collect in a different area and return to camp in the evening, and the day after that, they would collect closer to camp.

We then gathered back at our cabin, one of several small one-room huts made of logs and corrugated metal roofs, which was shared by three households. Staying in this cabin were my host father Adong, his wife, the village leader, and Adong's young cousin from another village household. While Adong's wife prepared dinner, others used toothbrushes to clean the fungi they had found. Everyone put their cleaned fungi in individual cloth wraps and then all together in a basket with a lid. Adong's cousin kept a record book for everyone, noting how much each person had collected every day, since profits would be allotted to each household, and three households were sharing a hut and fungus storage container. As I later sat chatting with the village leader during dinner, he explained how the village has a sophisticated system for managing the collecting of fungi and access to the land. He has been the leader for twenty-two years and worked to develop this system, since before his time the price was low and very few people collected caterpillar fungus.

Beginning in the early 2010s, the village completely banned all outsiders from this area where we were collecting. Enforcement of these regulations is communal and seasonal. Because community members are present at various temporary camps in the collecting grounds throughout the entire season, they will know if anyone from outside shows up and will force them out or require them to pay a fee if it is a collecting site where outsiders are permitted. In the off-season, when there is no fungus, access is not enforced. In another site over the ridge, outsiders with connections to the village can collect. The cost there is ¥1,500 (US$207) per person for the whole season. This fee is paid to the village leader, who then distributes all proceeds equally among the households. There is also another pasture that a village in the neighboring Tibetan Autonomous Region leases for ¥30,000 (US$4,142), the fee for which is shared among everyone in Mei-lishi. Since my host from Adong, with whom we hiked partway up the mountain, had married out of Meilishi, he could not collect in this place, Huding, so he and his wife had split off from us earlier in the day to collect in Yejaw. He now pays ¥600 (US$83) per year to collect there, since he was born in Meilishi, while his wife pays ¥1,500 (US$207) as a total outsider but with a marriage connection. They explained that the highest-quality fungus is found in Huding, hence the total ban on collection by outsiders.

The leader explained that since he took office there appears to be less fungus every year, but he believes this is because it is being divided up among more people, not because there is less growing. My research assistant asked whether they would ever consider closing the mountain for a year, but the leader explained that if they did not collect fungus, someone from outside would just steal it. He also explained that if they do not collect the fungus, it opens and dries and then is wasted economically. In reality, the fungi left behind by villagers reproduce and release fungal spores for the following year, whereas most of what is harvested is likely dug up before the spores are released (Winkler 2010). Meilishi's villagers' sophisticated management of caterpillar fungus land has also largely prevented environmental degradation by limiting the number of people collecting each year and requiring the removal of garbage and waste at the end of each season (the remote location makes it accessible only on foot over one to two days), but there is concern elsewhere across the Tibetan plateau. Encroachment by vehicular traffic, permanent and semi-permanent collection housing, and garbage have all damaged ecosystems in connection with fungus collection (see Ptáčková 2020).

The next day, villagers slept past 9:00 a.m. because a light overnight snow on the ground delayed collecting. By 10:00, the women had all gotten up to cook, while the men were still sleeping. For breakfast we drank butter tea and then set out around 11:00. This day, the collecting area was a very steep grassland slope at the back of the valley, along the top of a ridge. Collecting areas are chosen each day by the village leader and rotated every few days throughout the season as the fungi continue to emerge. As soon as we arrived, the villagers dispersed on the slope. It was a long climb, so I initially stuck with the people in the tail end of the group, who began collecting lower down. I followed three women, one older and two younger. One of the younger women was skilled (and perhaps lucky) and found three fungi within about ten minutes. Of my three companions, two found only one or none initially, while the skilled young woman found at least six. After almost two hours, I finally found one myself, which one of the younger women helped me dig out with her handpick. She then found another one right next to mine, so I gave her mine to make a pair.

I moved along the slope, interacting with different villagers before eventually meeting up with my host father. I followed him for a bit, and then he called to me when he found a fungus. With his finger, he drew a circle in the ground around the fungus and asked me to find it. Even though I knew where to look, the fungus was incredibly difficult to spot when partially buried in the grass and soil. He explained this was just the group's first day collecting in this location and that there were few fungi because many were still sprouting. In five to six days, there would be a lot more. The next few days, the group would move and collect in different parts of the valley before returning to this spot. The collection period would span up to one and a half months, with some families returning home sooner. Although all hike up the mountain together, to give everyone an equal chance at collecting, at the end of the season people return home on their own schedule. I remained on the mountain with villagers for over a week.

A month or so after the collecting trip, I returned to Adong Village after some time spent in other areas, including Cizhong and Bu, to see how people had fared once the collecting season had ended. My host father there, who had collected in the area for married-out Meilishi residents, found five hundred pairs of fungi for the year. A young man in the village explained how everyone knew about my host's remarkable find, and several teased him for not buying a new expensive motorcycle, as they had done. They said he got five hundred because he collected at Meilishi, instead of in the mountains around Adong, where people found only about two hundred pairs each. They explained that the quality of the fungi in the two locations is the same, and they sell them for the same price, but

FIGURE 17. Adong digging up a caterpillar fungus, 2015.

that the mountains around Meilishi have more. The evening provided an interesting post–collecting season scene, with men of different ages displaying and working on the new motorcycles they had bought with caterpillar fungus money. In many ways, it was a show of conspicuous consumption, with men decorating their bikes with Tibetan regalia and blasting music through their new stereos.

People in Adong return to the mountain to collect caterpillar fungus each year for the sake of livelihood continuity, community, and a sense of freedom from capitalistic work and modernity and to express community ownership of the landscape of common pool resources. They do so because the types of labor they are required to engage in when working for the Moët winery are drastically different and alienating. For those newly endowed with the livelihood given to them by Moët's arrival and land leases, spending one to two months on the mountain each year is not economically necessary, yet they choose to do so. Moët as an international firm with a new model of business has brought a kind of agrarian change to Northwest Yunnan that is different from the typical dragon head model experienced elsewhere in rural China and with wine and viticulture projects (Luo, Andreas, and Li 2017; Zhang, Oya, and Ye 2015). Under Moët's system and the exclusive contract over household land negotiated by the local government and village leaders without much consent, villagers have lost direct control and decision making over their land for at least fifty years (the duration of Moët's land leases) and have become alienated day laborers. Of course, most if not all in the community are in favor of this system and the long-term income and social security it provides versus the earlier volatility of growing grapes and selling them to Shangri-La Winery on an annual basis. Despite these positives, having to work as contracted labor leaves people with a desire for escape and for maintaining livelihood continuities with the mountains following the loss of seasonal agropastoralism and yak herding, a desire that is fulfilled by collecting caterpillar fungus.

Grapes and wine in many ways in this community have completely altered patterns of life and land ownership, unlike in the rest of Deqin and

Shangri-La, where household land tenure and individual labor remain intact despite the changing landscape of vineyards and the income and food insecurities that growing grapes has created. Returning each year as a community to the mountains, where land is co-managed to protect the availability of caterpillar fungus equally for all members, is a response and a methodology by which the people of Adong Village have found their own way of indigenizing the modernity that has been brought to the region by viticulture and of resisting the corporate co-optation of their use as a regulated labor force.

In the communities of Adong and Meilishi, compared to others in the region that collect caterpillar fungus, the preservation of social and community relations is an important part of this process. The geographer Michelle Olsgard Stewart (2014) conducted ethnographic work on caterpillar fungus collecting elsewhere in Diqing Prefecture and Deqin County and describes two very different situations in terms of the sociality of this activity. In one community, social relations, as she refers to them, remain embedded in the economy of the fungus and its collection. This community manages and privileges access to collecting grounds, along with collecting as a community together, as in Adong and Meilishi. In the other community, which has seen the construction of a new national highway proceed directly through its collecting grounds, the social relations that previously existed with fungus collection have disappeared or become dis-embedded. There is no longer managed access, with the area now open for anyone to collect, and collecting as a community has been abandoned. Dis-embedding in traditional social relations surrounding agriculture and land tenure in Adong has similarly occurred following Moët's arrival, where household production has been replaced by a capitalist form of work, which is controlled and managed beyond the bounds of the community. Previously, as observed in other communities throughout the region, while household agricultural production was an individual household endeavor, villagers shared labor between households and co-operated on a regular basis. With the arrival of daily wage-based vineyard work, this has disappeared.

Returning to the mountains each year provides an escape from this managed work, which villagers find adapting to difficult. Caterpillar fungus collection offers a sort of "freedom," which Tsing (2015b, 75–76) has also referred to with mushroom collection. It creates a chance for people to interact once more as a cohesive community and collect or generate a commodity that will earn them capitalist value but from the soil and experiences that they manage and control on their own land as a community. The dis-embedding of one section of the economy thus in a way has reinforced the embeddedness of social relations in another as a coping mechanism for the former. Much as wine ties more and more into identity downstream in Cizhong, the collection of caterpillar fungus allows the maintenance of identity by Adong people in the face of the social disruptions brought by vineyards and capitalist agrarian change.

I wish to suggest a cautionary critique. Emily T. Yeh (2013b) reminds us that the state's alteration of landscapes in Tibet as a form of development for local people is something worthy of heavy scrutiny. Under most measures of success, Moët Hennessy's project might be framed as a total success compared to earlier state and corporate ventures with Shangri-La Winery. On the surface, Moët has essentially alleviated concerns related to the environment and food insecurity with its project in Adong. Moët's vineyards are all organic, and it guarantees an income for land and employment to rural farmers regardless of its success or failure. However, its introduction of a completely new and foreign form of capitalist work on land that has been leased away from households to a foreign company has had unrealized effects. Clearly, there are impacts on the ways the community perceives itself and how they view agricultural labor. With the wine boom in both Shangri-La and greater China expected to continue to grow and with increasing international interest in China as a wine-producing region, caution toward how local communities are affected is needed as foreign firms continue to intercede and reconfigure long-standing community ties and forms of social relations in the globalization of this economy and region.

CHAPTER 5

Resisting and Indigenizing Modernity

Now, the yogic way to drink beer is this:
The first swig is for the Reality Body, Clear and Pure.
The second is for the Enjoyment Body, Perfect Buddhahood.
The third is for the Emanation Body, Manifesting Every Form.
Lucky initiates will drink the insipid first-strain of beer
As an unbroken stream of nectar,
Unlucky non-initiates will have no chance to drink this way.

Milarepa (Tibetan saint and poet, 1052–1135 CE)

I can easily recall my first encounter with Ani Dom in Bu Village. While his daughter Zhouma and I sat in her living room discussing the local agricultural and wine economy in the village, an elderly man in a wide-brim hat appeared with a beautiful strand of Tibetan *mala* (prayer beads) in his hand. He said that he had just heard a foreign researcher had arrived in the village and that he was eager to speak with me. This was Ani Dom. I listened, captivated, as he talked about the region, the sacred mountain Khawa Karpo, Buddhism, the forest, his previous career as a hunter, and the pollution occurring with viticulture. "Grapes and the wine industry are terrible for nature and are destroying this most sacred place and Khawa Karpo," he stated. I would later discover that his and others' perceived impacts of agrochemical pollution were connected with local climate change realities. This first meeting with Ani Dom opened my eyes to new environmental concerns among local people created by the expanded use of agrochemicals in viticulture and winemaking in Deqin County. His awareness was guided by Buddhist worldviews and the sacred landscapes' teachings, needs, and reactions to agrochemical pollution. As he further explained: "Buddhism and belief are very important for protecting the environment and for sustainability. If you believe in Buddhism and you believe in your heart and pray, this helps us to protect our mountain, the glacier, the forests, and the river and water." Our discussion that first day would be the first of many insightful conversations I had with Ani Dom during my time in Bu Village.

My encounters with Li Weihong were less accidental but just as enlightening.[1] One day while I was staying in Bu Village, I received a phone call from a friend recommending that I contact a prominent organic winemaker and environmentalist named Li Weihong, who had won awards for her community organizing work on organic viticulture, including a national-level environmental award in Beijing from the Nature Conservancy. She had also traveled around China promoting a documentary film she produced about her village and her organic viticulture. I called her, and we made plans to meet the next afternoon for lunch.

My conversations with Ani Dom and Li inform my thinking about religiously motivated action against viticulture and about local understandings of the impacts of pollution and climate change on sacred landscapes. These environmentalist activities take place alongside forms of entrepreneurial identity that respond to pollution by configuring viticulture to be both sustainable and profitable, as opposed to merely destructive for local landscapes and spirits. Another entrepreneur, Songtzen (Sonny) Gyalzur, owner of the Shangri-La Highland Craft Beer Company, also known as Shangri-La Beer, provides an example of an alternative business model that invests in local landscapes, people, and livelihoods.[2] These stories represent ways of indigenizing modernity that exist in contradistinction to state and corporate operations such as Shangri-La Winery and Moët.

What drives some rural Tibetan grape growers and brewers to pursue alternative, ecologically and socially conscious business strategies, in lieu of merely profit-oriented approaches? Their motivations include observations of chemical degradation of sacred animate land, Buddhist ethics, and ideas about ecologically friendly forms of commodity production. In the case of Shangri-La Beer, social and familial ties motivate entrepreneurs to give back to local communities and Shangri-La's natural environment and rural economy. These activities promote what Ani Dom calls a "real Shangri-La or Shambhala" (a place of divine serenity in Tibetan Buddhism), rather than a fake one, in reference to the Chinese government's renaming of the region in 2001. Although the government agricultural production incentives that promote growing grapes for Shangri-La Winery tend to overlook sustainability, some villagers and businesses are aware of and very concerned about the effects of viticulture on the ecological health of local environments and sacred landscapes. In some cases, farmers alter new state- and corporate-based wine commodity schemes to promote ecologically sound practices and a healthier environment in which to live. Contrary to many, these individuals are interested in sustainability and social responsibility, and in their pursuit of these values they practice viticulture and brewing beer in ways they consider to be compatible with indigenous cosmologies and local farmers' needs and desires. Their approach runs counter to that of the many grape growers and vintners in Deqin who have merely accepted growing grapes, and using the agrochemicals introduced with them by the state, as a means of economic livelihood improvement. Scholars have made similar observations about communities elsewhere in Tibet where new markets and livelihoods—in particular, the collection of caterpillar fungus—once viewed as destroying sacred lands and gods are now morally acceptable forms of natural resource extraction in the eyes of local villagers, given the rising economic value of such commodities within capitalist market society (Woodhouse et al. 2015).

In what ways do Tibetan Buddhist practitioners' and entrepreneurs' engagements with local cosmologies, spirits, the landscape, and rural farmers provide new insights into understanding pollution, climate change, and alternative forms of economic integration through wine and beer production? With respect to climate change, one important observation by others in this region and across the Himalayas is that for Tibetan villagers, pollution and climate change are seen as local issues that stem from two factors: a lack of devotion and reverence for mountain gods and goddesses, which has accompanied the influx of new "modern" forms of agriculture with grapes, and Chinese tourists who are not in harmony with sacred mountains and pollute them through littering and a lack of understanding and respect (Coggins and Yeh 2014; Salick, Byg, and Bauer 2013; Sherpa 2014).

Although most villagers in Diqing are indigenizing modernity by engaging with the new market economies that have come with viticulture, this does not necessarily involve following ecologically sound practices. For Li, however, ecological practices are a vital component of such endeavors and involve the integration of viticulture into local indigenous and Buddhist worldviews. Many around Li and Ani Dom produce grapes and wines marketed and labeled as "Tibetan" and with imagery of the sacred mountain Khawa Karpo and the local landscape. Yet villagers who grow grapes and sell them to Shangri-La Winery use conventional fertilizers and pesticides in a lack of consideration for the local spirit landscape and sacred mountain. In the minds of local lay Buddhists such as Ani Dom and Li, this is a poor choice. According to these two devout Buddhists, such a decision represents a lack of interest among everyday farmers in preserving Khawa Karpo's Buddhist nature, while instead choosing to utilize the mountain and the cultural values surrounding it to make profits. Consequences from these actions are "killing the mountain," in the words of Ani Dom. These differing opinions and actions toward the mountain also create tension among local Tibetans over their exploitation of Khawa Karpo and Tibetan "authenticity." These conflicting values can be observed through state- and market-driven change elsewhere in Tibet as well. As the anthropologist Charlene Makley (2018) discusses, people in Amdo in northeast Tibet believe that mountain deities have become active and exhibit agency in response to environmental disasters and destruction during contestations between Tibetan villagers and the government over land development as the Chinese state appropriates Tibetan culture for economic development purposes.

Some villagers in Deqin have expressed concern over the effects of agricultural chemical use on human health and the natural environment, including perceived pollution impacts on the sacred peak of Khawa Karpo, where glaciers are rapidly retreating. They have responded by producing their own chemical-free wines, which they insist are healthier not just for people, but also for the mountain, the god for which it is named, and the local ecology. This coincides with and reflects the problematic ignorance that Buddhist environmentalists perceive on the part of today's average Tibetan farmers who are disregarding centuries (including pre-Buddhist and prior Bön ideologies) of thought and practice with respect to landscape and mountain deities.[3] Ani Dom, Li, and others like them in a long-standing Tibetan tradition acknowledge the "ecological" agency and actions of nonhumans in the form of mountain deities in hopes of generating a more sustainable future (Bellezza 2005, 330). Lay Buddhists believe that by propitiating mountain deities for generations, people have preserved the ecology and beauty of the region's landscape. They question why their own children and other humans would seek to break relations with the mountain in favor of a future in which long-term sustainability (and economic productivity) is uncertain.

The sacred landscape of the mountain deity Khawa Karpo and its many lesser guardian deities is inhabited by a multitude of animate beings whom local villagers consider close neighbors. Spirits who dwell within and throughout the landscape, and whom villagers seek to move into the fold of local environmental politics, are viewed by Tibetans not only as neighbors but as superior to humans. A lack of devotion and care for these deities through the modernization of agriculture with chemicals and other forms of "development" is, in the minds of lay Buddhists, leading to negative impacts. These are particularly apparent regarding the impact of climate change in the region, including glacier retreat. The deities are thought to provide abundant natural resources and good weather for growing crops when people treat them with respect. Bad weather is similarly often viewed in Tibetan spiritual ecology as a direct agentive response by deities to the negative behavior of humans.

In Northwest Yunnan, mountain deities are ascribed with similar agency, and Buddhists believe that phenomena such as glacier retreat and disease among fruit trees are negative repercussions for mistreatment of the deities (Coggins and Hutchinson 2006; Coggins and Yeh 2014). In response to pollution and climate change, Tibetan Buddhist environmentalists are agitating against some of the state-initiated agricultural development schemes involving viticulture. Their stated intent is to provide agency in environmental decision-making to nonhuman spirit beings within the lands of Khawa Karpo. Some might suggest that nonhuman approaches do not provide sufficient grounded practical applications to solving environmental problems. However, local Tibetans opine that it is precisely this lack of attention and care for the nonhuman beings living within sacred landscapes that has caused rampant pollution and environmental destruction. For some Tibetan Buddhist grape growers in Yunnan, humans are indeed seen not as exceptional, but as only one small part of a much larger world and way of knowing.

Today, China is at the center of the world's crises of pollution from economic development, and Tibet and the Himalayas are experiencing pronounced climate change impacts with receding glaciers, expanding alpine tree lines, and warming temperatures (Baker and Moseley 2007). Among Buddhist pastoralists and farmers in Ladakh, for example, the anthropologist Karine Gagné (2018) illustrates how observable climate change impacts, in particular glacier retreat, lead locals who have lived on the same lands for generations to believe that they have morally failed in their obligations to the landscape. The same response is seen among lay Buddhists in Deqin, in reaction to agrochemical pollution occurring simultaneously with climate change.

Tibetan Landscape Animism, Cosmology, and Climate Change beyond the Human

Contemporary Tibetan Buddhism and mountain deity worship combines elements of Buddhism, pre-Buddhist Bön (a combination of shamanistic practices and spirit worship), and mountain deity or cult beliefs that pre-date Bön. Natural features contain spirits whom practitioners propitiate to maintain natural harmony. Various geomantic points and homes of deities exist in the Tibetan landscape—for example, mountain passes, lakes, springs, and trees—that maintain balance for even mundane activities such as hunting, fishing, and gathering food and medicines (Bellezza 2005, 330; Karmay 1994, 1996). Within Tibetan cultural areas, there exist mountains, lakes, and rivers that are named after the gods and spirits who are believed to inhabit them, and it is the role of humans to ensure that these deities are kept content through propitiation. Tibetan sacred sites and landscapes are multi-scalar and include entities as small as single trees and stones and as large as entire mountains ranges.

Engagement with the spirit world through natural landscapes extends beyond religious beliefs and includes local ideals and mythologies about landscapes, as well as a sense of place (Woodhouse et al. 2015). Today in Deqin, people represent themselves through the area's natural and economic resources, including ideal land for viticulture and fungi collection that the landscape provides. However, for some, such as Ani Dom and Li, using the land for economic benefit without providing reverence and respect to the mountain will lead to a problematic future. Khawa Karpo is a god and a deeply important landscape for both local and larger Tibetan Buddhist practice, and reaping economic benefit from the land at the god's expense through modern practices, including chemically intensive viticulture and hunting, is disrespectful. In addition to Buddhist ethics, localized "Tibetan" environmental efforts are likely also influenced by changing state policies toward environmental protection and by communication with Western environmental organizations (Woodhouse et al. 2015; Yeh 2014). Prior to 2008, several transnational conservation organizations and domestic Chinese environmental NGOs actively worked in collaboration with local Tibetan communities to promote biodiversity conservation and the value of sacred landscapes.

In Tibetan cosmology, mountains are the most important sacred objects in the natural world. The 22,113-foot Khawa Karpo represents two types of sacred mountains in Tibetan beliefs. It is both a *néri* (*gnas ri*), a mountain and god revered throughout the Tibetan cultural region and absorbed into Buddhist practice, and a *shidak* (*Gzhi bdag* or *yul lha*), which is a locally sacred mountain worshipped secularly by villagers and laypersons in forms of practice predating both Buddhism and Bön.[4] In greater cultural Tibet, Khawa Karpo is one of eight highly sacred *néri*. It is the most sacred among Kham Tibetans (in eastern Tibet) and arguably the second most revered in Tibetan Buddhism after Mount Kailas in western Tibet (Buffetrille 2014; Coggins and Hutchinson 2006). Thousands of pilgrims circumambulate the mountain range every year, and every twelve years tens of thousands visit during the auspicious Tibetan year of the sheep. As Katia Buffetrille, an anthropologist of Tibet, describes, mountain cults surrounding Khawa Karpo (and other *néri* like it) historically underwent a process of "Buddhicisation" (1998, 30), in which its role as a *shidak* was drawn into Buddhist practice and pantheon, leading it to be viewed as a site for pilgrimage as a "holy" mountain rather than just the object of a local secular cult.

The name Khawa Karpo refers to the range's highest peak and is the most common Tibetan name for the mountain range. The range in its entirety is named Menri (Medicine Mountains), reflecting the area's rich diversity of plants used in traditional Tibetan medicine (Salick and Moseley 2012). The most commonly used colloquial name for the mountain range, the Chinese name Meili Xueshan (Meili Snow Mountain), is a transliteration of Menri, originally coined by the People's Liberation Army during mapping of the region in the 1950s (Coggins and Hutchinson 2006; Salick and Moseley 2012). Sacred geography around Khawa Karpo is important for motivating humans to conserve a variety of habitats, landscape features, and old-growth forests through various prohibitions, including cutting certain trees, hunting, disturbing water sources, and removing items from deity-protected areas of mountains (Anderson et al. 2005).

Historically, a religious management system existed among villagers in the region, in which people divided the mountain into two sections, above and below approximately 13,000 feet in elevation. This system was abolished by the Chinese government in the 1950s, but since the 1980s local villagers, including Ani Dom, have been gradually reinstituting it. In local religious perception, the section below 13,000 feet makes up the mundane world, though this area is still full of sacred sites and spaces that people protect and conserve for religious and cultural purposes, with some sites significant only at the village and household levels and others that are pan-Tibetan sacred spaces. Ani Dom's sacred juniper grove in Bu Village is an example of one such lower-elevation pan-Tibetan site. Above approximately 13,000 feet, one crosses the *ri-gua*, or "door of the mountain." This marks the boundary between the human world and the divine world of the mountain gods, who live at higher elevations and where humans must take nothing from the landscape so as not to upset the spirits who dwell in these high elevations. If humans commit transgressions against the gods above the *ri-gua* (including hunting, fishing, or cutting trees), the gods will exact revenge on them for breaking their contractual relationships. In these relationships, the gods and Khawa Karpo serve as patrons and guardians to the local villagers of the region (Coggins and Hutchinson 2006; Litzinger 2004). Khawa Karpo and other nearby deities possess an agency that has been ascribed to them by local Buddhist villagers, in which the deities look upon the actions of local people and evaluate them either positively or negatively. When villagers show the mountain proper respect and propitiation, the gods provide good weather and abundant forest resources and medicines. But when villagers commit transgressions against the sacred landscape, the spirits are likely to instigate natural disasters, catastrophe, and environmental decline.

There are both lay and monastic examples of perceived local failures to appease the gods. One was when Chinese and Japanese climbers attempted to summit the mountain in 1991 and were killed by an avalanche, which locals viewed as revenge from the gods for disturbing their sacred realm. Another perceived failing in devotion to the gods is climate change and its effects on the landscape. Khawa Karpo's largest glacier, Mingyong, has retreated over the past eighty to one hundred years, as documented through photo replication of the works of early Western explorers in the region. Villagers and monks who see the glacier as a sacred site, traditionally marked by temples at its base, have observed this retreat. Because the glacier has continued to shrink, monks who worship at the Mingyong temple have begun to express concern that either they are not praying enough to appease the gods or local villagers are failing in their devotion (Baker and Moseley 2007; Salick and Moseley 2012). Similarly, local village elders have noted the glacier's retreat as a local phenomenon and a violation of sacred space: "Especially after the year 2000 there are more people coming; the pollution is serious and now there's electricity. These three problems put together make the situation really bad. In the past, people couldn't even go up [the glacier]. Now even the cows can make it up. If there were no people going up, no littering, and no electricity use, the glacier could recover naturally. If the current situation continues, the glacier will continue to recede" (Nima 2002; quoted in Coggins and Yeh 2014, 6).

These feelings and relationships between locals and Khawa Karpo and its glaciers reflect indigenous observations elsewhere in the Himalayas and the world, where local practice, cosmology, and worship intimately connect with glaciers as animate speaking objects. Often, such relationships with glaciers reflect more than responses to phenomena such as climate change as perceived by Western science.[5] For example, the anthropologist Julie Cruikshank (2010) explores a variety of oral histories and stories surrounding glaciers in the Yukon region of Canada, where glaciers themselves are actors and speakers in the changes that occur in the landscape. Some people, especially coming from a Western scientific background, would attribute such changes (including glaciers receding) to climate change, while indigenous populations suggest that other nonhuman agents might also be at play. Grounded in her research in the Yukon, then, Cruikshank (2010) asks if glaciers listen. Conversely, for Ani Dom and others such as the monks residing at the foot of Mingyong, the glacier is speaking, and locals are not listening or responding.

A perspective on appeasement of the mountain through more sustainable practices can be framed using what the anthropologist Giovanni Da Col (2007, 2012) has called "economies of fortune" in Deqin. Da Col frames this work around a sense of fortune, hospitality, and spirit-mediated vitality among local people at Khawa Karpo. His is an intriguing analysis, integrating traditional Tibetan views about the local landscape regarding merit and fate while also addressing how these views interplay with modern economies.[6] While Da Col suggests that many villagers' economic activities still often mediate their relationships with Khawa Karpo and the local spirit world today, this argument still does not take sufficient account of the pragmatic views practiced by local village farmers. Individuals such as Ani Dom and Li are unusual in exclusively maintaining such beliefs in mitigating their relationships with the mountain and the sacred landscape. For them, the health and prosperity of Khawa Karpo is paramount over any other concerns, including economic prosperity. Many villagers I have interacted with have accepted the economic prosperity and gains that come with modernity and things such as viticulture and tourism profits, with less attention or devotion given to cosmology and spirit worship. Some explain that they have reverence for the mountain, spirits, and landscape but are not necessarily as keen to allow such care to come between them and economic prosperity. This coincides with emerging local moral acceptance of fungi collection on sacred lands in Tibetan areas of Sichuan (Woodhouse et al. 2015). Yet, while their views may be exceptional, the actions and behaviors of Tibetan environmentalists demonstrate an important form of environmental consciousness that has been activated by the landscape changes instigated by wine production and transnational capitalism.

Many of my regular interlocutors in Deqin often seem to care less than Ani Dom and Li about Khawa Karpo's spirit world and its protection. Ani Dom's own family, daughter, and wife, in particular, hope he might quit being a conservationist. In their minds, these activities do nothing more than alienate him from the rest of the village and waste the family's money. When he was a famous hunter through the mid-1980s, everyone loved him. Now, most in the community, according to many interviews throughout the community, despise him. Li's family sees some profit in her activities, especially the documentary film making and the cash awards she has won for it, but many households in her community see no real benefit in devoting more time to organic viticulture when they can more easily spray pesticides and spread chemical fertilizers. To be organic takes more effort, and many are less inclined to expend the extra time and energy or acquire the learning required. I have seen many villagers engage in environmentally destructive activities, from excessive littering to cutting down forest trees simply to reach the wild fruit at the top. I have seen many trees cut down, and people often give no second thought to this activity when asked about it. Many local villagers indicate that Khawa Karpo and its surrounding landscape is sacred and important to them as their homeland and to larger Buddhist practice but see no problem with cutting down a few trees to harvest fruit or to improve their home or property.

According to Da Col, like the pilgrims who visit Khawa Karpo to gain merit, seek forgiveness for sins, and move toward reaching their own enlightenment, some more active Buddhist villagers in the region are constantly working to mediate and maintain a positive relationship with the local landscape to obtain good economic fortune, another way of indigenizing modernity. Acts such as cutting trees, even when necessary to protect one's own home, are still seen by active Buddhists as being negative for one's merit because they may interfere in humans' relationships with their patron gods in the mountain (Da Col 2012).

Much of the fortune and merit building that Da Col describes is based on what he calls "cosmoeconomics," a practice of managing fortune and luck while simultaneously appeasing the spirit world around Khawa Karpo (2012, 75–76). Villagers share this vital energy with spirits and the landscape of Khawa Karpo and believe incorrect actions can easily push it out of balance (also see Makley 2018). In this case, Da Col discusses the ways that maintaining a balance between traditional beliefs about fortune and modern economic prosperity can create conflicts, for example, through villagers' responses to discovering matsutake mushrooms. At first, they are often happy that their fortune and vital energy must be in a good place for them to have made such a discovery. However, such a fortunate discovery may also imply future challenges. For instance, finding many mushrooms all at once is often an indicator that their market value and price are about to drop. Therefore, in the economies of fortune and merit, luck is not always as beneficial as it might appear, and villagers are consistently leery of it (Da Col 2007). Ani Dom in particular exhibits this type of reverence and cautiousness in his relationships with the local landscape, warning that without proper propitiation of the god and spirits, any human activities can be harmful to Khawa Karpo and its landscape. Li also cares deeply for her village spirit landscape and the mountain, though if she can keep this relationship positive through organics and sustainable methods, then expanding her economic profits and gains is not a mutually exclusive act.

Ani Dom and Compassion for Life

During my days in Bu Village, Ani Dom explained to me much about local Buddhist practice and the cosmologies surrounding Khawa Karpo (both the mountain and the god for which it is named). Ani Dom is a Buddhist with a deep reverence for life, the mountain, and the local environment and culture. He was not, however, always a Buddhist, and did not adopt these beliefs until a near death experience, which he recounted for me. Until 1986, he was a great hunter. That year, during a twenty-five-day sleepless trance brought on by a heart attack, he had a vision in which the spirits of all the animals he killed came back for revenge. Next he saw the god Khawa Karpo. It was then that he devoted himself to conservation for the rest of his life. The god told him to throw his hunting dog in the river (which he did), and he turned his gun in to the police. During his career as a hunter, he had killed 15 bears, 17 deer, over 70 wild yaks, 200–300 blue sheep, and numerous rabbits and birds. His wife, however, did not support his hunting and even called him a devil for killing so many animals. For the broader community, though, these feats as a hunter earned him the name Áni Dom (Grandfather Bear).

Upon his conversion to Buddhism and his later turn toward environmental activism, Ani Dom's life was transformed. Many villagers in Bu, including members of his own family and the village leader, now think of him as a nuisance for interfering in their economic activities and success growing grapes and making wine. The village leader explained to me that he does not get along with Ani Dom because of his fight against chemical usage and against Sunspirit Winery, which buys its grapes from village households. As the leader of the community, he is primarily concerned with income and livelihood success, and he thinks that using chemicals is better for money and livelihood, contrary to Ani Dom. Today Ani Dom devotes all his time to working with NGOs to preserve and protect Khawa Karpo and the village environment. People have come to know him for his work protecting a sacred old-growth juniper grove in Bu Village, where he also worked to build a small temple commemorating Khawa Karpo, using funds generated through donations from NGOs and Buddhist monasteries.

Ani Dom's stories about his work with various NGOs and his Buddhist teachings are important to understanding his actions. His seniors' group, the Khawa Karpo Traditional Knowledge and Ecological Conservation Association, teaches villagers to plant grapes more organically and sustainably in collaboration with the Hong Kong NGO Partnerships for Community Development. For Ani Dom, this work became important when he began to notice that the overuse of pesticides on grapes was harming walnut and other fruit trees, which were starting to look sick and unhealthy, and that the soil degraded after many years from people spraying pesticides and applying chemical fertilizers. He advocates for organic wine, but most do not follow him. On the basis of his observations and knowledge collected from international NGOs, he explains that pesticides are harmful for the air, earth, soil, and water and all life (not just humans) and that to care about these things is what traditional Buddhist philosophies teach: all life is sacred.[7] Ani Dom first developed these concerns about sustainability in his collaborations with the Nature Conservancy and with the

Khawa Karpo Culture Association in the 2000s.[8] One major problem for Ani Dom and others like him has been that the national government will not allow them, as Tibetans, to accept money for conservation projects from foreign NGOs anymore. This is an aftereffect of the 2008 crackdowns after mass rioting in Tibet. Organizations such as the Nature Conservancy previously supported many conservation projects in Tibetan Yunnan, but today local environmental activists are on their own, without the same funding and resources they once enjoyed.

When I asked Ani Dom about the idea of developing a "Tibetan" Shangri-La wine brand, marketed as sustainably produced, he explained:

> Grapes and wine are not part of traditional Tibetan culture. That culture has been lost to the chemicals and garbage that come with grapes. Grapes and wine are from foreigners. The French could not convert the Tibetans in this area, so they chose Cigu [just downstream from Cizhong] and later Cizhong as multicultural places to preach and proselytize. The church in Cigu was burned and then rebuilt in Cizhong. The Buddhists did not agree with the government giving the French so much land, so the people said they could have only as much land as that covered by a cow's skin. The French then cut this skin up into threads to create a larger space of land to take. Tibetan scripture says no killing, protect the environment, and live in peace even with those from other religions, which includes the Catholics.

On the future and any link between grapes and Tibetan identity, he stated, "If pesticide use continues, things will be bad, and the soil will be destroyed. I do not think the grape industry is promising for Deqin's future."

Ani Dom's story is important to understanding the environmental movement that exists among perhaps a few dozen villagers in the region as a response to modern market economies. One evening, while visiting a sacred juniper grove and the temple built there after the 1991 climbing accident on Khawa Karpo, Ani Dom explained that the sacred junipers around the temple connect the area symbolically to the Samye Monastery in Tibet, an important historical religious center south of the Tibetan capital of Lhasa. The government had wanted to log this grove of junipers, but Ani Dom worked with other elders in the village to protect it as a sacred site. He explained that although the trees themselves do not speak, if they are cut, the spirits in them will be disturbed, and disasters would ensue.

The oldest tree in the grove is twelve hundred years old, the same age as the Samye Monastery. Legend has it that during the Tang dynasty an emperor who was a supporter of Tibetan Buddhism sent representatives to journey westward to Tibet. These Chinese imperial representatives brought a tribute of juniper seeds and met and traveled with the Tibetan king, who intended to plant the trees at the monastery, which was currently being built. When they came to Khawa Karpo, a raven tricked them, telling them that because the Samye Monastery in Tibet had already been built, junipers were not needed there. The travelers consequently planted their seeds at Khawa Karpo instead, creating a forest. People collect bark from the trees to use as medicine, and overharvesting has killed some of the trees. Some trees accidentally burned when the road through the village was built in 1988. Before that, there were never any floods, but afterward a flood washed away a small shop, killing the owner. Villagers found three holes in the man's hat and believed that these were from the tiger god, who came down from the mountain and killed the man as punishment for the building of the road through the sacred trees. Inside the temple in the sacred grove of junipers, on the wall behind a central altar, a fresco depicts the Khawa Karpo range. Ani Dom explains that when the climbers died in the avalanche, it was because Khawa Karpo's guardian spirits were protecting the mountain from the climbers, so he then built this temple to commemorate and show the god respect.

During an evening prayer session at the temple, Ani Dom explained more to me about his Buddhist and environmental philosophies:

> Things like mining and pesticides are not good for the five elements
> of nature and for Khawa Karpo. They destroy the natural balance
> of the elements. China has lost a lot of its Buddhist philosophy

and is very confused now. Buddhism is important for protecting the environment and for sustainability. There have been too many campaigns and too much violence in China with the civil war, the Great Leap Forward, the Cultural Revolution, and current environmental destruction. This is why in my early years I was a hunter—I had no guidance toward the cultural values that were lost in all this turbulence. Buddhism is two thousand years old, but today human practices of destruction overpower conservation. Placing statues to honor the mountain is not enough. Humans are too greedy to satisfy their own needs and end up destroying each other. If you [outsiders] believe in Buddhism in your heart and pray, this helps us villagers to protect our mountain, forests, and water.

Another morning, as we walked down to the temple, we choose to go through the vineyards rather than on the road, and Ani Dom talked more about the ideas of Buddhism and ecology. He remarked that under the government pest control program, techniques such as zapper lamps in the vineyards kill all the insects, not just the pests, so it is bad for the ecosystem's health and biodiversity. For Ani Dom, local knowledge is better and more important for protecting the environment than are laws and policies. He believes that nature (Ch: *ziran*) is the state that exists without the interference of human activities. He claims to have developed this belief and way of thinking on his own. However, given that several transnational conservation NGOs have worked closely with villagers including Ani Dom for many years, his way of thinking about nature today is likely influenced by those interactions. He says that being Buddhist must come from one's heart and that people must have compassion for nature and all living things. Everyone has a life, and Buddhism is about protecting all the life that exists on earth. Some local people resist his protectionism, but he explains that because everything is connected, things like pesticides affect not just one thing, but everything, including water and rivers. He believes that the government does not actually care about the health and biodiversity of Khawa Karpo. It does not give money to biodiversity protection or the village because those are not moneymakers. The tourism investment company managing the Khawa Karpo National Park makes significant sums of money but gives nothing to the environment or the local people.

Near the end of our conversation, Ani Dom drew a diagram of the earth with charcoal on an incense cairn next to the temple, explaining to me about how the five elements of the world work and how we humans have disrupted their cycle, perhaps eventually destroying ourselves. These elements cycle in the earth around the sun, but it is his belief that we are destroying this process through environmental destruction and a loss of care for the natural world. As Ani Dom talks about reverence and caring for all sentient life and the natural elements, including animals, trees, and the Mekong River, he regularly portends that the pollution that comes from viticulture makes the god of Khawa Karpo angry (as seen through the retreat of Mingyong glacier) because it destroys these natural elements and life-forms.

Li Weihong and Ecological Entrepreneurialism

Li Weihong's work is different from that of Ani Dom, in that while also motivated by Buddhist thought and care for the local environments around Khawa Karpo, she also uses her work for financial benefit, perhaps more effectively indigenizing modernity. Unlike Ani Dom, she actively pursues viticulture and winemaking as an economic livelihood but uses entirely organic methods. She may thus be described as an ecological entrepreneur. She and Ani Dom have actively worked with two of the same NGOs, the Hong Kong Partnerships for Community Development and the Khawa Karpo Culture Association, which in the past has often collaborated with participatory ethnographic filmmakers of the Yunnan Academy of Social Sciences.

According to Li, in the early 2000s the government introduced grapes to her village, Gushui, and elsewhere in Deqin, encouraging villagers to grow them to sell to the Shangri-La Wine Company. At that time, the gov-

FIGURE 18. Ani Dom discussing the sacred juniper trees next to his temple, 2014.

ernment also introduced chemical fertilizers and pesticides to use for the grapes. Over time, Li noticed that the health of the local environment was degrading and that the walnut trees around the vineyards looked especially sick. As a Buddhist with a particular fondness for and connection with the god and landscape of Khawa Karpo, she was concerned about the trees' health. She wrote a letter describing these worries to the Khawa Karpo Culture Association and a professor at the Yunnan Academy of Social Sciences who had been working with the organization. After hearing about the environmental problems with pesticides, an American agriculture professor working in Kunming came to teach Li and others about using sprays made from cigarette and grass ash as organic forms of pest control, along with using various forms of manure as fertilizers. She also connected with the Hong Kong Partnerships for Community Development, which sent a viticulture expert from the Philippines, who trained her in organic methods developed in Bordeaux using natural chemical sprays. This was the same training program that Ani Dom helped organize in Bu Village.

After the American professor visited Gushui and taught Li about organics, she tried to pass this knowledge on to other village members and nearby villages, encouraging them to follow. Today, twelve of twenty households in Gushui are completely organic, including Li's, while others still use chemicals. She has also worked with villages in other parts of Deqin County that have expressed interest. When the government began the grape programs in 2002 and requested that villagers grow only grapes, her family had still grown barley. Li wanted to keep some of the barley fields, but eventually acquiesced to her mother's insistence that they grow solely grapes. Her fields are now all vineyards, but she keeps greater spacing between the vines than the government recommends and grows grains between them, as she still worries that she may at times not have enough money to buy rice and barley.

In Gushui, as elsewhere in Deqin, most families have fewer yaks and cows than before they planted grapes, but Li still has fifteen yaks—many more than most families—because they provide organic fertilizer and, she said jokingly, her husband likes animals. She explained these types of "traditional" agricultural practices to me during our first conversation: "I like living as people did in past times, with things being less modern, including not using chemicals. Using old horses and living in old-style Tibetan homes." By effectively mobilizing herself (and a few fellow villagers) to take up organics, she has developed a niche market for her wine and, with her filmmaking, an ethnographic interest in her lifestyle. These endeavors economically and financially allow her to maintain what she calls more traditional forms of living, while avoiding the large-scale corporate and transnational forms of viticulture that she feels are polluting her village and the local landscape.

Li's work with organics and community organizing has won government recognition on both national and provincial levels. Her award from the Nature Conservancy in 2013 included a trophy, a certificate, and ¥50,000 (us$6,903). She explained to me at our first meeting that in the past her parents and husband both made fun of her, with all her organic experimentation, as she was making less money from grapes than were other families. However, since the government sent her to Beijing and gave her a large sum of money, her family is now more supportive. Li also explained that, like her father, who introduced mushroom cultivation to Gushui, she enjoys experimenting and trying new things; she often tries out the new pesticides she creates on local plants and has developed her own winemaking method through experimentation. She first began making wine in 2008 and refined the practice by 2011. In 2012, her first year selling wine, she made ¥1,000 (US$138); in 2013, ¥7,000–¥8,000 (US$966–$1,105); and in 2014, ¥14,000–¥16,000 (US$1,933–$2,209). Many foreigners and Chinese have also come to her village to buy her organic wine.

Li's other primary project is her filmmaking. In 2011, as part of a participatory documentary film program, Chinese professors from the Yunnan Academy of Social Sciences taught her how to use video cameras and edit film. At that time, she wanted to make a film about planting and caring for grapes, but the professor running the program said it would be very difficult to film and explain this whole process, and he suggested she instead film her village's Tibetan New Year festival. She filmed both, and when the professor returned the next year and watched both films, he said the one about grapes and village life was better. She has traveled all over China and screened the film in many places, including at universities in Beijing and various ethnographic film festivals. She now spends about ninety days per year out of the village for various engagements showing her film and promoting organics. When she leaves, she worries that her neighbors will start using chemicals, which bothers her because she wants to produce pure wine and grapes. Her fears are well-founded since other villagers do use more chemicals when she is absent.

Li believes that because more and more people are concerned about the importance of organics, her reputation has grown around Deqin County. I also observed how, overall, her vineyards and the surrounding ecosystem look much healthier than elsewhere in Deqin. There are more birds, more greenery, and indeed more weeds. In addition to her organic projects being environmentally friendly, their profit potential

FIGURE 19. Li Weihong in her vineyard, 2014.

and the desire among more people in China for things that are organic and centered on Tibetan culture also motivate her. On several occasions, she mentioned to me that she plans to make a lot of money making documentary films. Various TV stations in China have expressed interest in buying her films.

Shangri-La Beer

Tibetans have long produced a local barley beer known as *chang*, associated with hospitality. Information on when or how the practice of making this drink began is lacking. Recent archaeological work suggests that barley arrived on the Tibetan plateau and even more prominently in the Sino-Tibetan borderlands as an adaptation to colder climates sometime between 2500 BCE and 1499 BCE, although there is some disagreement among researchers (F. Chen et al. 2015; Guedes et al. 2015). It is also suggested that barley production may never have been as widespread in highland central Tibet as in the borderlands, including Yunnan, where today the variety of indigenous hull-less barley is extensive, with up to fifty-four different varieties in Shangri-La alone (Y. Li et al. 2011; Guedes, Manning, and Bocinsky 2016). Indeed, Sonny Gyalzur, the owner of today's Shangri-La Beer, explained to me that when he first began to experiment with local hull-less barleys, he had difficulty achieving any consistency with his beers. It was not until a Swiss brewmaster came to work with him and pointed out he had been using different varieties of barley that the beers then developed some consistency. The incredible diversity of Tibetan barleys has been attributed to the work of generations of village farmers in Shangri-La perpetuating and promoting this crop (Y. Li et al. 2011). Certainly, at some point after the introduction of these crops historically, the making of *chang* began.

Today the production of *chang* seems heavily to have died out, leaving most villagers producing only hard alcohols from barley. Magnus Fiskesjö (2010) suggests that in southern Yunnan (and I suspect in Tibetan Northwest Yunnan as well), rather excessive distillation and purchasing of hard liquors have resulted from the introduction of these items and Chinese liquor (*baijiu*) in markets and that locally brewed and fermented beers are quickly disappearing. Among the Wa ethnic group in southern Yunnan, until the 1950s there was very little consumption of hard liquors, whereas the local beer was consumed heavily in social and ritual situations. I believe the same may be true in the Shangri-La region, with *chang* having previously been more widely produced. Indeed, Gyalzur explained to me that in area villages where he has relatives residing, people claim that they used to produce *chang* using barley and local ancient yeast starters but say that these practices have died out. Interestingly, recent archaeological and biological research has proposed Tibet as the origin of ancient lager beer yeasts still used today and dating back to the fifteenth century in eastern Europe. Upon their introduction in Europe, these yeast strains, likely those found among *chang* brewers in particular, allowed lagers to ferment at colder temperatures. Quite a fitting adaptation given the climate of Tibet (Bing et al. 2014).

A thorough culling of Tibetan literary sources by religious studies scholars Kurtis R. Schaeffer, Matthew T. Kapstein, and Gray Tuttle (2013) suggests that beer in Tibet was indeed a large part of society historically, produced as an economic commodity and used for ritual, for medicinal purposes and as a preeminent social drug across many facets of life (447). One of Tibet's most famous Buddhist philosophers, Longchenpa (1308–1363 CE), produced a wonderful song in which he highlighted all the various aspects of beer in Tibetan society and sociality, reflecting on its use among rulers, religious leaders, and commoners and its association with divinity, healing, joy, and bliss among all who drink it.

Botanists Yali Li et al. (2011) note in their study on indigenous barley varieties and local knowledge in Shangri-La that the making of *chang*— they call it *qiang*, using some form of Chinese transliteration—is still common among some local villagers. Li and colleagues also use this terminology, though, side by side with the Chinese *qingkejiu* (barley liquor); having spent much time in this part of Tibet, I can say these are not the same thing. However, the brewing process they describe is certainly that of making *chang* rather than distilling *qingkejiu*, which I have witnessed the local winemaker and distiller Wu Gongdi doing many times in Cizhong. This leaves me wondering where in Shangri-La the authors witnessed this practice, as I have only seen it in one place. I am dubious of their suggestion that it is widespread, and I believe the confusion came from their mixing Chinese and Tibetan names for these drinks and in mistaking widespread *qingkejiu* distillation with limited *chang* brewing and fermentation:

[*Qingkejiu* (or *Qiang*)]: *Qingkejiu* is the major alcoholic beverage in Tibet. It is also called *Zajiu* and the Tibetan name is called *Qiang*. The preparation of *Qiang* begins with cleaning and washing raw hulless barley kernels. Currently many brewers mix malting barley with hulless barley in a 1:2 ratio. This specially prepared barley grain is boiled in water for 2–5 h. When the boiled barley grain is cooled, powdered yeast is added and the mixture is allowed to ferment for 3–5 days. There is no free liquid remaining at this point. This

fermented barley grain is known as Lenmar and can be directly consumed in small quantities or sometimes fried in a little oil and eaten
as a delicacy with sugar. Lenmar is usually put in an earthenware
pot with water and steeped for 6–10 h; it is then filtered to produce
Qiang. The water is added 3–4 times and the alcoholic content of
Qiang depends on the number of times to add water. Alcohol content of the first run of *Qiang* is usually about 7%, and the second is
about 5%. People normally drink *Qiang* at about 5% alcoholic content or less. (Y. Li et al. 2011, 651)

In one rather well-known village, popular among more intrepid travelers and trekkers and a bit off the beaten path, where I previously worked
for an NGO in ecotourism development with local households, barley
chang is still actively produced in the method described by Li et al. I always look forward to visits there, not just for the amazing scenery but also
for the *chang*, which is served warm and is incredible. In Nizu, or Niru,
a village a few hours east of Shangri-La, the hospitality that comes with
serving *chang* remains alive and well, modernized and perpetuated by
Sonny Gyalzur with Shangri-La Beer, whose products are enjoyed today
across China and now in Europe and Australia as well.

Founded and chaired by Gyalzur, Shangri-La Beer illustrates in many
ways how production of wine and beer can connect more directly with
Tibetan culture as a method of indigenizing modernity. Gyalzur is not motivated directly by sustainability or concerns over sacred landscapes and
ecology, but like Ani Dom and Li Weihong he presents himself through
an alternative lens more in line with Tibetan cultural and social values, in
contradistinction to other major players in the wine economy. Gyalzur and
his partners make promoting Tibetan culture and identities a priority not
only through the company's advertising and marketing but also by using
local Tibetan ingredients in their beer. This kind of commodity production is of interest to the local people of Shangri-La as they seek to play a
role in "shangrilazation" by indigenizing modernity on their own terms.

I have gotten to know Gyalzur well during my years living off and on in Shangri-La and consider him a good friend. I like his product and appreciate the structure and culture of his company. Though hailing from mountainous Switzerland, Gyalzur has deep roots in Shangri-La. His parents immigrated to Switzerland, his father from Gyalthang and his mother from another region of Tibet, during the period of Tibetan exile in the 1950s. The impetus for Shangri-La Beer began for Gyalzur in 2009, when he traveled to his family's homeland and visited a local orphanage that had been run by his mother for many years. Drawing on his real estate background in Switzerland, Gyalzur decided to give back to the community in Shangri-La by opening a restaurant, which he named Soyala. It was in Shangri-La's old town, and Gyalzur employed and trained former orphanage residents. In running this social enterprise, Gyalzur developed the idea to begin a local brewery, inspired by customers' asking whether any local brews were available in Shangri-La. After some research, Gyalzur learned that most Chinese beer is made using large quantities of rice, compared to Western brews he knew and enjoyed, so he engaged a Swiss brewmaster to come to Shangri-La and work with him to develop beers using the local Tibetan highland barleys. They opened a small brewery, which sold its bottled beers mostly to local restaurants in the old town area, in small quantities.

These efforts expanded to include a large industrial brewery facility, which opened in summer 2015. They initially made Tibetan Lager, Tibetan Pale Ale (brewed with local ancient Tibetan yeast strains), Black Yak (described as a light porter with some hints of coffee and chocolate), and Supernova (a strong flavorful ale with hints of local wild berries and licorice). The beers are all brewed using a combination of local indigenous hull-less, or naked, highland barley and imported Belgian and German malts. Today's beers from the new brewery include the Tibetan lager renamed Yalaso, Tibetan Pale Ale, Black Yak, Songha (a sweet flavorful Belgian-style ale), Supernova, Fat Dolma (a strong fruity wheat ale brewed using local wheats), and, most recently, Buddha's Hand, a New England IPA blending local pinewood essence with a citrus fruit from tropical southern Yunnan, from which the beer takes its name. Gyalzur and his team also produce seasonal limited-release microbrews, including some cask-aged ales brewed in oak barrels purchased from the Moët winery, part of a new small-batch local-ingredients program called the Shangri-La Beer Farmhouse project, meant to return to some of the roots of their original small brewery.

Following the initial local success of Gyalzur's original, though unofficial and unlicensed, brewery, the local government offered to support him in starting up a much larger officially licensed operation as a good way to work with local farmers in selling their barley crops. This "support," however, turned out to refer neither to funding for the new brewery or company nor to an open invitation to do business. Now, with the new brewery, two of the management staff work full-time as government liaisons, cultivating *guanxi* to keep all parties happy. Gyalzur stresses that to do business effectively and successfully in China, one needs to be able to work closely with the government and actively nurture relationships with officials.

The official opening ceremony of the new facility on June 20, 2015, was a spectacular event, with many notable dignitaries, both local and foreign, in attendance and, of course, free beer for all. Entertainment included a recorded video interview with Gyalzur introducing the brewery and the process of brewing good beer. Performances of Tibetan singing and dancing were featured, and signing ceremonies with distributors from cities and towns throughout Yunnan took place. The opening was paired with two other notable events in Shangri-La over the same weekend: the annual horse racing festival and the celebration of Shangri-La's establishment as an official city or municipality (its former designation was as a county capital/town). To capitalize on this weekend of activities, Gyalzur and his company also worked to make their event part of the Shangri-La celebration by formally establishing a sister city relation with the skiing town of Arosa, in Switzerland. The opening celebration for the new brewery included live speeches of recognition from both the Swiss ambassador to China and the local mayor of Shangri-La. The idea of establishing a sister city project was first pitched to Gyalzur as a way to establish good government relations. He was familiar with Arosa from skiing trips there and found it similar in look and feel to Shangri-La. The local city governments were both supportive of this idea and of using the brewery as a vehicle to support it, and fortunately, with much effort, the government in Beijing came through to support the idea as well.

Before taking me on a tour around the brewery, Gyalzur described the taste, nature, and quality of his beers and what makes them Tibetan beer and special as a local product. His brewmaster guesses that the local spring groundwater they use is over one hundred years old when it comes out of the ground, which gives it a unique local character. For Shangri-La Beer, brewing is less about hops, which have become especially popular among American microbreweries. Gyalzur's team is more interested in malts for flavor as well as development and utilization of local Tibetan yeasts and highland barley. Their beer has no additives or stabilizers, and they believe in being all-natural and green—Gyalzur claims that their beer cannot be any greener. Shangri-La Beer makes its products with all local highland barley in combination with imported Belgian malts, and they return the leftover barley mash to local farmers for animal feed.

Shangri-La Beer is a local company, employing local people, about 80 percent of them former orphanage residents, who now earn some of the highest salaries in the region. Gyalzur believes their beer is Tibetan beer, made by Tibetan people with local Tibetan raw materials. Tibetan people also drink local barley beer, or *chang,* so he feels that their innovation in making a local barley beer can spread the traditional Tibetan hospitality of *chang.* He believes that these characteristics keep the company's beers unique and distinctly Tibetan amid the increasing number and popularity of microbrews in China. I wish to note here the blending of cultures to appeal to Chinese middle-class and luxury consumers, with whom a Western-style microbrew is a growing trend in China, paired with what some view as exotic or pure and natural Tibetan culture. Much of the marketing of the beer that Gyalzur and his team engage in directly advertises the Tibetan aspects of the beer with traditional Tibetan religious *thangka* paintings (in a style and method of Tibetan art often used for frescos in monasteries) designed by one of his partners, a professionally trained *thangka* artist, whose illustrations appear on the bottle labels. Gyalzur and his company also carry out online social media campaigns that highlight the natural and cultural aspects of the beer. This connects the beer with consumers and drinkers by employing the language and semiotics from the company's marketing, with terroir even mentioned in reference to the local water and ingredients used in the beer.

With the new brewery, Shangri-La Beer has moved beyond the scale of a microbrewery, but its managers are committed to maintaining the quality and uniqueness of their craft beer. Gyalzur explains that to make a legally bottled micro-style beer is very difficult due to the required quantities, but I have been drinking Gyalzur's beer since it entered the market and can attest that he and his team have gone beyond achieving this feat. Obtaining their official health and bottling license from Beijing took a lot of investment and effort, given that the minimum production capacity required for such a license is twenty thousand bottles per day. Even at such quantities, Shangri-La Beer's products remain as good as some of the best microbrews I have come to love in the United States. Gyalzur's support of and work with local farmers around Shangri-La City continues to grow and expand, as does his and his brewmaster's work and experimentation with more local varieties of highland barley. Farmers from nearby villages now not only sell barley to the brewery at competitive rates but also take part in various nontechnical production activities such as boxing and packaging beer. In 2016, the brewery established a barley experimentation program, working directly with some of the local villagers, and they are now creating their own malts using the local highland barleys.

Gyalzur and Shangri-La Beer are part of a recasting of transnational connections with France and Switzerland in the formation of the region's contemporary landscape. Certainly, his family's roots in the area differ from those of the MEP or the Saint Bernard fathers, having resulted from the political upheaval in the 1950s that led to a large expatriate population of Tibetans in Switzerland. It is telling, though, that almost all the wine and beer projects in Shangri-La are linked with France and Switzerland and the intertwined histories between these regions, whether through colonialism or family connections, which are working to form this economy today. Contemporary wine and beer livelihoods and identities in Shangri-La are largely driven by new forms of global capital with historical European ties.

The following company mission statement by Gyalzur captures his and the brewery's aspirations:

> Shangri-La is a magical place and we're dedicated to brewing a magical beer. Life is tough and we think everyone deserves to find their own Shangri-La.
>
> All of our beers are inspired by Shangri-La, that's why we use only all-natural Tibetan Mountain Spring Water, heirloom Qingker Barley and Imported German Hops. It doesn't take a lot of ingredients to get to Shangri-La, only 3 perfect ones.
>
> But our mission is more than just making beer. We're in this to build a sustainable business that helps local farmers and businesses grow. Every single Shangri-La Beer comes from our community to yours.
>
> We're also proud of our unique heritage. With a majority Swiss-Tibetan executive team we're proud to partner with the city of Arosa, Switzerland our sister city. The Swiss dedication to craft and precision impacts everything we do. More importantly, we think you'll be able to taste the difference.
>
> At the end of the day, our mission is incredibly simple. Make Shangri-La in a Bottle.
>
> Respectfully,
> Sonny[9]

Gyalzur talks about how, living in Switzerland, he enjoyed good Swiss and German beers, so he wished to be able to do the same in Shangri-La, while adding Tibetan characteristics to reflect his family's story and the local landscape. Drinking for enjoyment and especially through sharing beer with visitors to the brewery's tasting room, in local restaurants, and

FIGURE 20. Sonny Gyalzur and his family, with children from his
mother's orphanage, at the ceremony celebrating the opening
of the new Shangri-La Beer brewery, 2015.

during special events are part of brewers' experience and business practices. Drinking Shangri-La Beer's products is an experience of embodiment of the local Tibetan landscape and culture not just for consumers
but also for Gyalzur and the local Tibetans working in the brewery who
make this beer.

I discovered another story about these sorts of transnational connections between Tibet and Switzerland through wine and beer during
my visit to the Saint Bernard archives in the Valais region of Switzerland
in June 2016. While reading some materials on Valais viticulture and its
history, I learned that the Dalai Lama also owns a small vineyard in the
Martigny district of Valais, where the Saint Bernard Hospice is located.
His vineyard there is officially the world's smallest, with only three vines,
and is named after a Swiss Robin Hood from the nineteenth century,
Joseph-Samuel Farinet, a local folk hero known for his counterfeiting of
money to give to the poor. The small vineyard honoring him was planted

on a mountainside in the mid-1980s, and after passing through different ownership, it was given by the last owner, Abbé Pierre, a French Catholic priest and anti-poverty campaigner, to the Dalai Lama in 1998, after the two visited the site together. The Tibetan leader has owned it ever since, and the wine produced from the vines there are sold each year to generate funds for a Tibetan children's charity, much like Gyalzur's work with his mother's orphanage in Shangri-La (Wallace 2014, 51–54; Zufferey-Perisset 2010, 498).

The work of both Ani Dom and Li Weihong to promote environmentalism through viticulture connects with their care for the animate local landscape surrounding Khawa Karpo, though in some ways they are in opposition. Li is an environmentally conscious entrepreneur, and like Sonny Gyalzur with Shangri-La Beer, has mastered the art of coexistence and collaboration with the state by negotiating niche markets and indigenizing modernity outside of state-run capitalism. For Li, to be both indigenous and modern means to recognize and maintain balance with the sacred landscape around her while engaging with the emerging viticulture and market economy taking shape within the region. For Gyalzur, crafting Tibetan beer involves a similar negotiation within and around contemporary markets and consumer preferences and draws on transnational business acumen. While engaging in such negotiations, Gyalzur seeks to highlight and enhance appreciation for local Tibetan ingredients and to give back to local communities and the landscape. Others around Li, including some of her fellow villagers, do not take this view, and they use agrochemicals and methods introduced by the state without localizing these practices to conform in a way that does not pit them against the wishes of local mountain spirits.

Counter to Li and Gyalzur, Ani Dom does not engage with modernity or markets and contrarily retreats from, resists, and avoids the authorities as much as he can. No real amount of economic prosperity is acceptable to him if it harms the spirit world of Khawa Karpo. However, both his and Li's motivations remain based on Khawa Karpo's renown throughout the

Tibetan world and the local cosmologies that Tibetans follow with respect to the mountain and its deities. Both Ani Dom and Li seek to acknowledge the agency of the mountain deity and other nonhuman beings because of the potential negative ecological ramifications of not doing so. Indeed, in Ani Dom's view, the shrinking of Mingyong glacier may be in direct response to agrochemical pollution associated with viticulture, and most villagers in the region now see the mountain and local landscape as an economic resource, as Li does, rather than a sacred site. Li remains the exception, however, in that, compared to many others, she maintains her reverence for the mountain while strategically engaging with new market economies and listening and observing how the mountain and spirits are directing her toward a more ecocentric way of living with modernity and markets.

Contrasting Ani Dom's and Li's actions with those of other villagers in some ways exemplifies an inverse "economy of fortune" (Da Col 2007, 2012), wherein villagers feel endowed with certain riches given by the environment around them. For others, concerns over trespassing the sacredness and animate landscape to benefit from this fortune are mostly nonexistent in the modern economy. Being a resident of a community with access rights and tenure to this landscape gives people the right to use natural resources as they wish. Today, quality of life and standard of living drive economic success in Deqin. The production and sale of grapes is vital to this standard of living, as villagers attest. This goes hand in hand with collecting and marketing items such as valuable fungi, which, like wine, are highly desired not by local Tibetans themselves but by Chinese consumer classes or, in the case of matsutake, consumers in Japan.

The modern economic success of people living in Shangri-La is largely a product of global capitalism and national and transnational commodity chains. In addition, major agricultural shifts have occurred in which villagers abandon crops traditionally grown for subsistence and for religious and cultural practices, such as wheat and barley, in exchange for cash crops that are more lucrative. In response to these national and transnational economic pressures, Gyalzur has worked to create a continuing niche market for local barley varieties to allow villager farmers to maintain livelihood continuity and perpetuate and modernize Tibetan culture for consumption, by brewing his beer with this barley. What is clear and prevalent throughout the region is that engagement with outside markets through agriculture and forest products is redefining local perceptions of and connections to the landscape. Ani Dom, Li, and Gyalzur have each responded to these changes initiated by the state and globalization with alternative possibilities.

Taking up viticulture, collecting fungi for sale internationally, and commercializing barley beer are some ways that most of the region's villagers have indigenized modernity. Ani Dom's, Li's, and Gyalzur's practices and ways of doing so, however, remain more exceptions to these methods. The first two seek to maintain balance in luck and fortune with Khawa Karpo and its spirit world. For the third, motivations are more personal and familial than ecological. However, all three carry a hope of mitigating negative social and environmental impacts from the transnational capital that has come to Shangri-La.

Conclusion

In wine there is wisdom,
In beer there is freedom,
In water there is bacteria . . .

Blackboard outside a pub in London

Wine and viticulture, together with the global influences that have come with them, have worked to reconfigure perceptions of self, landscape, and community among Tibetan villagers and other actors in Shangri-La. While in many situations, local individual agency is lost in this process of landscape change and economic "development" at the hands of the state and corporate interests, in other cases agency remains in the hands of local villagers and actors in the production and development of Shangri-La as a wine region. In Cizhong, many households have explicitly moved to dedicate themselves to what a landscape of vineyards and winemaking should look like, building on the history of French and Swiss missionaries and particular methods of production "inherited" from them. In doing so, villagers have indigenized modernity to create an image of themselves and their community reflective of an ideal of terroir to give wines made in Cizhong a "taste of place" based on locale, history, and production methods. This project has been carried out differently than in other communities, where landscape transformation related to wine production has been part of a larger process of statecraft, incorporation, and "shangrilazation" (Yeh and Coggins 2014a). But in both Cizhong and the larger wine landscapes across greater Shangri-La, relevant actors have drawn on the history of French wine in the region to promote today's developments. Although archival work reveals that it was the Swiss missionaries in later years who engaged in viticulture and winemaking at a significant scale, the French concept of terroir remains central to this story.

By deploying the idea of terroir and winemaking as projects in place making and identity formation together with the semiotics of drinks as a form of "embodied material culture" (Manning 2012), I have illustrated the ways that village winemakers, the state, corporate interests, and small entrepreneurial winemakers all seek to capitalize on the niche market of embodying Tibetan culture and the landscape of Shangri-La. In Cizhong, villagers such as Wu Gongdi and Hong Xing draw on their identity as both Tibetans and Catholics within the context of Shangri-La to give their wine and landscape of Rose Honey vineyards a distinctive identity. Moving outside the bounds of the state's larger process of "shangrilazation," Cizhong people say their wine and wine landscapes are authentic and unique in ways that others in the larger region are not. These are traits they point out to illustrate the ideal of Cizhong wine's having a special terroir. Elsewhere, actors including the state/Shangri-La Winery, Moët, Sonny Gyalzur's Shangri-La Beer, and villager cooperatives in Weixi utilize the imagery of Shangri-La's landscapes and various aspects of Tibetan culture to create their own terroirs within the larger context of Shangri-La. Shangri-La Winery and Moët adhere to more traditional associations of terroir with climate, geography, and regionality, with Tibetan "culture" and imagery tacked on as marketing ploys rather than directly associated with local people. Outside of Cizhong and Weixi, many local farmers do nothing more than grow grapes and sell them to the wineries or grow grapes as contracted plantation-style labor. Their lives and livelihoods have been transformed by wine, but their role as Tibetan people in creating a terroir for these wines is nonexistent even though they are connected to the wines through corporate and state marketing and imagery.

There also remains a sort of transnational loop, rooted in history, with ties between Shangri-La, France, and Switzerland that emerges in almost all the wine- and beer-producing projects and ventures in Shangri-La today. Historically, intoxicants and simulants such as wine and tea have worked to set up interactions in the Sino-Tibetan borderlands and elsewhere in Asia between different actors, and such connections are appearing in new modes of global capitalism. This repeating circuit exemplifies the ways that transnational flows of commodities, stimulants, and intoxicants in particular have shaped livelihoods and identities historically and continue to do so. Many populations, including the Tibetans of today's Shangri-La, are unknowingly part of far older and significant transnational connections as they produce their own contemporary livelihoods and identities. As with the earlier tea trade, in Shangri-La and across the Sino-Tibetan borderlands, wine and beer work to make connections with both China and the West, similar to the way matsutake as a commodity has created new transnational links with Japan (Hathaway 2014). However, while some of the links built by wine are reworkings of older connections, matsutake lacks the historical connections and conversations that wine evokes and enlivens.

Shangri-La brand wine and the local state have worked to "develop" the village agricultural landscape in the region to raise farmers out of poverty, but perhaps more importantly, to bring them into the fold of the larger transnationalized Shangri-La landscape and region. These activities have associated the wine with having an important French history. Even among knowledgeable villagers such as Wu Gongdi and foreign wine-makers who are aware of the paramount Swiss influence, most choose to make the history French because among Chinese wine consumers this is the known commodity (Mustacich 2015; Ross and Roach 2013). Tibetan culture and the potential fulfillment that it provides in escaping an increasingly polluted China is also becoming a major draw, which both local village Tibetans themselves and urban transnational Tibetans with local connections, such as Gyalzur of Shangri-La Beer, are quick to respond to in the production of their goods. In all these ventures, local realities meld with larger global perspectives and histories. Craft beer is a global and predominantly Western trend for instance, and Shangri-La

Beer markets itself as (and in fact is) China's first officially licensed craft brewery, using Tibetan ingredients and characteristics.

While on the surface the entrance of transnational corporate interests into Shangri-La's wine landscape with Moët appears positive, there have been drawbacks. Adong villagers are happy with the deal they received for their land and prefer it to their prior arrangement of selling their grapes to Shangri-La Winery. Yet the introduction of capitalist labor has disrupted customary household and community activity in ways not yet fully realized. Caterpillar fungus collection as a community activity and the management of the land on which this other luxurious or conspicuous "Tibetan" resource grows contrasts with paid labor in Moët's vineyards on village land. However, caterpillar fungus collection remains a community-wide annual pilgrimage and shared family activity.

These new drinks and the landscapes that are appearing with them are also changing drinking as a practice among local Tibetans. Today, especially in Cizhong and Bu Villages, locally produced grape wine is slowly making its way into festivals and daily consumption. While butter tea remains the dominant drink of hospitality, for Cizhong Tibetans this is changing fast with every household producing grape wine. With the arrival of Shangri-La Beer, Gyalzur is perpetuating and expanding the traditional hospitality of Tibetan beer across China and beyond. The beer brings both the idea and a physical part of Shangri-La, through ingredients such as water and local highland barley, to the palate of those who would like a chance to experience the region and culture by embodying it through drink. These are powerful moves of agency by the likes of Gyalzur and Wu Gongdi in the strategic deployment of the terroir of Shangri-La as a physical place.

Despite agentive and strategic deployments of terroir and their role in the perpetuation of local actors in the continued crafting of the Shangri-La landscape, problems remain in the state's use of viticulture to make rural villagers contributing citizens of Shangri-La. As Ani Dom and Li Weihong remind us, there is perhaps more at stake in the development of viticulture and wine in Shangri-La in terms of long-term sustainability and the sacred landscape of Khawa Karpo. The culture, traditions, biodiversity, and environment surrounding this mountain are extensive and are central to articulating the indigenous spiritual ecology of the region (Coggins and Hutchinson 2006; Salick and Moseley 2012). Yet these traditions remain important only to the few individuals who perpetuate them, such as Ani Dom. As he points out, the long-term viability of this sacred place and these traditions seems to have taken a backseat to the economic gains that have come with viticulture and its landscape transformations. Li, however, has demonstrated that environmental and cultural preservation of the landscape does not need to exclude making viticulture a viable form of economic production. Through educating herself and organizing local communities as an ecological entrepreneur, she demonstrates that growing grapes can indeed be a "green" and economically productive industry.

Two conceptualizations frame the landscape of wine in Shangri-La: the strategic deployment of terroir as a form of indigenizing modernity and the hybrid forms of capitalism in contemporary China. The production of terroir itself can be described as a picturesque assemblage of human and nonhuman factors (Paxson 2010). In Shangri-La, these factors include histories and a sort of "placiality," a space that is known to and familiar to the people living there (Cons 2016; Hardy 2000), that is melded together with a variety of factors and individual ideals among various wine producers and the state to create working "assemblages of coordinations within a dynamic history" (Tsing 2015a, 6).

Shangri-La's many wine and beer makers rely and call on images from the history and temporality of the region's landscapes as they craft their drinks as commodities for market. The histories are built on a variety of transnational connections with Europe that are being re-envisioned today to illustrate a specific image of wine, linking Shangri-La and the larger Sino-Tibetan borderlands with the rest of China and the outside world. In doing so, some maintain a strict adherence to state-organized markets and capitalism, or "socialism with Chinese characteristics," while others have branched out from these state visions of Shangri-La as a wine landscape using their own individual imagery, ideals, and entrepreneurial spirit. Outside of state interventions, and even working to reconfigure them in response to their potential environmental and economic consequences, all winemakers and grape growers in Shangri-La have used these new conceptions of landscape and commodity production as a way of adapting to and indigenizing the modernity that wine has brought. People are recrafting modernity in their own image. Wine and viticulture have brought agentive power to the people of Shangri-La as development tools alongside profound changes in livelihood production and cultural identity.

Afterword

Wine is sunlight, held together by water.

Galileo Galilei

Many changes have taken place in the landscape of wine in Shangri-La since my original fieldwork was concluded in 2016 and since my last visit in 2018. Of course, China and the world were upended by the COVID-19 pandemic, which prevented me from returning since that time. But I have stayed in touch with many friends and kept abreast of happenings over WeChat and social media.

Shortly after my last visit in summer 2018, Wu Gongdi passed away unexpectedly from acute pancreatitis. This came as a shock to his family and the entire community of Cizhong. Had it not been for him, the community's winemaking identity might not have ever come to fruition. When I last saw him, I fortunately had been able to present him with a Chinese book on foreign and local perspectives on Shangri-La (compiled to celebrate the fiftieth anniversary of Diqing Prefecture), to which I had contributed. My chapter tells the story of the French and Swiss missionaries and Wu Gondi and his family in creating Cizhong's and the larger prefecture's wine industry. I was comforted to know that before he passed away, he had been able to read a portion of the story I had been learning from him over many years.

Hong Xing has continued to carry on his father's winemaking tradition with rigor. In his forties, much to his family's joy, he finally married, opened a wine shop next to the church, and built a new house, winery, and guesthouse situated in the middle of the family's vineyards, upslope from the paternal home. He works annually with expert winemakers from Xiaoling Estate, and he has increased his skills and equipment to run a very professional bottling operation and now ships his wines throughout China via online sales on WeChat. His wines receive rave reviews from visitors to Cizhong, both foreign and domestic, and he has thoroughly built his new married life around winemaking in the image and memory of his father.

Major state-initiated alterations occurred in 2019, however, upending everyone's life in Cizhong. Despite all the features that make the village unique religiously and in terms of agriculture—with its wetland paddy rice grown by Tibetans, grapes, and wine—changes disrupted both agriculture and religious harmony. While Cizhong sits on a small plateau approximately 130 feet above the banks of the Mekong River, high enough to avoid flooding, another upstream community called Yanmen, Cizhong's administrative township, which was situated closer to the riverbank, was inundated by the 990 megawatt Wunonglong Dam 25 miles downstream. Yanmen has been relocated to what had been Cizhong's carefully cultivated and terraced rice paddy fields, bulldozed to accommodate the move.

In addition to losing land and the ability to practice rice agriculture and irrigation techniques, which had been developed over centuries, Cizhong has been merged with several hundred wheat- and barley-growing Buddhist households from outside the community and with no understanding or knowledge of local Catholic practice and rice agro-ecology. Overnight, Cizhong's Catholic (and Buddhist) rice growers have become minorities on their own land and have lost access to what had been their mode of self-sufficient food production with rice growing. Similarly, unique localized Tibetan irrigation and water management techniques and relationships with water are quickly disappearing. As villagers have often told me, what makes the rice grown in Cizhong special for them is that it is organic, which cannot be guaranteed with any rice purchased from markets, and that they themselves produce it. While Yunnan-based Tibetans living upstream in locales such as Yanmen and elsewhere have been known to consume rice via trade for quite some time, guaranteeing where this rice comes from today and whether it can be relied on to be clean and healthy have become concerns.

Given the state's promotion of Cizhong within the larger Shangri-La tourism circuit, its essential destruction as an agricultural hamlet with a particular religious identity is further concerning. Much of the community's recognition comes with its name, which, though still unclear in terms of policy, may be lost now because Yanmen, as a township, is higher up in the administrative structure, and Yanmen may be the name that will be used moving forward. Many villagers are also quite concerned about the arrival of so many Buddhists, who will disrupt the precarious religious harmony in the village. The Buddhist households in Cizhong lived side by side harmoniously with the Catholics for over one hundred years, but Yanmen's people have no grasp of Catholic Tibetan culture. Common tropes of understanding and conceptions among Catholics and Buddhists in Cizhong are that Catholics do not know how to effectively make money off their church and unique religion as a tourism resource and that the Buddhists who live near the church profit too much off Catholicism, as illustrated in remarks by villagers:

> Catholics don't know how to run businesses. Otherwise, we could make more money from restaurants, hotels, and entertainment venues near the church.
>
> Tibetan Buddhists are favored by the local government. The vineyard next to the church was our property, but the government hasn't returned it to our church, and instead rented it out to a Buddhist family to manage and market the vineyards there.

These ideas are expressed by villagers in a tongue-and-cheek manner, and, in fact, intermarriage between Catholics and Buddhists is quite common. However, the remarks reveal a tension that has been carefully negotiated and managed over time. Catholics worry that these issues will be exacerbated with the arrival of more Buddhists who are unaware of these differences of opinion and approach regarding religion. They are concerned about Buddhists viewing the village church and Catholicism as an economic resource.

Additionally, with tourism making up the majority of Cizhong household incomes through wine sales and the operation of household guesthouses, the picturesque image that has drawn tourists to the community has very much disappeared. The new homes located on top of all the paddy fields are built in an urban concrete style rather than the Tibetan architectural styles previously used in the community. As there is not enough land now to serve the agricultural needs of all the new households in addition to the old ones, everyone will have their official household registration changed from rural to urban, meaning that they will now be expected to look for wage-based labor outside of the community to make a good livelihood and generate profits. They will need to purchase grain and other food to eat, with no more land on which to grow subsistence crops.

For many villagers, the repercussions from the loss of land, trees, and crops are twofold: they view the compensation provided by the state as inadequate, and they feel a sense of loss with respect to the paddy fields and irrigation canals that had been created by the community by hand over several centuries, before communist China existed. Many elders reported crying when they first heard about the destruction of the paddy fields. Older generations are most defiant toward the government about land requisition. As a seventy-three-year-old grandmother from one well-off Catholic family explained to me: "¥30,000 per *mu* plus 260 per month compensation for our rice fields will be given, but that is not enough. Without our land, we have no history, and it won't be the same Cizhong that we have always known. We won't have a *xiaokang* life.[1] I wish they would make the other villages and the township being relocated move to the mountain above Cizhong instead of in our fields. I don't really care about the money. It's the land that is important to me."

Many households have lost 100- to 200-year-old walnut trees along roads or at the edges of fields to make way for widening the roads to accommodate the new township. Compensation for these trees has ranged from ¥300 to ¥10,000 (US$41–$1,381) per tree, while some trees produce up to ¥10,000 (US$1,381) in annual profits and take decades to reach full maturity. Road projects have also led to the loss of vineyard space, with compensation matching the profits made from only one year of grape or wine sales.

These changes and impacts are being felt even in outlying areas beyond the central village due to road widening and other infrastructure projects associated with dam construction and the relocation of Yanmen Township to Cizhong. While Wu Gongdi and Hong Xing's family did not lose their paddy lands, they were unable to grow rice for two years because road construction prevented their use of irrigation canals. Fortunately, one rice crop provides enough to last a household for two years, but other households that have completely lost their lands are not so fortunate.

I have mentioned the 2018–19 land requisition here in brief only, but it has had a great impact on the community.[2] Most vineyard land was spared from these changes, so winemaking continues. Conversely, at the site of the original French church downstream in Cigu, which is also Tibetan and Catholic, vineyards and winemaking are seeing expansion at the hands of foreign endeavors with Xiaoling Estate and Château Roduit, which are working with villagers to plant more vineyards and engage in vocational training for vine care. Family connections exist as well. The Swiss Valais owner of Roduit works closely with his wife, who comes from Badong Village in the Cigu area. These types of collaborations between professional winemakers and local farmers are great ways to improve the industry and the quality of wines in China, as suggested by wine studies colleagues Pierre Ly and Cynthia Howson, who have examined wine and economic development throughout China and who, on my recommendation, spent time with Hong Xing, Wu Gongdi, and others in villages around Deqin County (Howson and Ly 2020).

By working together, winemakers can refine and develop terroir and taste and also learn to improve sustainability and organic methodologies, which have become a major focal point for foreign winemakers in Shangri-La, including Xiaoling, Château Roduit, and Moët. Shangri-La Winery still sends village grape farmers large annual pesticide and fertilizer packets rather than investing in sustainability training. As I have suggested previously (Galipeau 2015), vocational training in winemaking to diversify outlets for grape sales beyond Shangri-La Winery could be an effective means to improving sustainability and food and economic security. It is thus heartening to see the boutique foreign wineries forging more cooperation with local communities.

More broadly, the development of wine and vineyard landscapes has continued apace throughout Shangri-La and Diqing. Moët still releases new vintages (at the same high prices) every year, receiving rave reviews from international critics such as Robert Parker. More accolades are being given both within China and abroad for Xiaoling Estate, Château Roduit, and other wines as more independent wineries pop up throughout the region. Shangri-La Winery now produces drinkable wines across a variety of price ranges, with some of their best wines, such as A3, now selling quite reasonably for ¥120 (US$17). While this company was always a bit of a black hole and difficult to fully capture ethnographically given its close association with the government, my understanding is that it has liberalized to some extent in response to increasing wine tourism in the region and has now opened its facilities to visitors for tastings and direct purchases. I visited the winery in 2014, when it was not open to the public, and received an icy reception. I hope to return and experience the new visitor facilities (and those of other wineries) soon. A full winery operation that regularly caters to visitors is now also up and running for white dry and ice wines in Hada Village and appears headed for continued success and expansion.

With wine and beer achieving such marvelous success through "shangrilazation," it was only a matter of time before another form of spirits jumped on the band wagon. A friend of Sonny Gyalzur's, a New Zealander who previously worked at Goose Island Beer's brewpub in Shanghai, has started Shangri-La Youyun Distilling, going by the brand name the Rambler. This establishment is named after the famous British plant hunter George Forrest, who, like the Rambler's owner, was born in Scotland,

and who is lauded for his efforts as an explorer in Yunnan. The Rambler hopes to be a pioneer, distilling with local Yunnan ingredients and flavors (Playfoot 2021). With four gins on the market, major sales throughout China, and international awards, the Rambler continues to push wine and spirits from Shangri-La into the national and international spotlight and highlight the unique traits of this place as a potential landscape of wine, beer, and sprits, all crafted in the "Tibetan" image of the landscape of Shangri-La and its peoples and natural resources.

Glossary

Chinese (modern pinyin romanization)	Alternate romanization	Chinese characters	Tibetan (romanized)	English
Cigu	Tsu-kou Cikou	茨姑		Cigu (village in Yunnan)
Cizhong	Tsu-chung Tsechung	茨中		Cizhong (village in Yunnan)
dong chong xia cao		冬虫夏草	yartsa gunbu	caterpillar fungus (*Ophiocordyceps sinensis*)
fengtu		风土		terroir
song rong		松茸	beshing shamo (be sha)	matsutake mushroom (*Tricholoma matsutake*)
Xianggelila		香格里拉	Rgyalthang	Shangri-La (city formally known as Zhongdian in Chinese and Rgyalthang in Tibetan)
Yanjing	Yerkalo	鹽井	Tsha kha lho	Yanjing or Yerkalo (village in Tibet)

Notes

Introduction

Epigraph: From *The Nine-Eyed Agate*, translated by Heather Stoddard.

1. For more on the unique history, development, and governance of Diqing, see Hillman 2003, 2010; Mortensen 2019.

2. The Chinese state and other actors have heavily reified "Shangri-La" as an actual place with actual people in Northwest Yunnan today. The term as a name and a place has a powerful, constructed nature. I do not wish to reify Shangri-La in this way but instead comment on this process of invention of place throughout this book. Beyond these initial paragraphs, I do not enclose Shangri-La in quotation marks as James Ferguson (1994) does in his work critiquing the constructed nature of the term *development*. Nevertheless, readers should remain wary of the reification of this name. The process of constructing Shangri-La has captivated numerous scholars. For examples, see Coggins and Yeh 2014; Hillman 2003; Kolås 2011; Smyer Yü 2015.

3. Other scholars have suggested that I refer to Shangri-La using the Chinese transliteration of Xianggelila in this work to perhaps more properly address the Chinese name given to the place. Since this Chinese name is a transliteration of a made-up English name, I have chosen to use the English spelling. There is also the question of referring to the place using the original Tibetan name of Rgyalthang in recognition of the region's indigenous Tibetan vernacular. Given that today even local Tibetans largely use Shangri-La as the name of the city, county, and larger region, and that the topics of wine and terroir in this book are heavily linked to this name, I have decided to stick with this title throughout the book while fully recognizing its problematic and reified nature.

4. Transnational conservation projects of the Nature Conservancy, the World Wildlife Fund, Conservation International, and other NGOs and their entanglements with local Tibetan villagers and livelihoods in the early 2000s have been the focus of extensive ethnographic scholarship, engagement, and discussion. For some examples, see Coggins and Hutchinson 2006; Grumbine 2011; Hathaway 2013; Litzinger 2004; Moseley and Mullen 2014; Zhou and Grumbine 2011; Zinda 2014.

5.   For a few particularly good examples of ethnographic and scholarly treatments of ethnic minorities and *minzu* studies focused on Yunnan, Southwest China, and Tibet, see Brown 1996; Harrell 1996, 2001; Mueggler 2001; Mullaney 2011; Yeh 2013a. These are just some of many works in this field.

6.   For some examples of such scholarship, see Cattelino 2010; Lambert 2007; Povinelli 2002; Yeh 2007b.

1. Wine in Tibet from Catholic Colonialism to Global Capitalism

Epigraph: From *The Hundred Thousand Songs of Milarepa*, translated by Ben Joffe.

1.   For a general overview of the history of the modern Chinese wine industry, see Anderson 1990; Jenster and Cheng 2008; Z. Li 2011; Shu 2016.

2.   In the case of Tibet, my discussion focuses on Catholic missionaries who traveled and spent time in Northwest Yunnan, nearby western Sichuan, or central Tibet, including the capital of Lhasa. Catholic missionary activity was also prevalent in the Sino-Tibetan borderlands of northwest China in today's Qinghai and Gansu Provinces as well as in the south along the border of Tibet with India. For information on Catholic history in the northwest, see Horlemann 2013, 2014, 2015. For work on Catholics in northern India, including the Missions Étrangères de Paris (MEP) and other orders, see Bray 2011, 2014; Raignoux 2010.

3.   See, for example, Bonet 2006 and Deshayes 2008, two general historical works on both the MEP and the Saint Bernard missions written using primarily archival materials. Also see the official chronical of the mission written by Adrien Launay (1909), a father of the MEP in Paris. Contrary to other primary missionary works, which include many geographical and ethnographic details, Launay's is written much more from a religious perspective, focusing on the struggles and issues faced by the French fathers as missionaries rather than chronicling the peoples and places they encountered.

4.   See Kilpatrick 2015, which extensively chronicles the work of the MEP fathers (and a few other notable figures) not only as missionaries but also as botanical explorers who made the first introductions of thousands of species of plants from China to Europe.

5.   Accounts of the work of Forrest, Rock, and others, including Frank Kingdon Ward, who was a prolific writer himself, are abundant. For two excellent examples, see Glover et al. 2011 and Mueggler 2011.

6.   The Patriotic Catholic Association of China is the official Catholic Church recognized and organized by the Chinese government, which does not openly acknowledge the authority of the pope and Vatican.

2. Landscape Change, Tibetan Identity, and Terroir in Cizhong Village

Epigraph: From Ward, *The Land of the Blue Poppy*.

1. I use Wu Gongdi's real name rather than a pseudonym, at his own request. Wu Gongdi is a bit of a public figure in Cizhong. He and his son Hong Xing are both especially proud of their family's winemaking and viticulture, something people know them for, and they have asked me to use their family members' real names when writing about them because they want people to know about their wine and their family's story.

2. For examples of scholarly work on this topic, see Hansen 1999; Harrell 2001; Jinba 2014; McCarthy 2009.

3. In other parts of highland Asia and Yunnan, drinking is often predominantly a ritual activity. For examples, see Dove 1988; Fiskesjö 2010; Kirsch 1973.

4. For an analysis of Christmas in Cizhong and an examination of Cizhong's religious practices, see Galipeau 2018.

3. Producing "Tibetan" Wine and Altering Landscapes and Livelihoods

Epigraph: "Song of the Grape," translated by author and Yi Ma.

1. Liu Jiaqiang is an easily identifiable public figure as the owner of Sunspirit, and therefore I use his real name.

2. For an extensive analysis of these vulnerability issues in a village upstream from Bu, see Galipeau 2015.

3. Readers should note that ethnographic access was and remains an issue with Shangri-La Winery, as it is a quasi-state-owned company. Access to officials and interest on their part in participating in research and interviews was limited despite official government-issued research permits. For a fuller story of villagers growing grapes for Shangri-La Winery and the economic and environmental struggles they face, see Galipeau 2015.

    In this chapter and elsewhere herein, I often refer to the "state," as I do Shangri-La, much in the same way that Ferguson (1994) frames "development." Readers should not necessarily conflate the state with Shangri-La Winery but recognize that, compared to other wineries, this semi-government-owned entity largely represents and operationalizes the wishes of the local state to utilize grape agriculture and winemaking as a rural and economic development initiative alongside tourism promotion and "shangrilazation."

4. On dragon head enterprises' state-driven agricultural transformation in rural China, see Schneider 2017; Luo, Andreas, and Li 2017; Zhang and Donaldson 2008; Zhang, Oya, and Ye 2015.

5. Litsing Gerong is an easily identifiable public figure, like Liu Jiaqiang, and was featured in an article from 2012 in *China Daily*, which credited him with putting

Deqin on the map as a wine region; I use his real name, therefore, since he may be identified just by that description (Xiao and Li 2012).

6. For a detailed discussion about some of these individuals, whom I call ecological entrepreneurs, and their identities related to grapes and wine, see chapter 5.

7. For more details on Moët's Ao Yun and other regional wineries, see Anson 2015; Mustacich 2015; Robinson and Lander 2014; Xiao and Li 2012.

8. For an in-depth look at household and community land tenure and management in Adong and the changes that have arrived with Moët's lease and work program, see chapter 4.

9. In more recent years, it seems Shangri-La Winery's monopoly has been further relaxed by the prefectural government, but these changes took place after my research, so I only mention them here as a note.

10. See Schmitt (2014) for a discussion about a similar process that he calls de-swiddening among Ersu Tibetans in western Sichuan, where traditional subsistence grains are replaced with monocropped vegetables, connecting village economies with the provincial capital.

4. Free in the Mountains or Home in the Vineyard

Epigraph: From *Songs of the Sixth Dalai Lama*, translated by Ben Joffe.

1. Adong is my longtime host father in Meilishi Village, not to be confused with the village Adong, also discussed in this chapter.

2. For more extensive analysis of smallholders and agrarian change in rural China, see Luo, Andreas, and Li 2017; Schneider 2014; Tilt 2008; Zhang, Oya, and Ye 2015.

3. Village collectors in Yunnan always count, price, and sell their caterpillar fungus by pairs to the first initial market buyers. At higher levels of the commodity chain, people usually sell the fungi by gram weight or other methods of pricing, including in expensive gift boxes. The reason collectors sell the fungi by pairs is not known, but the geographer Michelle Olsgard Stewart (2014), who conducted fieldwork on collection in Yunnan, suggests it may have to do with finding the male or female mate for each collected fungus, since pairs often are found close to each other.

5. Resisting and Indigenizing Modernity

Epigraph: From *The Hundred Thousand Songs of Milarepa*, translated by Ben Joffe.

1. I use the real names of both Ani Dom and Li Weihong, as they are easily identifiable merely by description and have already been written about elsewhere.

2. Sonny Gyalzur is an easily identifiable public figure as the owner of Shangri-La Beer, and therefore I use his real name.

3. For more on the history and background of Tibetan mountain deity worship, see Karmay 1994, 1996; Buffetrille 1998, 2014.

4. For more on the various types of mountain deities and their roles in society, see Coggins and Hutchinson 2006; Diemberger 1998; Huber 1999; Karmay 1994, 1996.

5. For examples of specific work on glacier retreat as an animate spiritual response to climate change, see Cruikshank 2010; Drew 2012; Gagné 2018.

6. Also see the discussion by Makley (2018), who, drawing from Da Col, examines the in-depth ways that struggles over land and Tibetan cultural resources between local villagers, the state, and modern market economies have created what she calls "battles of fortune." In Makley's work in the Tibetan region of Rebgong in Qinghai Province, and as I observed in Deqin, some local villagers readily collaborate with the state and take up modern market economies, while others resist them, sometimes leading to intervillage conflicts and discord between the state and local mountain deities.

7. Of course, there remains an ambivalence in Ani Dom's actions and beliefs about the sanctity of life given that he killed his dog upon converting to Buddhism. When I asked about this, he explained that in his vision, according to the god Khawa Karpo, throwing his dog into the river was required as part of his redemption and conversion process to Buddhism and that his Buddhist forms of thinking are directed by the teachings of Khawa Karpo.

8. The Nature Conservancy was active in the region through the mid-2000s through many projects involving local knowledge experts and village conservation practitioners, including Ani Dom. For detailed analyses of the organization, see Litzinger 2004; Moseley and Mullen 2014; Salick and Moseley 2012. The Khawa Karpo Culture Association is an environmental and cultural NGO started by a local Tibetan.

9. Shangri-La Highland Craft Beer Co., Ltd., "Our Mission," accessed January 10, 2023, http://shangrilabeer.cn/mission/#:~:text=Shangri%2DLa%20is%20 a%20magical,Barley%20and%20Imported%20German%20Hops.

Afterword

1. *Xiaokang*, literally "small comforts," a Chinse concept referring to basic comforts beyond food and shelter, has been part of national development rhetoric in rural China for the past several decades. For more thorough analysis and ethnographic examination of this term and its use in rural China, see Ingman 2012; Tilt 2011.

2. I document the story of land requisition in Cizhong in more detail in Galipeau 2022.

References

Allerton, Catherine. 2009. "Introduction: Spiritual Landscapes of Southeast Asia."
   Anthropological Forum 19 (3): 235–51.
"Analyse de vin, Cépè de Bacot, apporté de Tsechung à Taiwan par le Père Gabriel
   Délèze et de Taiwan en Suisse en été 1999, 1 p. A4." 1999. Archives du Grand-
   Saint-Bernard. AGSB MIS F2 k10.3.
Anderson, Danica M., Jan Salick, Robert K. Moseley, and Ou Xiaokun. 2005.
   "Conserving the Sacred Medicine Mountains: A Vegetation Analysis of Tibetan
   Sacred Sites in Northwest Yunnan." *Biodiversity and Conservation* 14 (13): 3065–
   91. https://doi.org/10.1007/s10531-004-0316-9.
Anderson, E. N. 1990. *The Food of China*. New Haven, CT: Yale University Press.
Anson, Jane. 2015. "Anson on Thursday: Vineyards on the Roof of the World."
   Decanter, April 30, 2015. http://www.decanter.com/news/blogs/anson/588248
   /anson-on-thursday-vineyards-on-the-roof-of-the-world.
Atwill, David G. 2005. *The Chinese Sultanate: Islam, Ethnicity, and the Panthay
   Rebellion in Southwest China, 1856–1873*. Stanford, CA: Stanford University Press.
Baker, Barry B., and Robert K. Moseley. 2007. "Advancing Treeline and Retreating
   Glaciers: Implications for Conservation in Yunnan, P.R. China." *Arctic, Antarctic,
   and Alpine Research* 39 (2): 200–209.
Bellezza, John Vincent. 2005. *Spirit-Mediums, Sacred Mountains and Related Bon
   Textual Traditions in Upper Tibet: Calling Down the Gods*. Leiden: Brill.
Bernard, H. Russell. 2011. *Research Methods in Anthropology*. 5th ed. Lanham, MD:
   AltaMira Press.
Besky, Sarah. 2013. *The Darjeeling Distinction: Labor and Justice on Fair-Trade Tea
   Plantations in India*. Berkeley: University of California Press.
Bing, Jian, Pei-Jie Han, Wan-Qiu Liu, Qi-Ming Wang, and Feng-Yan Bai. 2014.
   "Evidence for a Far East Asian Origin of Lager Beer Yeast." *Current Biology* 24
   (10): R380–81. https://doi.org/10.1016/j.cub.2014.04.031.
Boesi, Alessandro. 2003. "*dByar rtswa dgun 'bu* (*Cordyceps sinensis* Berk): An
   Important Trade Item for the Tibetan Population of Li thang County, Sichuan
   Province, China." *Tibet Journal* 28 (3): 29–42.

Bonet, André. 2006. *Les chrétiens oubliés du Tibet*. Paris: Presses de la Renaissance.

Booz, Patrick. 2014. "In and Out of Borders: The *Beifu* 背夫 Tea Porters Encounter Tibet." *Cahiers d'Extrême-Asie*, no. 23: 253–69.

Bourdieu, Pierre. 1984. *Distinction: A Social Critique of the Judgement of Taste*. Translated by Richard Nice. Cambridge, MA: Harvard University Press.

Bray, John. 1995. "French Catholic Missions and the Politics of China and Tibet, 1846–1865." In *Tibetan Studies: Proceedings of the 7th Seminar of the International Association for Tibetan Studies*, edited by Helmut Krasser et al., vol. 1, 85–95. Vienna: Verlag der Österreichischen Akademie der Wissenschaften.

———. 2011. "Sacred Words and Earthly Powers: Christian Missionary Engagement with Tibet." *Transactions of the Asiatic Society of Japan* 3: 93–118.

———. 2014. "Christian Missionary Enterprise and Tibetan Trade." *Tibet Journal* 39 (1): 11–37.

Brown, Melissa, ed. 1996. *Negotiating Ethnicities in China and Taiwan*. Berkeley: Institute of East Asian Studies, University of California, Berkeley.

Buffetrille, Katia. 1998. "Reflections on Pilgrimages to Sacred Mountains, Lakes and Caves." In *Pilgrimage in Tibet*, edited by Alex McKay, 18–34. Richmond, Surrey: Curzon Press.

———. 2014. "The Pilgrimage to Mount Kha ba dkar po: A Metaphor for *Bar do*?" In *Searching for the Dharma, Finding Salvation—Buddhist Pilgrimage in Time and Space*, edited by Christoph Cueppers and Max Deeg, 197–277. Lumbini: Lumbini International Research Institute.

Cattelino, Jessica R. 2010. "The Double Bind of American Indian Need-Based Sovereignty." *Cultural Anthropology* 25 (2): 235–62.

Chan, Selina Ching. 2012. "*Terroir* and Green Tea in China: The Case of Meijiawu Dragon Well (*Longjing*) Tea." In *Geographical Indications and International Agricultural Trade: The Challenge for Asia*, edited by Louis Augustin-Jean, Hélène Ilbert, and Neantro Saavedra-Rivano, 226–38. New York: Palgrave Macmillan.

Chen, F. H., G. H. Dong, D. J. Zhang, X. Y. Liu, X. Jia, C. B. An, M. M. Ma, et al. 2015. "Agriculture Facilitated Permanent Human Occupation of the Tibetan Plateau after 3600 B.P." *Science* 347 (6219): 248–50. https://doi.org/10.1126/science.1259172.

Chen, Jia-Ching, John Aloysius Zinda, and Emily T. Yeh. 2017. "Recasting the Rural: State, Society and Environment in Contemporary China." *Geoforum* 78 (January): 83–88. https://doi.org/10.1016/j.geoforum.2016.03.014.

Clifford, James. 2001. "Indigenous Articulations." *Contemporary Pacific* 13 (2): 467–90.

Coggins, Chris, and Tessa Hutchinson. 2006. "The Political Ecology of Geopiety: Nature Conservation in Tibetan Communities of Northwest Yunnan." *Asian Geographer* 25 (1–2): 85–107.

Coggins, Chris, and Emily T. Yeh. 2014. "Introduction: Producing Shangrilas." In Yeh and Coggins 2014a, 3–18.

Coggins, Chris, and Gesang Zeren. 2014. "Animate Landscapes: Nature Conservation and the Production of Agropastoral Sacred Space in Shangrila." In Yeh and Coggins 2014a, 205–28.

Cons, Jason. 2016. "Conclusion: The Placial Imagination." *Journal of Environmental Studies and Sciences* 6 (4): 788–89.

Croidys, Pierre. 1949. *Du Grand-Saint-Bernard au Thibet: "Sur la Terre des Esprits"; Une équipe héroique s'en va batir a 3000 mètres un nouveau Saint-Bernard*. Paris: Spes.

Cruikshank, Julie. 2010. *Do Glaciers Listen? Local Knowledge, Colonial Encounters, and Social Imagination*. Vancouver: University of British Columbia Press.

Da Col, Giovanni. 2007. "The View from Somewhen: Events, Bodies and the Perspective of Fortune around Khawa Karpo, a Tibetan Sacred Mountain in Yunnan Province." *Inner Asia* 9 (2): 215–35.

———. 2012. "The Elementary Economies of Dechenwa Life: Fortune, Vitality, and the Mountain in Sino-Tibetan Borderlands." *Social Analysis* 56 (1): 74–98.

Dangl, Gerald. 2011. "Tales from the FPS Plant Identification Lab." *FPS Grape Program Newsletter* (Foundation Plant Services, University of California, Davis), October 2011.

Davies, Henry Rodolph. 1909. *Yün-nan: The Link between India and the Yangtze*. Cambridge: Cambridge University Press.

Decanter Asia Wine Awards. 2016. "Results: Himalaya Development Group, Tsekou, Yunnan Plateau, Yunnan, China (Mainland), 2014." https://awards.decanter.com /DAWA/2016/wines/660035.

Demossier, Marion. 2011. "Beyond *Terroir*: Territorial Construction, Hegemonic Discourses, and French Wine Culture." *Journal of the Royal Anthropological Institute* 17 (4): 685–705.

———. 2018. *Burgundy: A Global Anthropology of Place and Taste*. New York: Berghahn Books.

Desgodins, C. H. 1872. *La mission du Thibet de 1855 à 1870. D'après les lettres de m. l'abbé Desgodins*. Verdun: Imprimerie de Ch. Laurent.

Deshayes, Laurent. 2008. *Tibet (1846–1952); Les missionnaires de l'impossible*. Paris: Indes savantes.

Desideri, Ippolito. 1932. *An Account of Tibet: The Travels of Ippolito Desideri of Pistoia, S.J., 1712–1727*. Edited by Filippo De Filippi. London: George Routledge and Sons.

———. 2010. *Mission to Tibet: The Extraordinary Eighteenth-Century Account of Father Ippolito Desideri, S.J.* Translated by Michael J. Sweet. Edited by Leonard Zwilling. Boston: Wisdom Publications.

Dickinson, Chris, dir. 2012. *The St. Bernard Mission to Tibet*. Hong Kong: China Exploration and Research Society and Wildlife Asia.

Diemberger, Hildegard. 1998. "The Horseman in Red: On Sacred Mountains of La stod Iho (Southern Tibet)." In *Tibetan Mountain Deities, Their Cults and Representations*, 43–56. Vienna: Verlag der Österreichischen Akademie der Wissenschaften.

Dinaburg, Jennifer. 2008. "Making the Medicine Mountains: The Politics of Tibetan Doctors and Medicinal Plant Management in the Meilixueshan Conservation Area, Yunnan Province, PRC." Master's thesis, Prescott College, Prescott, AZ.

Douglas, Mary. 1987. "A Distinctive Anthropological Perspective." In *Constructive Drinking: Perspectives on Drink from Anthropology*, edited by Mary Douglas, 3–15. Cambridge: Cambridge University Press.

Dove, Michael. 1988. "The Ecology of Intoxication among the Kantu of West Kalimantan." In *The Real and Imagined Role of Culture in Development: Case Studies from Indonesia*, edited by Michael Dove, 139–82. Honolulu: University of Hawaii Press.

Drew, Georgina. 2012. "A Retreating Goddess? Conflicting Perceptions of Ecological Change near the Gangotri-Gaumukh Glacier." *Journal for the Study of Religion, Nature and Culture* 6 (3): 344–62.

Emerson, Robert M., Rachel I. Fretz, and Linda L. Shaw. 2011. *Writing Ethnographic Fieldnotes*. 2nd ed. Chicago: University of Chicago Press.

"Émile Monbeig, 1876–1942." n.d. Archives of the Paris Foreign Missions (MEP). Document identifier 2587. Accessed April 30, 2024. https://irfa.paris/en /missionnaire/2587-monbeig-emile.

Ferguson, James. 1994. *Anti-Politics Machine: Development, Depoliticization, and Bureaucratic Power in Lesotho*. Minneapolis: University of Minnesota Press.

Fiskesjö, Magnus. 1999. "On the 'Raw' and the 'Cooked' Barbarians of Imperial China." *Inner Asia* 1 (2): 139–68.

———. 2002. "The Barbarian Borderland and the Chinese Imagination: Travelers in Wa Country." *Inner Asia* 4 (1): 81–99.

———. 2010. "Participant Intoxication and Self–Other Dynamics in the Wa Context." *Asia Pacific Journal of Anthropology* 11 (2): 111–27. https://doi.org /10.1080/14442211003720588.

Freeman, Michael, and Selena Ahmed. 2011. *The Tea Horse Road: China's Ancient Trade Road to Tibet*. Bangkok: River Books.

Fuchs, Jeff. 2008. *The Ancient Tea Horse Road: Travels with the Last of the Himalayan Muleteers*. Toronto: Renouf Publishing Company.

Gagné, Karine. 2018. *Caring for Glaciers: Land, Animals, and Humanity in the Himalayas*. Seattle: University of Washington Press.

Galipeau, Brendan A. 2014. "Socio-ecological Vulnerability in a Tibetan Village on the Mekong River, China." *Himalaya, the Journal of the Association for Nepal and Himalayan Studies* 34 (2): 38–51.

———. 2015. "Balancing Income, Food Security, and Sustainability in Shangri-La: The Dilemma of Monocropping Wine Grapes in Rural China." *Culture, Agriculture, Food and Environment* 37 (2): 74–83.

———. 2018. "A Tibetan Catholic Christmas in China: Ethnic Identity and Encounters with Ritual and Revitalization." *Asian Ethnology* 77 (1–2): 335–70.

———. 2022. "Rice, Wine, Grapes, and Land in Shangri-La: The Politics of Land and Water Loss in a Catholic Tibetan Village." *Global Food History* 9 (1): 72–91. https://doi.org/10.1080/20549547.2022.2145755.

Gaonkar, Dilip Parameshwar. 1999. "On Alternative Modernities." *Public Culture* 11 (1): 1–18.

Glarey, Lea. 2009. *Alla ricerca di altre nevi: Una missione alle porte del Tibet (1933–1952)*. Turin: Museo regionale di scienze naturali.

Glover, Denise M., Stevan Harrell, Charles F. McKhann, and Margaret Byrne Swain, eds. 2011. *Explorers and Scientists in China's Borderlands, 1880–1950*. Seattle: University of Washington Press.

Goodman, Jim. 2001. *The Exploration of Yunnan*. Kunming: Yunnan People's Publishing House.

———. 2010. *Grand Canyon of the East*. Kunming: Yunnan People's Publishing House.

Goré, Francis. 1939. *Trente ans aux portes du Thibet interdit*. Paris: Éditions Kimé.

———. 1943. "Ephemerides de Tsechung: Janvier—février—mars, 1943." Archives du Grand-Saint-Bernard. AGSB MIS F2 c.3.4.1.1/3.

———. 1946a. "Ephemerides de Tsechung: Journal du Père F. Goré, M.E.P." *Grand-Saint-Bernard Thibet*, no. 3, 52–55.

———. 1946b. "Ephemerides de Tsechung: Journal du Père F. Goré, M.E.P." *Grand-Saint-Bernard Thibet*, no. 4, 71–72.

Gros, Stéphane. 2001. "Ritual and Politics: Missionary Encounters with Local Culture in Northwest Yunnan." Paper presented in the panel "Legacies and Social Memory: Missionaries and Scholars in the Ethnic Southwest," Association for Asian Studies Annual Meeting, Chicago, March 2001.

———, ed. 2019a. *Frontier Tibet: Patterns of Change in the Sino-Tibetan Borderlands*. Amsterdam: Amsterdam University Press.

———. 2019b. "Foreword and Acknowledgments." In Gros 2019a, 9–17.

———. 2019c. "Frontier (of) Experience: Introduction and Prolegomenon." In Gros 2019a, 41–83.

Grumbine, R. Edward. 2011. *Where the Dragon Meets the Angry River: Nature and Power in the People's Republic of China*. Washington, DC: Island Press.

Gudeman, Stephen. 2001. *The Anthropology of Economy: Community, Market, and Culture*. Malden, MA: Blackwell.

Guedes, Jade A. d'Alpoim, Hongliang Lu, Anke M. Hein, and Amanda H. Schmidt. 2015. "Early Evidence for the Use of Wheat and Barley as Staple Crops on the Margins of the Tibetan Plateau." *Proceedings of the National Academy of Sciences* 112 (18): 5625–30.

Guedes, Jade A. d'Alpoim, Sturt W. Manning, and R. Kyle Bocinsky. 2016. "A 5,500-Year Model of Changing Crop Niches on the Tibetan Plateau." *Current Anthropology* 57 (4): 517–22. https://doi.org/10.1086/687255.

Hall, Stuart. 1996. "Introduction: Who Needs 'Identity'?" In *Questions of Cultural Identity*, edited by Stuart Hall and Paul du Gay, 1–17. Thousand Oaks, CA: Sage Publications.

———, ed. 1997. *Representation: Cultural Representations and Signifying Practices*. London: Sage Publications in association with Open University.

Hansen, Mette Halskov. 1999. *Lessons in Being Chinese: Minority Education and Ethnic Identity in Southwest China*. Seattle: University of Washington Press.

Hardy, Stephen. 2000. "Placiality: The Renewal of the Significance of Place in Modern Cultural Theory." *Brno Studies in English* 26 (1): 85–100.

Harrell, Stevan. 1996. "Introduction: Civilizing Projects and the Reaction to Them." In *Cultural Encounters on China's Ethnic Frontiers*, edited by Stevan Harrell, 3–36. Seattle: University of Washington Press.

———. 2001. *Ways of Being Ethnic in Southwest China*. Seattle: University of Washington Press.

———. 2014. "Foreword." In Yeh and Coggins 2014a, vii–iv.

Hathaway, Michael J. 2013. *Environmental Winds: Making the Global in Southwest China*. Berkeley: University of California Press.

———. 2014. "Transnational Matsutake Governance: Endangered Species, Contamination, and the Reemergence of Global Commodity Chains." In Yeh and Coggins 2014a, 153–74.

Hessler, Peter. 2010. *Country Driving: A Journey through China from Farm to Factory*. New York: Harper.

Hillman, Ben. 2003. "Paradise under Construction: Minorities, Myths and Modernity in Northwest Yunnan." *Asian Ethnicity* 4 (2): 175–88.

———. 2010. "China's Many Tibets: Diqing as a Model for 'Development with Tibetan Characteristics'?" *Asian Ethnicity* 11 (2): 269–77. https://doi.org/10.1080/14631361003779604.

Hilton, James. 1933. *Lost Horizon*. London: Macmillan.

Himalaya Development Group. 2016. "About Us." https://www.linkedin.com/company/himalaya-development-group.

Horlemann, Bianca. 2013. "Christian Missionaries in Qinghai and Gansu: Sources for Tibetan and Mongol Studies." *Xiyu lishi yuyan yanjiu jikan* 西域历史语言研究集刊 (Historical and philological studies of [China's] western region) 6: 163–91.

———. 2014. "Xixiang, a Historic Catholic Mission Station in Northwest China." *Religion and Christianity in Today's China* 4 (2): 40–49.

———. 2015. "The Catholic Missionary Enterprise in Late 19th/Early 20th Century Qinghai, Gansu and Xinjiang as Perceived by Chinese and Western Travellers." In *History of the Catholic Church in China: From Its Beginning to the Scheut Fathers and 20th Century*, edited by Ferdinand Verbiest Institute, 363–92. Leuven: Ferdinand Verbiest Institute K.U. Leuven.

Howson, Cynthia, and Pierre Ly. 2020. *Adventures on the China Wine Trail: How Farmers, Local Governments, Teachers, and Entrepreneurs Are Rocking the Wine World*. Lanham, MD: Rowman and Littlefield.

Huber, Toni. 1999. *The Cult of Pure Crystal Mountain: Popular Pilgrimage and Visionary Landscape in Southeast Tibet*. New York: Oxford University Press.

Huc, Évariste-Régis. 1928. *Huc and Gabet: Travels in Tartary, Thibet, and China, 1844–1846*. Translated by William Hazlitt. Edited by Paul Pelliot. 2 vols. London: George Routledge and Sons.

Ingman, Mark Christian. 2012. "The Role of Plastic Mulch as a Water Conservation Practice for Desert Oasis Communities of Northern China." Master's thesis, Oregon State University.

Ingold, Tim. 1993. "The Temporality of the Landscape." *World Archaeology* 25 (2): 152–74.

———. 2000. *The Perception of the Environment: Essays on Livelihood, Dwelling and Skill*. London: Routledge.

Jangbu. 2010. *The Nine-Eyed Agate: Poems and Stories*. Translated by Heather Stoddard. Lanham, MD: Lexington Books.

Jenster, Per, and Yiting Cheng. 2008. "Dragon Wine: Developments in the Chinese Wine Industry." *International Journal of Wine Business Research* 20 (3): 244–59. https://doi.org/10.1108/17511060810901055.

Jinba, Tenzin. 2014. *In the Land of the Eastern Queendom: The Politics of Gender and Ethnicity on the Sino-Tibetan Border*. Seattle: University of Washington Press.

———. 2017. "Seeing like Borders: Convergence Zone as a Post-Zomian Model." *Current Anthropology* 58 (5): 551–75. https://doi.org/10.1086/693731.

Karmay, Samten. 1994. "Mountain Cults and National Identity in Tibet." In *Resistance and Reform in Tibet*, edited by Robert Barnett, 112–20. Bloomington: Indiana University Press.

———. 1996. "The Tibetan Cult of Mountain Deities and Its Political Significance." In *Reflections of the Mountain: Essays on the History and Social Meaning of the Mountain Cult in Tibet and the Himalaya*, edited by Anne-Marie Blondeau and

Ernst Steinkellner, 59–75. Vienna: Verlag der Österreichischen Akademie der Wissenschaften.

Kilpatrick, Jane. 2015. *Fathers of Botany: The Discovery of Chinese Plants by European Missionaries*. Chicago: University of Chicago Press.

Kirsch, A. Thomas. 1973. *Feasting and Social Oscillation: A Working Paper on Religion and Society in Upland Southeast Asia*. Ithaca, NY: Southeast Asia Program Publications.

Klein, Jakob A. 2014. "Connecting with the Countryside? 'Alternative' Food Movements with Chinese Characteristics." In *Ethical Eating in the Postsocialist and Socialist World*, edited by Yuson Jung, Jakob A. Klein, and Melissa L. Caldwell, 116–43. Berkeley: University of California Press.

Klingberg, Travis. 2014. "A Routine Discovery: The Practice of Place and the Opening of the Yading Nature Reserve." In Yeh and Coggins 2014a, 75–94.

Kolås, Åshild. 2011. *Tourism and Tibetan Culture in Transition: A Place Called Shangrila*. London: Routledge.

Kopytoff, Igor. 1988. "The Cultural Biography of Things: Commoditization as Process." In *The Social Life of Things: Commodities in Cultural Perspective*, edited by Arjun Appadurai, 64–91. Cambridge: Cambridge University Press.

Lambert, Valerie. 2007. "Choctaw Tribal Sovereignty at the Turn of the 21st Century." In *Indigenous Experience Today*, edited by Marisol de la Cadena and Orin Starn, 151–70. Oxford, UK: Berg.

Latour, Bruno. 2015. "'Fifty Shades of Green': Bruno Latour on the Ecomodernist Manifesto." *ENTITLE Blog—a Collaborative Writing Project on Political Ecology*, June 27, 2015. https://entitleblogdotorg3.wordpress.com/2015/06/27/fifty -shades-of-green-bruno-latour-on-the-ecomodernist-manifesto.

Launay, Adrien. 1909. *Histoire de la mission du Thibet*. 2 vols. Paris: Missions Étrangères de Paris.

"Les missionnaires vous donnent des nouvelles." 1948. *Grand-Saint-Bernard-Thibet*, no. 1, 29.

Li, Tania Murray. 2000. "Articulating Indigenous Identity in Indonesia: Resource Politics and the Tribal Slot." *Comparative Studies in Society and History* 42 (1): 149–79.

Li, Yali, Chunlin Long, Kenji Kato, Chunyan Yang, and Kazuhiro Sato. 2011. "Indigenous Knowledge and Traditional Conservation of Hulless Barley (*Hordeum vulgare*) Germplasm Resources in the Tibetan Communities of Shangri-La, Yunnan, SW China." *Genetic Resources and Crop Evolution* 58 (5): 645–55. https://doi.org/10.1007/s10722-010-9604-2.

Li, Yongxiang, and Bryan Tilt. 2007. "In Search of Solvency: Changing Agricultural Governance in an Ethnic Minority Autonomous Region of Southwest China." *International Journal of Agricultural Resources Governance and Ecology* 6 (6): 626–41.

Li, Zhengping. 2011. *Chinese Wine*. Cambridge: Cambridge University Press.

Lim, Francis Khek Gee. 2009. "Negotiating 'Foreignness,' Localizing Faith: Tibetan Catholicism in the Tibet-Yunnan Borderlands." In *Christianity and the State in Asia: Complicity and Conflict*, edited by Julius Bautista and Francis Khek Gee Lim, 79–96. London: Routledge.

Litzinger, Ralph. 2004. "The Mobilization of 'Nature': Perspectives from North-West Yunnan." *China Quarterly* 178 (June): 488–504. https://doi.org/10.1017/S030574100400027X.

———. 2014. "Afterword: The Afterlives of Shangrila." In Yeh and Coggins 2014a, 279–86.

Liu, Wenzeng, dir. 2002. *Christmas Eve in Cizhong, Cizhong Red Wine* (Cizhong shengdan ye, Cizhong hongjiu 茨中圣诞夜， 茨中红酒). Kunming: Baima Mountain Culture Research Institute.

Loup, Robert. 1956. *Martyr in Tibet: The Heroic Life and Death of Father Maurice Tornay, St. Bernard Missionary to Tibet*. Translated by Charles Davenport. New York: David McKay Company.

Lovey, Angelin. 1942. "Extraits d'une lettre écrite par le p. Lovey à ses parents le 7 juillet 1942, et arrivée à Orsières le 24 décembre." Archives du Grand-Saint-Bernard. AGSB MIS G9.D1/9.

Luo, Qiangqiang, Joel Andreas, and Yao Li. 2017. "Grapes of Wrath: Twisting Arms to Get Villagers to Cooperate with Agribusiness in China." *China Journal* 77 (January): 27–50. https://doi.org/10.1086/688344.

Makley, Charlene. 2018. *The Battle for Fortune: State-Led Development, Personhood, and Power among Tibetans in China*. Ithaca, NY: Cornell University Press.

Manning, Paul. 2012. *Semiotics of Drink and Drinking*. New York: Bloomsbury Academic.

McCarthy, Susan K. 2009. *Communist Multiculturalism: Ethnic Revival in Southwest China*. Seattle: University of Washington Press.

McGovern, Patrick E. 2009. *Uncorking the Past: The Quest for Wine, Beer, and Other Alcoholic Beverages*. Berkeley: University of California Press.

McLean, Brenda. 2009. *George Forrest: Plant Hunter*. Suffolk, UK: Antique Collectors' Club.

Melly, Marie. 1944. "Vigne." Archives du Grand-Saint-Bernard. AGSB MIS H1.b.

———. 1947. "Culture de la vigne au Thibet." *Grand-Saint-Bernard Thibet*, no. 3, 47–49.

Michaud, Jean. 2007. *"Incidental" Ethnographers: French Catholic Missions on the Tonkin-Yunnan Frontier, 1880–1930*. Leiden: Brill.

Monbeig, Emile Cyprien. 1906. "Voyage dans le Thibet de Ta-tsien-lou Oui-si." *Annales de la Société des Missions Étrangères*, no. 51, 1–14. https://irfa.paris/en/ancienne_publication/annales-de-la-societe-des-missions-etrangeres-1906/annales-n-51.

Mortensen, Eric D. 2019. "Boundaries of the Borderlands: Mapping Gyelthang." In Gros 2019a, 115–39.

Moseley, Robert K. 2011. *Revisiting Shangri-La*. Beijing: China Intercontinental Press.

Moseley, Robert K., and Renée B. Mullen. 2014. "The Nature Conservancy in Shangrila: Transnational Conservation and Its Critiques." In Yeh and Coggins 2014a, 129–52.

Mueggler, Erik. 2001. *The Age of Wild Ghosts: Memory, Violence, and Place in Southwest China*. Berkeley: University of California Press.

———. 2011. *The Paper Road: Archive and Experience in the Botanical Exploration of West China and Tibet*. Berkeley: University of California Press.

Mullaney, Thomas. 2011. *Coming to Terms with the Nation: Ethnic Classification in Modern China*. Berkeley: University of California Press.

Mustacich, Suzanne. 2015. *Thirsty Dragon: China's Lust for Bordeaux and the Threat to the World's Best Wines*. New York: Henry Holt.

Nima, Zhaxi, dir. 2002. *Glacier* (Bing chuan冰川). Kunming: Baima Mountain Culture Research Institute.

Oi, Jean C. 1995. "The Role of the Local State in China's Transitional Economy." *China Quarterly* 144 (December): 1132–49. https://doi.org/10.1017/S0305741 000004768.

———. 1999. "Two Decades of Rural Reform in China: An Overview and Assessment." *China Quarterly* 159 (September): 616–28. https://doi.org/10.1017 /S0305741000003374.

Orwell, George. 1934. *Burmese Days*. New York: Harper and Brothers.

Osburg, John. 2013a. *Anxious Wealth: Money and Morality among China's New Rich*. Stanford, CA: Stanford University Press.

———. 2013b. "Global Capitalisms in Asia: Beyond State and Market in China." *Journal of Asian Studies* 72 (4): 813–29. https://doi.org/10.1017/S00219118 13001629.

———. 2020. "Consuming Belief: Luxury, Authenticity, and Chinese Patronage of Tibetan Buddhism in Contemporary China." *HAU: Journal of Ethnographic Theory* 10 (1): 69–84. https://doi.org/10.1086/708547.

Paxson, Heather. 2010. "Locating Value in Artisan Cheese: Reverse Engineering *Terroir* for New-World Landscapes." *American Anthropologist* 112 (3): 444–57. https://doi.org/10.1111/j.1548-1433.2010.01251.x.

Playfoot, Neil. 2021. "How Rambler Gin Came to Be Made in Shangri-La." *Asian Beer Network* (blog), March 21, 2021. https://www.asianbeernetwork.com/how -gin-came-to-be-made-at-the-top-of-the-world.

Pomplun, Trent. 2010. *Jesuit on the Roof of the World: Ippolito Desideri's Mission to Tibet*. New York: Oxford University Press.

Povinelli, Elizabeth A. 2002. *The Cunning of Recognition: Indigenous Alterities and the Making of Australian Multiculturalism*. Durham, NC: Duke University Press.

Ptáčková, Jarmila. 2020. *Exile from the Grasslands: Tibetan Herders and Chinese Development Projects*. Seattle: University of Washington Press.

Raignoux, Remy. 2010. *The South Tibet Mission (1880–1929)*. Kathmandu: Foreign Missions Society of Paris, France.

Reuse, Gaetan. 2007. "Sur les traces des missionnaires catholiques au Tibet et dans les Marches tibétaines." *Asdiwal: Revue genevoise d'anthropologie et d'histoire des religions*, no. 2: 108–23.

Robinson, Jancis, and Nicholas Lander. 2014. "Finding Shangri-La in Yunnan, China." *Financial Times*, June 20, 2014. https://www.ft.com/content/61ef6470 -f73e-11e3-8ed6-00144feabdc0.

Rock, Joseph F. 1947. *The Ancient Na-khi Kingdom of Southwest China*. Cambridge, MA: Harvard University Press.

Ross, Warwick, and David Roach, dirs. 2013. *Red Obsession: The Vintage of the Century in the Year of the Dragon*. Sydney: Lion Rock Films.

Roux, Émile. 1999. *Searching for the Sources of the Irrawaddy: With Prince Henri d'Orléans from Hanoi to Calcutta Overland*. Translated by Walter E. J. Tips. Bangkok: White Lotus Press. Originally published as *Aux sources de l'Irraouddi, d'Hanoï à Calcutta par terre* in *Le Tour du Monde* (Paris), n.s., 3, nos. 17–23 (1897): 193–276.

Ruffle, Chris. 2015. *A Decent Bottle of Wine in China*. Hong Kong: Earnshaw Books.

Sahlins, Marshall. 1994. "Cosmologies of Capitalism: The Trans-Pacific Sector of 'The World System.'" In *Culture/Power/History: A Reader in Contemporary Social Theory*, edited by Nicholas B. Dirks, Geoff Eley, and Sherry B. Ortner, 412–55. Princeton, NJ: Princeton University Press.

———. 1999. "What Is Anthropological Enlightenment? Some Lessons of the Twentieth Century." *Annual Review of Anthropology* 28: i–xxiii.

———. 2010. "The Whole Is a Part: Intercultural Politics of Order and Change." In *Experiments in Holism: Theory and Practice in Contemporary Anthropology*, edited by Ton Otto and Niles Bubandt, 102–26. Chichester, West Sussex: Wiley-Blackwell.

Saint Macary, Jean René. n.d. *Le Père Théodore Jean Monbeig: Missions Étrangères de Paris, 1875–1914*. Paris: Missions Étrangères de Paris.

Salick, Jan, Anja Byg, and Kenneth Bauer. 2013. "Contemporary Tibetan Cosmology of Climate Change." *Journal for the Study of Religion, Nature and Culture* 6 (4): 447–76.

Salick, Jan, and Robert K. Moseley. 2012. *Khawa Karpo: Tibetan Traditional Knowledge and Biodiversity Conservation*. St. Louis: Missouri Botanical Garden Press.

Schaeffer, Kurtis R., Matthew T. Kapstein, and Gray Tuttle. 2013. *Sources of Tibetan Tradition*. New York: Columbia University Press.

Schmitt, Edwin A. 2014. "The History and Development of De-swiddening among the Ersu in Sichuan, China." *Himalaya, the Journal of the Association for Nepal and Himalayan Studies* 34 (2): 97–110.

Schneider, Mindi. 2014. "What, Then, Is a Chinese Peasant? *Nongmin* Discourses and Agroindustrialization in Contemporary China." *Agriculture and Human Values* 32 (2): 331–46. https://doi.org/10.1007/s10460-014-9559-6.

———. 2017. "Dragon Head Enterprises and the State of Agribusiness in China." *Journal of Agrarian Change* 17 (1): 3–21. https://doi.org/10.1111/joac.12151.

Scott, James C. 1987. *Weapons of the Weak: Everyday Forms of Peasant Resistance*. New Haven, CT: Yale University Press.

———. 2009. *The Art of Not Being Governed: An Anarchist History of Upland Southeast Asia*. New Haven, CT: Yale University Press.

Sherpa, Pasang Yangjee. 2014. "Climate Change, Perceptions, and Social Heterogeneity in Pharak, Mount Everest Region of Nepal." *Human Organization* 73 (2): 153–61. https://doi.org/10.17730/humo.73.2.94q4315211733t6.

Shu, Noel. 2016. *China through a Glass of Wine*. Virginia Beach, VA: Cafe con Leche Books.

Smith, Norman. 2012. *Intoxicating Manchuria: Alcohol, Opium, and Culture in China's Northeast*. Vancouver: University of British Columbia Press.

Smyer Yü, Dan. 2012. *The Spread of Tibetan Buddhism in China: Charisma, Money, Enlightenment*. London: Routledge.

———. 2015. *Mindscaping the Landscape of Tibet: Place, Memorability, Ecoaesthetics*. Boston: De Gruyter.

———. 2017. "Introduction: Trans-Himalayas as Multistate Margins." In *Trans-Himalayan Borderlands: Livelihoods, Territorialities, Modernities*, edited by Dan Smyer Yü and Jean Michaud, 11–41. Amsterdam: Amsterdam University Press.

Standing, Guy. 2014. "Understanding the Precariat through Labour and Work." *Development and Change* 45 (5): 963–80. https://doi.org/10.1111/dech.12120.

Stein, Rolf Alfred. 1972. *Tibetan Civilization*. Translated by J. E. Stapleton Driver. Stanford, CA: Stanford University Press.

Stewart, Michelle Olsgard. 2014. "Constructing and Deconstructing the Commons: Caterpillar Fungus Governance in Developing Yunnan." In Yeh and Coggins 2014a, 175–98.

Tilt, Bryan. 2008. "Smallholders and the 'Household Responsibility System': Adapting to Institutional Change in Chinese Agriculture." *Human Ecology* 36 (2): 189–99.

———. 2011. "Local Perceptions of Quality of Life in Rural China: Implications for Anthropology and Participatory Development." *Journal of Anthropological Research* 67 (1): 27–46.

Trubek, Amy B. 2009. *The Taste of Place: A Cultural Journey into Terroir*. Berkeley: University of California Press.

Tsing, Anna. 2009. "Beyond Economic and Ecological Standardisation." *Australian Journal of Anthropology* 20 (3): 347–68.

———. 2015a. "In the Midst of Disturbance: Symbiosis, Coordination, History, Landscape." Firth Lecture, given at the Association of Social Anthropologists of the UK and Commonwealth 2015 Conference, "Symbiotic Anthropologies: Theoretical Commensalities and Methodological Mutualisms," University of Exeter, April 2015. http://www.theasa.org/downloads/publications/firth /firth15.pdf.

———. 2015b. *The Mushroom at the End of the World: On the Possibility of Life in Capitalist Ruins*. Princeton, NJ: Princeton University Press.

Turner, Sarah, Christine Bonnin, and Jean Michaud. 2015. *Frontier Livelihoods: Hmong in the Sino-Vietnamese Borderlands*. Seattle: University of Washington Press.

Ulin, Robert C. 1995. "Invention and Representation as Cultural Capital." *American Anthropologist* 97 (3): 519–27.

———. 2002. "Work as Cultural Production: Labour and Self-Identity among Southwest French Wine-Growers." *Journal of the Royal Anthropological Institute* 8 (4): 691–712.

Voutaz, Jean-Pierre, and Pierre Rouyer. 2014a. *Discovering the Great Saint Bernard*. Martigny, Switzerland: Les Éditions du Grand-Saint-Bernard.

———. 2014b. *There Will Your Heart Be: The Treasury, Church, and Crypt of the Great Saint Bernard Hospice*. Martigny, Switzerland: Les Éditions du Grand-Saint-Bernard.

Walker, Adam, and Paul Manning. 2013. "Georgian Wine: The Transformation of Socialist Quantity into Postsocialist Quality." In *Wine and Culture: Vineyard to Glass*, edited by Rachel E. Black and Robert C. Ulin, 201–19. New York: Bloomsbury Academic.

Wallace, Ellen. 2014. *Vineglorious: Switzerland's Wonderous World of Wines*. Saint-Prex, Switzerland: EllenBooks.

Wang, Mingming. 2004. *The West as the Other: A Genealogy of Chinese Occidentalism*. Hong Kong: Chinese University Press.

———. 2009. *Empire and Local Worlds: A Chinese Model for Long-Term Historical Anthropology*. Walnut Creek, CA: Left Coast Press.

Ward, Frank Kingdon. 1913. *The Land of the Blue Poppy: Travels of a Naturalist in Eastern Tibet*. Cambridge: Cambridge University Press.

The Way to Tibet. 2004. Hong Kong: Audio Visual Center of the Catholic Diocese of Hong Kong.

Wilk, Richard. 1997. *Household Ecology: Economic Change and Domestic Life among the Kekchi Maya in Belize*. DeKalb: Northern Illinois University Press.

Wine-Searcher. 2022. "Baco Noir Wine." November 18, 2022. https://www.wine -searcher.com/grape-26-baco-noir.

Winkler, Daniel. 2005. "Yartsa Gunbu—*Cordyceps sinensis*: Economy, Ecology and Ethno-Mycology of a Fungus Endemic to the Tibetan Plateau." In "Wildlife and Plants in Traditional and Modern Tibet: Conceptions, Exploitation and Conservation." Special issue, *Memorie della Società italiana di scienze naturali e del Museo civico di storia naturale di Milano* 33 (1): 69–85.

———. 2008. "Yartsa Gunbu (*Cordyceps sinensis*) and the Fungal Commodification of Tibet's Rural Economy." *Economic Botany* 62 (3): 291–305.

———. 2010. "*Cordyceps sinensis*: A Precious Parasitic Fungus Infecting Tibet." *Field Mycology* 11 (2): 60–68.

Woodhouse, Emily, Martin A. Mills, Philip J. K. McGowan, and E. J. Milner-Gulland. 2015. "Religious Relationships with the Environment in a Tibetan Rural Community: Interactions and Contrasts with Popular Notions of Indigenous Environmentalism." *Human Ecology* 43 (2): 295–307.

Xiao, Xiangyi, and Yingqing Li. 2012. "High Ambitions." *China Daily*, August 31, 2012, sec. Business.

Yang, Fengyi. 2015. "Shangri-La Hosts International Icewine Culture Festival." China Wines Information Website, December 21, 2015. http://en.wines-info.com/html /2015/12/189-63957.html.

Yang, Mayfair Mei-hui. 1994. *Gifts, Favors, and Banquets: The Art of Social Relationships in China*. Ithaca, NY: Cornell University Press.

Yang, Ming-zhi, Hua-feng Yang, Jin-hai Luo, Xia Lu, and Jia-qiang Liu. 2007. "Yunnan gaoyuan bing putaojiu shengchan kexing xing lilun yu shijian" 云南高原冰葡萄酒生产可行性理论与实践 (Theory and practice of the possibility of producing ice grape wine in Yun'nan Plateau)." *Niangjiu keji* 酿酒科技 (Liquor-making science and technology) 5 (155): 42–44.

Yeh, Emily T. 2007a. "Exile Meets Homeland: Politics, Performance, and Authenticity in the Tibetan Diaspora." *Environment and Planning D: Society and Space* 25 (4): 648–67.

———. 2007b. "Tibetan Indigeneity: Translations, Resemblances, and Uptake." In *Indigenous Experience Today*, edited by Marisol de la Cadena and Orin Starn, 69–98. Oxford, UK: Berg.

———. 2013a. "The Politics of Conservation in Contemporary Rural China." *Journal of Peasant Studies* 40 (6): 1165–88. https://doi.org/10.1080/03066150.201 3.859575.

———. 2013b. *Taming Tibet: Landscape Transformation and the Gift of Chinese Development*. Ithaca, NY: Cornell University Press.

———. 2014. "The Rise and Fall of the Green Tibetan: Contingent Collaborations and the Vicissitudes of Harmony." In Yeh and Coggins 2014a, 255–78.

Yeh, Emily T., and Chris Coggins, eds. 2014a. *Mapping Shangrila: Contested Landscapes in the Sino-Tibetan Borderlands*. Seattle: University of Washington Press.

———. 2014b. "Constructing the Ecological State: Conservation, Commodification, and Resource Governance." In Yeh and Coggins 2014a, 95–104.

———. 2014c. "Contested Landscapes: Harmonious Society and Sovereign Territories." In Yeh and Coggins 2014a, 199–204.

———. 2014d. "Shangrilalization: Tourism, Landscape, Identity." In Yeh and Coggins 2014a, 19–26.

Yeh, Emily T., Kevin J. O'Brien, and Jingzhong Ye. 2013. "Rural Politics in Contemporary China." *Journal of Peasant Studies* 40 (6): 915–28. https://doi.org/10.1080/03066150.2013.866097.

Ying, Li-hua. 2014. "Vital Margins: Frontier Poetics and Landscapes of Ethnic Identity." In Yeh and Coggins 2014a, 27–50.

Zhang, Jinghong. 2014. *Puer Tea: Ancient Caravans and Urban Chic*. Seattle: University of Washington Press.

Zhang, Qian Forrest, and John A. Donaldson. 2008. "The Rise of Agrarian Capitalism with Chinese Characteristics: Agricultural Modernization, Agribusiness and Collective Land Rights." *China Journal* 60 (July): 25–47. https://doi.org/10.1086/tcj.60.20647987.

Zhang, Qian Forrest, Carlos Oya, and Jingzhong Ye. 2015. "Bringing Agriculture Back In: The Central Place of Agrarian Change in Rural China Studies." *Journal of Agrarian Change* 15 (3): 299–313.

Zheng, Xiangchun. 2019. "Narrating *Terroir*: The Place-Making of Wine in China's Southwest." *Food, Culture and Society* 22 (3): 280–98. https://doi.org/10.1080/15528014.2019.1596435.

Zhou, D. Q., and R. Edward Grumbine. 2011. "National Parks in China: Experiments with Protecting Nature and Human Livelihoods in Yunnan Province, Peoples' Republic of China (PRC)." *Biological Conservation* 144 (5): 1314–21.

Zinda, John Aloysius. 2014. "Making National Parks in Yunnan: Shifts and Struggles within the Ecological State." In Yeh and Coggins 2014a, 105–28.

Zufferey-Perisset, Anne-Dominique, ed. 2010. *Histoire de la vigne et du vin en Valais: Des origines à nos jours*. Sion: Infolio.

Index

Locators in *italics* refer to figures.

Culture, Place, and Nature
STUDIES IN ANTHROPOLOGY AND ENVIRONMENT

Crafting a Tibetan Terroir: Winemaking in Shangri-La, by Brendan A. Galipeau

China's Camel Country: Livestock and Nation-Building at a Pastoral Frontier, by Thomas White

Sustaining Natures: An Environmental Anthropology Reader, edited by Sarah R. Osterhoudt and K. Sivaramakrishnan

Fukushima Futures: Survival Stories in a Repeatedly Ruined Seascape, by Satsuki Takahashi

The Camphor Tree and the Elephant: Religion and Ecological Change in Maritime Southeast Asia, by Faizah Zakaria

Turning Land into Capital: Development and Dispossession in the Mekong Region, edited by Philip Hirsch, Kevin Woods, Natalia Scurrah, and Michael B. Dwyer

Spawning Modern Fish: Transnational Comparison in the Making of Japanese Salmon, by Heather Anne Swanson

Upland Geopolitics: Postwar Laos and the Global Land Rush, by Michael B. Dwyer

Misreading the Bengal Delta: Climate Change, Development, and Livelihoods in Coastal Bangladesh, by Camelia Dewan

Ordering the Myriad Things: From Traditional Knowledge to Scientific Botany in China, by Nicholas K. Menzies

Timber and Forestry in Qing China: Sustaining the Market, by Meng Zhang

Consuming Ivory: Mercantile Legacies of East Africa and New England, by Alexandra Celia Kelly

Mapping Water in Dominica: Enslavement and Environment under Colonialism, by Mark W. Hauser

Mountains of Blame: Climate and Culpability in the Philippine Uplands, by Will Smith

Sacred Cows and Chicken Manchurian: The Everyday Politics of Eating Meat in India, by James Staples

Gardens of Gold: Place-Making in Papua New Guinea, by Jamon Alex Halvaksz

Shifting Livelihoods: Gold Mining and Subsistence in the Chocó, Colombia, by Daniel Tubb

Disturbed Forests, Fragmented Memories: Jarai and Other Lives in the Cambodian Highlands, by Jonathan Padwe

The Snow Leopard and the Goat: Politics of Conservation in the Western Himalayas, by Shafqat Hussain